Know your God

Know your God

The doctrine of God in the Pentateuch

Linleigh J. Roberts

 EVANGELICAL PRESS

EVANGELICAL PRESS
Faverdale North Industrial Estate, Darlington, DL3 0PH, England

Evangelical Press USA
P. O. Box 825, Webster, New York 14580, USA

e-mail: sales@evangelicalpress.org

web: http://www.evangelicalpress.org

First published 2005

British Library Cataloguing in Publication Data available

ISBN 0 85234 582 8

Printed and bound in Great Britain by Creative Print & Design Wales, Ebbw Vale

To my young Brazilian colleague, Rodrigo Franklin de Sousa,
who, although young in the faith, has demonstrated spiritual
maturity and commitment beyond his years,
and to his lovely wife, Ana,
I dedicate this work.
Rodrigo served as my interpreter in north-eastern Brazil and,
because of his concern to establish believers in the faith and to
reach the lost for Christ, undertook to translate this and other of
my materials into Portuguese.

Contents

Introduction

During his imprisonment for political activism in Nazi Germany during World War II, Dietrich Bonhoeffer observed, in his *Letters and Papers from Prison,* that God was increasingly being edged out of life and would become irrelevant for people by the end of the twentieth century. Modern man, he suggested, is able to cope quite well without God. He believed that this would lead to 'religionless Christianity'. From outward appearances and for all practical purposes, Bonhoeffer's prediction has come to pass; God appears to be irrelevant for multitudes of people. Many, it seems, go through life without serious thought of their Maker or of their moral responsibility to him; they have the physical necessities and comforts of life, and that is all that seems to matter. How has this happened? What are the consequences of the loss of the knowledge of God? And why do we need to consider the truth about God?

The Protestant Reformation which swept through several countries of Europe in the sixteenth century was, in many ways, a rediscovery of the biblical doctrine of God. As a result, people began to investigate the world because they saw it as God's world. The more they learned of the creation, the more they acknowledged and worshipped the Creator. The Reformation gave birth to many modern movements: modern science, political democracy, and much, much more. Some of the greatest works of art, music and literature emerged from that era. Ironically, most, if not all, of these great developments which emerged from the Reformation have become antagonistic to the Reformation.

As with most religious revivals, succeeding generations took religion for granted and settled into a cold, formalistic ritual. When the Reformation fires subsided and people began to let their church do their thinking for them, the intellectual and spiritual climate was right for another major change. The new scientific era, which, ironically, had been brought to birth by the Reformation, led men to believe that they did not need God to explain the mysteries of the universe and of human existence. Hence, the Enlightenment dawned. Philosophers, like David Hume, believed that the world is ruled by natural law and human reason.

If God was no longer part of the equation, how did everything begin? Charles Darwin supplied the answer. Human beings originated from lower forms of life by a purely chance process. Because sinful men do not like to retain God in their thinking, Darwin's theory was immediately accepted as the *scientific* explanation. Some theologians, desiring to maintain academic respectability and credibility, embraced these 'enlightened' ideas. Since human beings had evolved from lower forms of life, they reasoned, religion must also be part of the evolutionary process. As the human mind developed and man began to think about things, he saw the need to explain the mysteries of his existence in terms of a higher power or deity. At first, sticks and stones were worshipped but, as the ideas were refined, men began to think in terms of a personal God. This meant, of course, that the Bible, instead of being a revelation *from* God (as men had believed for centuries) was merely a record of what men thought *about* God. On the basis of that notion, theologians thought it necessary to restructure the Bible to make it fit their presuppositions. Consequently, the so-called Enlightenment effectively divorced the Creator from his creation — it excluded God from his universe!

I was in my teens when I saw my first film; it was a black-and-white Western. I have forgotten what it was all about except for one scene. An old stagecoach was meandering along a hot, dusty track; the driver was half asleep and the horses were trotting

along at an easy gait. Suddenly, a gang of outlaws emerged from
an outcrop of boulders with their six-guns a-blazing. The coach
driver whipped the team to a gallop and the race was on. As the
outlaws were gaining, at a critical point, one of the wheels came
off the coach. It continued to hurtle on down the track until it
hit a rock; the rim flew off, the hub fell out, and what remained
was simply a small heap of sticks. God is, as it were, the hub (the
beginning and centre) and the rim (the circumference and the
end) of all things. If God is removed from his creation, as the
Enlightenment tried to do, all that remains is an assortment of
academic disciplines without meaning. People continue to study
the spokes of the wheel (from astronomy, biology, chemistry ...
all the way round to zoology) and, in many cases, some have a
very thorough knowledge of one or more of those disciplines.
Without God, however, we end up with a fragmented universe
that lacks significance or purpose.

Liberal theologians did not abandon the concept of God, of
course — they did not dare do that! Had they done so, they
would have lost their credibility entirely. Instead, they spoke of
loftier concepts and greater insights of God. Even within the
Bible they imagined a progression, or evolution, of the concept
of God — the God of the Old Testament was characterized as
cruel, harsh and relentless in his dealings with men, whereas the
God of the New Testament was presented as compassionate,
loving and kind. They did not admit, however, that they had
abandoned the only source of objective truth about God. If the
Bible is merely a record of what men thought about God, it does
not have much relevance, if any, for modern man. These
'enlightened' ideas have had a devastating effect on the church
and have left multitudes destitute of purpose, meaning and
hope.

Why do we need to know God?

Why should we study what God has revealed about himself? I have, of course, already alluded to a fundamental reason: God is the unifying, integrating factor in the universe and only as all things are seen in relationship to him do we find meaning and purpose for our existence. Though that is tremendously import-ant and practical, it might be regarded as a philosophical or academic matter. There are several other important reasons.

Firstly, since we are commanded to love the Lord God with all our heart, mind, soul and strength, *we need to know the object of our love*. If I had been asked in my early Christian life if I loved the people in Brazil, I would have replied without hesi-tation, 'Of course.' It was not that I knew anyone from Brazil but, so far as I can recall, I had no adverse feelings or racial prejudice towards anyone there. Having been to Brazil on several extended periods of ministry in recent years, I can still say that I love those people; the difference is, however, that I now know numerous wonderful people in that great land and I have an objective basis for my claim. Similarly, with God, the more we get to know him, the more objective base we have for our love to him.

Secondly, *to worship God acceptably*, we need to know him and what he requires. The word 'worship' comes from an old Anglo-Saxon root, meaning 'to recognize the *worth*'. While we cannot deduce the meaning of a word from its etymology, in this case it seems to fit; to worship God is to recognize his worth. All kinds of innovative ideas are being introduced to make church services appealing to sinners, but that which pleases men might be offensive to God. True worship consists of a sincere recog-nition of his worth and an acknowledgement of our unworthi-ness to approach him.

Thirdly, *the purpose for our existence* is 'to glorify God and enjoy him for ever'.[1] The more we know and understand the reason for our being in this world, the more meaning, purpose and satisfaction we find in fulfilling the purpose for which we were made.

Fourthly, *the answers to human problems are* not psychological (as many these days seem to think) but *theological*. Forgiveness for, and deliverance from, sin, relief from guilt and other deep spiritual problems are resolved satisfactorily only through the redemptive work of Jesus Christ on the cross. Management of stress and the pressures of modern living may be relieved temporarily through drugs or transcendental meditation but, as the prophet Isaiah says, those who keep their minds focused on the living God will be kept in perfect peace (Isa. 26:3).

Fifthly, our knowledge of God affects *our prayer life*. Often people cannot understand why God appears not to answer their requests. Many Christians, it seems, do not understand God's ways because they do not know him very well or grasp the fact that he is doing an important work in their lives. We can trust his judgement in all things when we know that he is righteous and true in all his ways and that his wisdom is infinite.

Sixthly, our knowledge of God affects *missionary endeavour*. Many false notions of God exist; indeed, there are many false gods. There is a constant danger, on one hand, if we do not know the true and living God, that we ourselves will be deceived, enticed and led astray. Our unbelieving hearts are readily attracted to falsehood; any idea of a god who demands nothing and permits everything is appealing and convenient. We need to grow in our knowledge of God to avoid this danger. On the other hand, we need to know God in order to introduce him to others; we cannot represent him adequately if we simply have vague notions about him. Further, it is a very serious matter to misrepresent God or give a false impression of him. Matthew Henry says, 'Those who undertake to speak to others of the things of God must have an insight into those things themselves.'[2]

Finally, we need to know God *in order to stand firm in times of trouble*. During a brief period of ministry in Malaysia in 1996, my wife and I were privileged to stay with a beloved Chinese-

Malay pastor and his family in Kuala Lumpur. He had been educated in England as an electrical engineer and had, for a time, held an important position in a prestigious Malaysian university. His burden for the masses of people without Christ became so great, however, that, eventually, he resigned his position to preach the gospel and plant Christian churches. Although Malaysia ostensibly has freedom of religion, ten years before our visit, he was arrested and thrown into prison for almost one year for conducting a Bible study in his own home. As he shared with us something of the trials of imprisonment, the stress of frequent, intense interrogation and the discouragement of watching others renounce their faith, the only thing which sustained him, he said, was the conviction that God is sovereign and knows what he is doing. Like Job, he knew that God can be trusted even though he were to slay him (Job 13:15).

In speaking of the 'abomination of desolation' (a time of terrible trouble), the prophet Daniel stated the principle when he said, 'The people who know their God shall be strong, and carry out great exploits' (Dan. 11:32).

According to our host, the other pastors who renounced their faith under the pressure had been trained by evangelical missionaries who evidently had taught a somewhat superficial, program-oriented kind of religion which, unfortunately, has become characteristic of much of Western Christianity. Those pastors had memorized Scripture, learned certain clichés and had pat answers to theological questions. As they were to discover, however, it is not merely an acquaintance with the Word of God which sustains one in times of trial; it is, rather, the personal knowledge of the God of the Word. Our host withstood the test, not because he was stronger or wiser than others, but because he had prepared himself in the day of opportunity by getting to know God personally.

Now that Global Information Service (GIS) and Global Positioning Service (GPS) are operational, instantaneous worldwide communication is a reality; universal surveillance and control of the entire world is no longer an idle dream or a

remote possibility. This technology in the hands of people who
deny absolute truth — and, as a result, have no moral standards,
no sense of moral responsibility and no moral restraint — means
that almost anything is possible. Consequently, anyone who
teaches or promotes anything contrary to the idealism of the new
world order, towards which present world leaders aspire, will
inevitably face intense pressure and hostility. Those who teach
the biblical doctrine of God, proclaim the uniqueness and
exclusiveness of Jesus Christ, oppose wicked practices such as
abortion and homosexuality and speak of judgement to come
will not be tolerated; already they are seen as an impediment to
progress and will, no doubt, be subjected to increased scrutiny
and pressure. 'Christians who believe that the Word of God is
objectively true and who are trying to share the good news of
Christ with people whose eternal salvation they desperately care
about can expect not just disagreement but personal resentment
and hostility.'[3]

'Behold your God!'

By the eighth century B.C., the social, religious and moral
conditions in Israel were comparable to those in our day — the
differences are mostly superficial and incidental. The covenant
with Abraham had been forgotten, the law of Moses was ignored, materialism had overtaken morality and the idolatry and
immorality of Baal worship had replaced the worship of Jehovah. In other words, Israel had forgotten her calling and purpose, she had set her own standards and had adopted sensual
and false religion. Into that context, God called his servant, the
prophet Isaiah.

At the outset, God gave Isaiah a vision of his holiness and
glory (Isa. 6). That vision brought a real sense of sin in his own
life and of the true spiritual condition of the nation. Isaiah
needed to know God intimately before he could speak for God.
Some scholars insist that there were two Isaiahs (or more)

because although the prophet lived around the time of the Assyrian Captivity in 722 B.C., he mentions King Cyrus. Cyrus, the Mede, however, did not appear on the scene for another two centuries; he issued the decree allowing the Israelites to return from captivity in 536 B.C. Obviously, to have the prophet refer to a king *by name* two centuries before he appeared presents a problem for those who do not understand divine revelation or are ignorant of the message of the prophet. The message and integrity of the book of Isaiah rest on this prior revelation.

As I have said, Israel had embraced Canaanite idolatry and, even in Babylon, they were impressed, no doubt, with the ornate deities of the Babylonians. Two centuries before the Israelites were taken into captivity, Isaiah showed the worthlessness of idols of wood and stone (Isa. 44:9-17). To prove their worthlessness, Isaiah challenged the idols to foretell and declare what is to come to pass (Isa. 41:21-24). Throughout chapters 40-48, the prophet says repeatedly, 'To whom then will you liken God? Or what likeness will you compare to him?' (Isa. 40:19,25; 46:5). The God of Israel was, and is, incomparable. For one thing, he knows precisely what will happen two hundred years hence and, if he chooses to do so, can name and identify individuals who are yet to be born. (Some think that the message of Isaiah was instrumental in causing Israel to turn from idolatry and to regard it as abhorrent. When Cyrus appeared, the Israelites realized that Jehovah had already declared what had come to pass.)

While Isaiah was severe in his denunciation of the sins of the people, his book is full of promise and comfort. He looked to the coming of the Messiah, who would, in the fulness of time, be 'despised and rejected by men, a Man of sorrows and acquainted with grief', and would be 'wounded for our transgressions [and] bruised for our iniquities' (Isa. 53:3,5). That wonderful prospect was absolutely certain because God had declared it. The redemption of sinful people depended on the greatness, goodness and grace of God. In contrast to sinners who, like grass, wither and fade, 'the word of our God stands for ever' (Isa. 40:6-8). To appreciate and rejoice in redemption from sin, we must know the God who has planned, initiated and accomplished it. For that reason, Isaiah says:

> Lift up your voice with strength,
> Lift it up, be not afraid;
> Say unto the cities of Judah,
> 'Behold your God!'

> (Isa. 40:9).

Similarly, the crying need in the church in our times is for Christians to 'behold [their] God'. This work is written simply, but with a deep burden for those who profess to know God but who, through the influences and pressures of contemporary society, have allowed God to be 'edged out' of their lives and know very little of a personal relationship to him. My concern is that they need to get to know God in the day of opportunity before the day of adversity comes. While I have written for the person in the pew, I hope also that ministers will recognize the importance of this material and be encouraged to 'lift up [their] voices with strength' and declare, 'Behold your God!' to this generation. What I have written is but a survey; sufficient material is introduced in these pages to provide the basis for many years of preaching — every chapter could easily be developed into a profitable series of sermons. My use of the *Westminster Shorter Catechism* is due to the fact that I regard it as one of the most accurate statements of biblical doctrine ever devised. It was fashioned by church leaders from several denominations, who were summoned by the English Parliament on 1 July 1643 and continued to meet for several years. My indebtedness to Matthew Henry (1663?-1714) will be obvious; I make no apology for consulting one so eminent in the Scriptures. His commentary on the entire Bible has been recognized as a non-technical, yet accurate, laymen's commentary for many years. Unfortunately, his work has been largely neglected by Christian workers in recent years. (Incidentally, he began to read the Bible for himself at three years of age.) His comment is appropriate:

'What God is himself, that he will be to his people; his wisdom theirs, to guide and counsel them; his power theirs, to protect and support them; his goodness theirs, to supply and comfort them.'[4]

1.
God's own introduction to his Word

In the only course offered in Bible at the liberal denominational college in Australia where I began my theological training, our teacher told us that we should leave all our preconceived notions and prejudices aside and approach the Bible in a scholarly manner. To study it scientifically, we were informed, we should approach it like any other book. Being young and immature, none of us thought to ask what I now consider to be an obvious question: 'Like *what* other book?' There is a vast difference between books. One does not approach a dictionary in the same way as a novel, a commentary as a song book, or a telephone directory as a biography. How a book is approached depends, of course, on the nature of the book. The difference between the Bible and all other books is the same difference that exists between Jesus Christ and all other men. Because the Bible is unique among books, it must be approached differently than all other books. Our teacher told us that the events recorded in the early chapters of Genesis are actually myths which had been transmitted by oral tradition for centuries. As tribal fathers told the stories to their grandchildren around campfires, they naturally exaggerated and embellished them to captivate the interest of wide-eyed youngsters. Whether those events actually happened is not important, we were told; it is the message which matters. Further, since the early chapters of Genesis are merely a conglomerate of oral traditions, Moses, it was affirmed, could not have been the author. None of us realized that these un-founded assertions were neither scholarly nor scientific; they were nothing less than an attack on the integrity of the Word of God. We did not realize that the foundations of Christianity were being subtly eroded and undermined. Being immature and impressionable, most of the students, who had come from evangelical homes and churches, adopted the stance that since salvation is in the Gospels, the historicity or authenticity of Genesis was not crucial. We did not realize that 'if the founda-tions are destroyed', the entire structure collapses. Because the Lord Jesus believed in both the historicity of Genesis and the Mosaic authorship of the Pentateuch, both his veracity and his deity are at stake. If he was mistaken, our salvation is in serious trouble.

Every book worthy of the designation has an introduction in which the author states his reasons for writing and shows the importance of his subject. The Bible is no exception; Genesis 1 - 11 is God's own introduction to his Word. In his book, *Genesis in Space and Time,* Francis Schaeffer says, 'I wish to point out the tremendous value Genesis 1 - 11 has for modern man. In some ways these chapters are the most important ones in the Bible.'[1]

The purpose of an introduction is to introduce. God's introduction to his Word is especially important in an era when many professing Christians ignore the principal subject ad-dressed in these chapters and one in which the church, by and large, has forgotten the reason for its existence. These eleven chapters are unique; failure to grasp the point, or to understand the essential message, will inevitably result in the failure to appreciate fully the message in the rest of the Bible. In other words, this introduction reveals the magnitude of the problem; the solution is revealed from Genesis 12 to Revelation 22.

These eleven chapters span the period of world history from creation to the call of Abraham. While we do not know the date of creation, we know that Abraham lived around the year 2,000 B.C. Over 300 years ago, by assigning a certain number of years to each generation listed in Genesis, Bishop Ussher calculated the date of creation to be 4004 B.C. Undoubtedly, that is the most conservative (and precise!) date one is likely to encounter. Many evangelical scholars today allow greater flexibility and place the date of creation as far back as 10,000 B.C. or earlier. Actually, we do not know. If, for the sake of argument, Bishop Ussher's date is adopted, 2,000 years of human history at least are covered in this brief section of God's Word. That is a longer period than that covered from Genesis 12 through the writing of Revelation 22.

God's introduction is unique, not only in the expanse of time covered, but also in its content or message. Within these chapters, there are four major events — all of which are *universal* in significance and importance. By way of comparison, Genesis 12-50 cover only about two hundred years and focus on four individuals of *particular* importance in God's great plan of redemption. What are these events, and what is their significance?

The creation (Gen. 1-2)

These two chapters contain just fifty-six verses. Obviously, this is not an exhaustive account of creation. Had God chosen to tell us everything about creation, I dare say that the U.S. Library of Congress would look like the collection of books in a kindergarten in comparison. Although this is not an exhaustive account by any means, it is *accurate*. What God has recorded is not intended to satisfy the curiosity of sinful creatures, but to inform us of our origin. As we shall see in the next chapter, in his majestic work of creation, God called all things into being out of nothing by his powerful word. That is a simple statement, yet how Godlike it is! Because God created the world and all that it contains, everything has design, order and purpose. If the

message of the Bible is to be appreciated fully, we must understand that the universe, and all that it contains, has a meaningful
origin.

There was one exception to God's creative word. To create
man, God formed him from the dust of the earth — man is,
therefore, directly *identified with* the creation. Having fashioned
man from dust, God then 'breathed into his nostrils the breath
of life; and [he] became a living being' (Gen. 2:7). By this special
act of creation man was *set apart from* the creation. To appreciate
fully the message of the Bible, we must understand that man is
unique and wonderful; he has been made *by* God and *like* God.
Further, we have been made *for* God: 'Man's chief end is to
glorify God, and enjoy him for ever.'[2] Because man has been
made by a special creative act of God, he has a meaningful
origin, a purpose for his existence and a realistic destiny. In
contrast, the evolutionary hypothesis, which is held so ten-
aciously and taught so dogmatically in contemporary society,
affirms categorically that everything emerged from primordial
slime by a purely chance process. If that were our origin and if
everything were here by chance, a meaningful origin, an objective purpose and a hope for the future are nothing but wishful
thinking. Meaning for our existence cannot be found in a
process of chance; it is impossible. The theory of evolution
destroys the possibility of a meaningful origin and a purposeful
existence. Though somewhat trite, the following little poem
expresses the absurdity of evolution:

> First, he was a tadpole, beginning to begin;
> Then, he was a frog with his tail tucked in.
> Next, he was a monkey in a banyan tree;
> Now, he is a doctor with a Ph.D.

To appreciate fully what God says in his Word, we must
begin with a biblical view of man; we must understand the truth
and implications of these three foundational facts:

- Man is made *by* God — he is wonderful; he is a special creation.
- Man is made *like* God — he is unique within the creation.
- Man is made *for* God — he is made for a wonderful purpose.

The fall of man (Gen. 3-4)

The entry of sin into the human race was achieved through the subtle temptation of 'that serpent of old, called the Devil' (Rev. 12:9). Satan approached Eve with the most insidious attack upon the being and character of God. He implied that God has ulterior and perverse motives in his dealings with men. He succeeded in his temptation and seduced Eve to partake of the forbidden fruit. Eve saw that the tree was:

- 'good for food' — it promised to meet man's *physical* needs;
- 'pleasant to the eyes' — it promised to meet the *aesthetic* needs;
- 'desirable to make one wise' — it promised to meet the *intellectual* needs (Gen. 3:6).

Our first parents imagined that they could be totally independent of God — and, if independent, they would be free to set their own moral standards and do as they pleased. The magnitude and enormity of Adam's disobedience towards God can be understood only in the light of creation. In other words, if the seriousness of the Fall is to be comprehended, man's uniqueness, as a being made in the image of God, must be understood. That is, to appreciate how far, or how *low*, man has fallen, one must first appreciate how *high* he was created. The enormity of the sin problem can be comprehended only when one realizes who it was that rebelled against his Maker. I believe that it was Charles Bridges who said, '[Man's] original dignity only serves to set out more vividly his present degradation.'

Adam stood at the head of the human race; he acted as our representative. By his disobedience to, and transgression of, the law of God, he incurred guilt, not only for himself, but for all his posterity. 'Through one man sin entered the world' (Rom. 5:12). The catechism says, 'The covenant being made with Adam [i.e., the covenant of life conditioned on perfect obedience], not only for himself, but for his posterity; all mankind, descending from him by ordinary generation, sinned in him, and fell with him, in his first transgression.'[3]

The consequences of sin are great. To begin with, human nature became corrupt and totally depraved. All men are sinners, not simply because we commit sinful acts, but because we are sinners by nature! We enter this world with the innate and vain notion that we are gods in complete control of our lives and that nothing matters other than our personal satisfaction. Sinful man sees himself as self-sufficient, self-determining and essentially good. Unacceptable behaviour is attributed to one's environment, some form of chemical imbalance, or low self-esteem. Violence, we are told, is merely a vestige of man's animal instincts. The sinfulness of man is expressed in his ingenuity and ability to avoid, excuse, minimize, rationalize and justify sin.

Many differences have arisen within the church because not all theologians have been prepared to admit or acknowledge the seriousness of the sin problem. Some even refuse to mention it in case it adversely affects the 'self-esteem' of people. Matthew Henry summarizes our condition when he says, 'In eating forbidden fruit, we have offended a great and gracious God, broken a just and righteous law, violated a sacred and most solemn covenant, and wronged our own precious souls by forfeiting God's favour and exposing ourselves to his wrath and curse; in enticing others to eat of it, we do the devil's work, make ourselves guilty of other men's sins, and accessory to their ruin.'[4]

In the introduction to his Word, God reveals the historical details of the *entry of sin* into the human race. Because we, as sinners, possess a corrupt nature, we transgress the law of God continually. Significantly, the account of the Fall is immediately followed by the record of Cain's heinous crime of murdering his brother Abel. In other words, chapters 3 and 4 belong together. Chapter 3 records the *entry* of sin into the human race and chapter 4 shows *the immediate consequences* of sin towards God and towards man. Cain did not take sin seriously. He thought that he could approach God on his own terms and ignore the instructions which God had evidently given. One would have thought that, when his offering was rejected by God, he would have sought the advice and help of his brother. But such is the nature of sin; instead of acknowledging his transgression, Cain reacted in anger and violence towards his brother. He broke the first and great commandment to 'love the LORD [his] God with all [his] heart, soul, and mind' and the second commandment, which is like it, to 'love [his] neighbour as [himself]' (Matt. 22:37,39). There are many aspects to Cain's sin; it was no single, simple act but a complex of attitudes and actions which increasingly compounded the problem. His sin began with an arrogant disregard for God and his Word; he acted as a 'god' determining his own approach to God. This was expressed in the following ways:

- Anger towards God and jealousy towards Abel. It is strange, is it not, how sin reacts towards the righteous and innocent?
- The text seems to imply that Cain enticed his brother into the field in order to murder him. By smooth, treacherous words, he led his brother to the place of his death.
- The sin of murder. Significantly, the first recorded expression of man's fallen nature was an attack on one who was made in the image of God (see Gen. 9:5-6).

- When God challenged Cain concerning the where-
abouts of Abel, he lied. He declared, 'I do not know'
(Gen. 4:9).

- Cain charged God with injustice by calling him to responsibility; he asked, 'Am I my brother's keeper?' (Gen.
4:9). He was the elder brother; he should have loved his
younger brother and protected him.

- When God pronounced judgement on Cain, the latter
was far more concerned about his punishment than about
the heinousness of his sin.

- Cain tried to solve his sin problem by further acts of
sin. He added sin to sin: 'He willingly renounced God
and religion, and was content to forego its privileges, so
that he might not be under its precepts. He forsook
Adam's family and altar, and cast off all pretensions to the
fear of God, and never came among good people, nor
attended on God's ordinances any more. Hypocritical
professors, that have dissembled and trifled with God
Almighty, are justly left to themselves.'[5]

So great was Cain's transgression that he is cited in the
Epistle of Jude as one of the primary examples of an apostate in
all history (Jude 11). He was, as the apostle John says, 'of the
wicked one' (1 John 3:12).

A genealogy (Gen. 5)

This is one of those passages which everyone loves to read! Why
did God place a genealogy in his introduction to his Word?
Certainly, he is not like a high-school student looking for 'filler
material'! Nor did he record this information to make the
reading of his Word boring or difficult. This chapter is very
important. First, it shows that the events recorded in these
chapters are not mythological; they concern real people who

actually lived in history. Some scholars claim that Adam was not a historical person; the name 'Adam', they say, is a generic term for the human race. That position is rather difficult to maintain if one reads the first five verses of chapter 5. (It is, nevertheless, the position espoused in the new *Catholic Catechism*.[6]) Further, this genealogy provides the important connecting link between events. As we have seen, a long period of time is covered in these chapters; God wants us to know that the events recorded in them were not isolated, but are related to, and connected by, real people. The historicity of these early chapters is exceedingly important. The reality of wickedness and violence in the world today demands an explanation; if such things exist, when, where and how did they originate?

The importance of this genealogy is seen in the message it contains. Several years ago, I read of a Christian man who invited his non-Christian neighbour to church; to his delight, the neighbour accepted. The Christian phoned his pastor to inform him that his friend would be coming to church the following Sunday. When they arrived at church everything went well; the people were friendly, the singing was enthusiastic and the prayers were brief. The Christian felt sure that his neighbour would be impressed. When the pastor announced the Scripture reading, however, his attitude changed dramatically. The pastor began, 'Our Scripture reading tonight is Genesis 5. So-and-so begat so-and-so and so-and-so begat so-and so, etc.' The Christian grew quite angry with the pastor, thinking to himself, 'The pastor knew that I was bringing my unsaved neighbour and he has to pick a passage of Scripture like that! My friend will think that we are all mad.' While he was inwardly angry, his friend listened and was wonderfully converted. Throughout the chapter, a little three-word phrase recurs repeatedly. After the summary of each individual's life, we are told, '... and he died.' The repetition of that phrase impressed itself on the unsaved man's mind; he realized that death is a reality and that he had better get right with God before he was called to give an account of his life. While Genesis 4 shows the *immediate* consequences of sin towards God and man, chapter 5 shows that those consequences *continue* throughout all generations. 'It is appointed for men to die' (Heb. 9:27). 'The wages of sin is death' (Rom. 6:23).

Noah and the Flood (Genesis 6-9)

Of the eleven chapters in God's introduction to his Word, four are devoted to the Flood. That suggests something of its tremendous importance. I confess that when I hear children being taught light-hearted songs about Noah and the Flood, it troubles me. This event has not been recorded as the basis for fun songs or as a children's bedtime story. In its ignorance, the world mocks Noah and treats the Flood as a joke, but Christians ought to take it very seriously. There are, incidentally, two Old Testament events which the world ridicules more than others — Noah and the Flood and Jonah and the fish. Significantly, the Lord Jesus identified himself with both events: he related Jonah to his resurrection and Noah to his Second Coming.

At the outset, God describes the conditions in the world which prompted him to act in judgement; we are told, 'The LORD saw that the *wickedness* of man was great in the earth, and that every intent of the thoughts of his heart was only evil continually' (Gen. 6:5, emphasis mine). A few verses later we read, 'The earth also was corrupt before God, and the earth was filled with *violence*. So God looked upon the earth, and indeed it was corrupt; for all flesh had corrupted their way on the earth' (Gen. 6:11-12, emphasis mine).

The world was characterized by both 'wickedness' and 'violence'. Wickedness concerns man's relationship to God; violence concerns his relationship to his fellow man. Again, the two basic commandments on which hang all the law of God were being broken. The extent of the wickedness, violence and corruption is expressed in the use of the words, 'every', 'great', 'continually' (v. 5), 'filled' (v. 11) and 'all' (v. 12). Corruption had not only affected *all* the earth, it affected the *whole* man: '...

every intent of the thoughts of his heart was only evil continually'
(Gen. 6:5). Men had excluded God from their thinking and
were expressing their wickedness, violence and corruption
openly and freely.

In giving us the account of the Flood, God has revealed the
extent of sin; it has infected the *whole man* and the *whole race.*
This description sounds all too contemporary; the fact that Jesus
declared that 'As the days of Noah were, so also will the coming
of the Son of Man be' (Matt. 24:36-39) suggests that the return
of our Lord might be closer than some realize. This event
reveals, not only the extent of human sin and corruption, but
also the sobering fact that sin comes under the judgement of
God; it shows *the ultimate consequences* of sin.

Although God was grieved over the corruption and depravity
of men, he did not send judgement immediately. God never acts
hastily or impulsively. In his mercy, he spared the world for
another 120 years while Noah built the ark. Noah, we are told,
was 'a preacher of righteousness' (2 Peter 2:5); the construction
of the ark was, in itself, a constant reminder of impending
judgement. Eventually, God was true to his Word; he kept his
covenant with Noah and he sent judgement on the wicked. God
always keeps his promises and his threats.

Some time during the nineteenth century, an atheist was
travelling around the United States giving popular lectures on
atheism. On one occasion, when he had his audience 'fighting
mad', he held up his pocket watch and exclaimed, 'If there is a
God, I defy him to strike me dead in sixty seconds.' After the
blasphemous things he had uttered, the audience sat tensely
expecting a bolt of lightning, or something equally dramatic, to
strike him on the spot. Each second seemed like an age; finally,
the minute expired and nothing had happened. He exclaimed
jubilantly, 'There you are: there is no God! He did not meet my
challenge.' In his next editorial, the editor of the local newspaper
wisely pointed out that God does not always settle his debts on
13 October 1834 (or whatever the date actually was). Though
men transgress the law of God, challenge and defy him, live in

wickedness, violence and corruption, and appear to get away
with it, it must never be forgotten that a day is coming when
God will settle his debts with exact justice. 'It is appointed for
men to die once, but after this the judgement' (Heb. 9:27). On
that day, God will not overlook or forget any sin which has not
been acknowledged, confessed and forsaken; indeed, men will
be held accountable for every idle word which has been uttered.
All sin is exceedingly serious and its consequences are great; it
comes under God's condemnation and judgement. The latter
end of the wicked is not to be envied, no matter what their
material prosperity or circumstances might be in this life (see Ps.
73).

The Table of Nations (Gen. 10)

This table serves as another important connecting link between
the events recorded in these chapters and, as with many of the
genealogical records of Scripture, is particularly important
concerning the Messianic line. In this table, many of the names
end in '-im' — that is the Hebrew plural and suggests that families
or groups of people are listed rather than individuals. (For this
reason, the period of time covered in these chapters might be
greater than Bishop Ussher calculated.) The emphasis here is on
nations: 'These were the sons of Shem, according to their
families, according to their *languages*, in their *lands*, according to
their *nations*' (Gen. 10:31, emphasis mine; see also vv. 5,20).

Of particular interest is the mention of Nimrod, who 'began
to be a mighty one on the earth' (Gen. 10:8). 'The beginning of
his kingdom,' we are told, 'was Babel [or Babylon]' (Gen.
10:10). That comment is important in that it introduces us to
the fourth major event in these chapters.

The Tower of Babel (Gen. 11:1-9)

In contrast to the amount of space given to the record of the
Flood, the account of the building of the Tower of Babel occupies only nine verses. From all the events which must have
occurred during those centuries, why did God include this one?
What was so important or significant about a building project
that God would record it for time and eternity? The building of
the tower was not the idea of a shrewd property developer, town
planner, or investor. The kingdom of Babylon, to which we are
introduced here, is most significant in that it appears throughout
the pages of Scripture, right through to the book of Revelation.

At the creation, God told Adam to 'be fruitful and multiply;
[and] fill the earth' (Gen. 1:28). To accomplish that objective,
people needed to scatter, rather than consolidate and settle in
one location. A primary objective in building the Tower of Babel
was to avoid being 'scattered abroad over the face of the whole
earth' (Gen. 11:4). The objective at Babel was to unify all men by
engaging them in a common project — one which was completely and diametrically opposed to the purpose of God and to
the fulfilment of his plan. If all people could be united in this
way, that generation would have been known as the generation
that solved the problem of sin without the help of God. The
concept is seriously flawed in that it reduces sin to external
circumstances or conditions. It implies also that sinful men are
able to save themselves by their own wisdom and effort. 'There
is a way that seems right to a man, but its end is the way of
death' (Prov. 14:12).

The kingdom of Babylon stands in stark contrast and in
direct opposition to the kingdom of God. All that Babylon
represented was epitomized in King Nebuchadnezzar, who,
centuries later, declared, 'I am, and there is no one else besides
me' (Isa. 47:8). Only the living God, the Maker of heaven and
earth, can make that statement truthfully — as the prophet Isaiah
shows so clearly! Nebuchadnezzar was so controlled by, and
identified with, Satan that Bible scholars have debated whether

Isaiah 14 was addressed to him or Satan. Since Satan motivated Nebuchadnezzar, probably both are in view. Sinful man is not ashamed or embarrassed to express his defiance of the living God.

The secular humanists of our day do not talk about building a city, but they are most anxious to reconstruct society, and the objective is to unify all people and bring in a new world order.[7] Even the pope, according to Malachi Martin, is uniquely and eminently qualified to lead the new world order.[8] The answer to all the ills of mankind, according to modern leaders, lies in the destruction of social evils through equality, unity and tolerance. The generation which achieves this ideal and unifies all people as the global family will make a name for itself. Actually, this modern solution is exactly the same strategy as that proposed at the Tower of Babel. The Tower of Babel is *man's solution* to his sin problem. God has recorded this event to inform us that a diverse ideology exists which seeks to solve the sin problem without reference to, or dependence on, God. Just nine verses are devoted to this event; that is all the space it merits! At the risk of being repetitious, let me say it again: if we fail to understand the importance and significance of this event, we shall not appreciate fully what God has said in his Word and what he has done for us in the person of his Son, Jesus Christ.

So then, in God's introduction to his Word, he has revealed:

- *The uniqueness of man.* He is made *by* God, *like* God and *for* God (Gen. 1–2).
- *The entry of sin* into the human race *and its immediate consequences* towards God and man (Gen. 3–4).
- *The continuing consequences of sin.* 'The wages of sin is death' (Gen. 5).
- *The extent of sin and the ultimate consequences.* Sin comes under the judgement of God (Gen. 6–9).
- *Man's solution* to his sin problem (Gen. 11:1-9).

God has shown us the nature, magnitude and consequences of the sin problem so that we might realize our desperate need of him.

Another genealogy (Gen. 11:10-26)

Besides providing another important connecting link between events, this genealogy introduces Abraham, the man whom God called from Ur of the Chaldees — which, significantly, is the region of Babel. God, in his mercy and grace, called a man 'out of [the kingdom of] darkness and into his marvellous [kingdom of] light' (1 Peter 2:9). When God took the initiative and approached Abraham to make his covenant with him, essentially he was saying, 'I have shown you the problem; now I will reveal my solution to you.' The problem of sin and its awful consequences must be understood before the gospel has any meaning or relevance. Those ministers who avoid referring to sin because it might be offensive and turn people away from the church are unfaithful to their calling; they have no good news to offer. It is no act of mercy or kindness to ignore the problem and thereby jeopardize the souls of sinners. God could have left us all to wallow in our sin and misery, or cast us all aside without any hope of eternal life. Instead, because he is a God of great compassion, abundant in mercy and plenteous in grace, he revealed the problem clearly and he has shown us the awful consequences of our sin. He has not merely stated the problem, of course; he has planned, initiated and executed a wonderful plan of redemption in which sinners, in spite of their corruption, rebellion and disobedience, are delivered from the penalty and power of sin — and, one day, will be delivered from its presence! When the problem of sin is understood, the greatness, goodness and grace of God are magnified. The realization of what God has done in Christ in redeeming his people should cause us to be 'lost in wonder, love, and praise'.[9]

God's solution to man's sin problem

When God declared to Abraham, 'I will make you a great nation
... and in you all the families of the earth shall be blessed' (Gen.
12:1-3), he began to unfold his great plan of redemption for
sinful men (although it was in effect long before that!). The
apostle Paul tells us that when God made that promise to
Abraham, he 'preached the gospel' to the patriarch (Gal. 3:8).
And, lest there be any misunderstanding, he quotes the promise.
What does Paul mean by 'the gospel'? In his first letter to the
Corinthians, he says that the gospel consists of the death, burial
and resurrection of Jesus Christ according to the Scriptures
(1 Cor. 15:3-4). Are we to conclude, then, that God told Abraham about the death of Jesus Christ?

As Abraham journeyed up Mt Moriah with his only son,
Isaac, obviously he knew the importance of obedience and
sacrifice. When he declared that 'God will provide for himself
the lamb' (Gen. 22:8), was he not looking in faith to 'the Lamb
of God who takes away the sin of the world'? (John 1:29).
Abraham understood that a substitutionary sacrifice for the
atonement of sin had to be made if sinful men are to stand in
the presence of God. Since the gospel consists also of the
resurrection of Jesus Christ from the dead, did Abraham know
about that? The author of Hebrews says that Abraham believed
that God would raise Isaac from the dead (Heb. 11:17-19);
where did he get that idea unless God revealed it to him? It is
clear that Abraham knew the gospel. Jesus himself said to the
Jews, 'Abraham rejoiced to see my day, and he saw it and was
glad' (John 8:56).

God promised Abraham that all the families of the earth
would be blessed in him. Several times in the book of Revelation, a great multitude from every tribe, nation, kindred and
tongue are seen gathered around the throne of God worshipping
the Lord Jesus, the Lamb slain for sinners (Rev. 5:9; 7:9). In
other words, what God promised Abraham in Genesis, he fulfils
in Revelation. When history reaches its culmination, God will

have accomplished exactly what he planned. What sinful man could never achieve through his wisdom and effort, God has accomplished through his Son. God's solution to the sin problem was, and is, to send his only Son into this world to '[bear] our sins in his own body on the tree' (1 Peter 2:24).

'Oh, the depth of the riches both of the wisdom and knowledge of God!' (Rom. 11:33).

Part I
Genesis — The sovereignty of God

2.
The sovereignty of God in his work of creation

While I was a student at Moody Bible Institute, I was privileged to teach a Bible class for schoolchildren on the south side of Chicago. One day, one of my twelve-year-old girls asked, 'Mr Roberts, which is more important, the book of Genesis or the Gospel of John?' In those days I knew all the answers, so, without hesitation, I replied, 'The Gospel of John.' She lit up with that victorious look which students get when they outwit their teachers and she said, in essence, 'How can we understand the meaning of re-creation if we do not know about creation?' I knew that I was in trouble. I have since learned that the truth concerning *creation* must be established and understood before *re-creation* has any real meaning. The facts of *generation* must be known before one can talk about *regeneration*.

Subsequently, during my student days, I was privileged to meet Joy Ridderhoff, the lady who established the mission organization, Gospel Recordings, Inc. She and her colleagues developed special techniques for recording gospel messages in unwritten languages. The messages were recorded on simple discs to be played on manually operated record players. Native tribespeople could sit all day cranking the handle and listening over and over to the message of truth. Miss Ridderhoff explained that when missionaries prepared recordings for an unreached tribe, they began with simple biblical teaching concerning creation. She and her colleagues understood that the doctrine of creation is an essential platform for the gospel.

More recently, I had lunch with the director of another missionary agency. His mission, having been built initially on Dispensational theology, had set aside the Old Testament as non-essential and unnecessary. Their missionaries were sent out simply 'to preach the gospel'. He told me that his mission had learned that the minds of primitive people could not be penetrated with the gospel and they could not be persuaded concerning the Lord Jesus Christ until they had first been taught the biblical doctrine of creation.

Several years ago, my wife assisted a team of missionaries in Japan for a few weeks. They were using opportunities for teaching English as a means to reach people for Christ. Part of each two-hour teaching session was devoted to studying the English Bible. At the time of our visit, the classes were studying the miracles of Jesus. At an appropriate time, I asked the missionaries why they were teaching the miracles. There is a place for that subject, of course, but I doubt that it is the starting point for reaching the lost — after all, most religions claim miracles of some kind. Though miracles might be impressive and evoke wonder, they do not generate true faith. As the apostle John says, 'Many believed in his name when they saw the signs which he did. But Jesus did not commit himself to them, because ... he knew what was in man' (John 2:23-25). The God of Christianity is unique; he bears an important relationship to all his creatures because he made them. The missionary responsibility is to teach people how they relate to him and what must be done for them to be reconciled to him. The biblical truth concerning God as Creator is the starting point for our understanding of just about everything.

The importance of origins

The question of origins is exceedingly important because, as we shall see, a meaningful and purposeful existence depends upon a meaningful origin. The question of origins, however, is one which many people prefer to avoid. Yet at every turn of their existence they are confronted with the existence of their Maker and their responsibility to him. To acknowledge God as Creator carries obligations which we, as sinners, prefer to avoid. So then, either God must be acknowledged as Creator, or an alternative explanation for our existence must be found. Because no alternative explanation is satisfactory, men have attempted to bury this fundamental question in the obscure and hazy mists of time. One subjective, pragmatic reason why evolutionists postulate billions of years for the age of the universe is ultimately to avoid the question of origins. If our origin can be made so remote that it goes unnoticed, responsibility towards our Maker can be ignored. But the question of our origin is one that will not go away. No matter how many billions of years are postulated, the question persists — how did it all begin?

In the issue of *Time* magazine published on 6 March 1995, the cover story was entitled, 'When did the universe begin?' In the article, astrophysicist Michael Turner said, 'Either we are close to a breakthrough, or we're at our wits' end.' A few years later, on 20 July 1998, *US News & World Report* carried a cover story entitled, 'What came before creation?' It states, 'While thinkers have often engaged the question of whether the cosmos is newly formed or unfathomably old, few have speculated on the head-spinning topic of what might have come before creation... Just as clergy may prefer to sidestep the issue of what caused God, the issue of what caused the universe has often been one the science world would rather skip.'

The article describes theories based on assumptions, supposition and speculation. It is stated, for example, that 'Today, mainstream researchers increasingly embrace the idea of a multiverse, in part because it might explain the life-favouring

features of the cosmos without reference either to the supernatural or to incredible chains of luck. The problem with
multiverse thinking is that so far there is no evidence other
universes or dimensions exist. Attributing the virtues of this
cosmos to unseen other universes is a little like attributing the
virtues of existence to God – in either case you might be right,
but you're assuming an article of faith.'

Obviously, science has not said the final word! The article
reveals something of the lengths to which people go to avoid the
issue. The problem is, however, that modern man begins with
'nothing-something', as Francis Schaeffer used to call it. That is,
modern man begins with that nebulous, indescribable, non-
substance substance referred to as 'primordial slime'.

Dr J. Oliver Buswell, Jr. used to point out to his students, of
whom I was privileged to be one, that only two alternatives
concerning the question of origins are possible: *either something
comes from nothing, or something is eternal.* In spite of concerted
efforts to do so, no one has yet produced any evidence to show
that something comes from nothing. To the contrary, science
has categorically affirmed that matter can neither be created nor
destroyed – though some scientists these days, it seems, are
trying to prove that something does come from nothing. The
only realistic alternative is that something is eternal.

Bertrand Russell, who was not noted for Christian piety, tried
to show the fallacy of believing in the existence of God by
declaring, 'If everything must have a cause, then God must have
a cause.' There is no problem with his logic; the problem lies
with his major premise. Is it necessary that everything, without
any exception whatsoever, must have a cause? Ironically, Russell
shoots himself in the foot, as it were, when he says in the same
paragraph that 'There is no reason why the world could not have
come into being without a cause.'[1] In refuting Russell's argument, Dr Sproul points out that 'If something may be self-
existent, then something may exist without a cause.'[2] If something may exist without a cause, surely it makes much more
sense to believe in an intelligent, wise, powerful and moral being

than in a non-intelligent force or glob of matter! Something is
eternal, and that something is the living God — the Maker of
heaven and earth. That is not a supposition based on speculation, but a conviction based on revelation. God, who created
all things, has revealed how it all began.

The opening verse of the Bible

Dwight L. Moody said, 'I do not know anything more difficult to
believe than just the first verse of the Bible. If we master this
verse, anything else that happened in the heavens or in the earth
which God created will not stumble us.'[3] Moody was not a
theologian in the formal sense, but what insight! He understood
the importance of this opening declaration of Scripture. The
Bible opens without apology; the first verse declares that 'In the
beginning God created the heavens and the earth.' Those ten
words (only seven in Hebrew, which incidentally, occupy less
than a single line in my Hebrew Bible, eight in Portuguese and
nine in Japanese) contain foundational facts of tremendous
importance. The first verse of the Bible reveals:

- *The starting point* — 'In the beginning'. There was a
point in time when this world and all that it contains
began.
- *The ultimate reality* — 'God'. He is the eternal being to
whom all things owe their being and existence.
- *The origin* — 'created'. Since God created it, the universe has purpose and meaning.
- *The phenomenal universe* — 'the heavens and the earth'.
The universe is not an illusion but a reality. The universe
exists because God created it.

At the same time, this simple statement denies all the major
false philosophies of men; it excludes:

- *Atheism* (the claim that there is no God). At the outset, God declares his existence without apology.
- *Polytheism* (the notion that there are many gods). This verse affirms the fact that there is only one God.
- *Pantheism* (the concept that everything is God and God is everything). The God of Genesis 1 is distinct and separate from his creation.
- *Agnosticism* (the idea that God is unknown and unknowable). In the creation, God's eternal power and deity are clearly seen so that all men are without excuse (Rom. 1:20).
- *Materialism* (the belief that matter is all that matters). This verse shows that matter is not self-sufficient; behind the creation, there is a Creator.
- *Humanism* (the notion that man is completely autonomous, independent and self-sufficient). This verse implies that man is dependent upon his Maker.
- *Evolution* (the theory that everything is the result of a chance process).

The nature of God

How remarkable that God, in one simple statement, can dismiss so many false ideas! *Who* and *what* is this God who has created all things? In the introduction to my book, *Let Us Make Man*,[4] I recounted the occasion when some students in a senior class in theology took the liberty to change an examination question from '*What* is God?' to '*Who* is God?' Later, I explained to them that there is a big difference between those two questions. If I ask a person *who* he is, I expect him to tell me his name. If, on the other hand, I ask him *what* he is, I expect him to tell me that he is a human being or, depending on the context, to state his profession, his citizenship, or his relationship. Most professing Christians know the name of God, but many, it seems, do not know *what* they profess to love and serve. It is, incidentally, an interesting question to ask of Jehovah's Witnesses; they claim to know the name of God but they do not know *what* God is!

What God is is revealed in his names and works. In biblical times, names had meaning and significance; they were an expression of character and/or characteristics. The name for God in Genesis 1:1 is *'Elohim'* — a name which appears thirty-five times in the creation account. (In chapter 1, it is used in every verse except verse 5.) This is not the only name by which God has revealed himself, of course. Entire books have been written on God's proper names (Elohim, Jehovah, El Shaddai, and others), his compound names (Jehovah-Jireh, Jehovah-Nissi, etc.), and his metaphorical names (Rock, Shepherd, Fortress, etc.). All these names are significant because they express different aspects of *what* God is and does; they are not the personal preferences of different authors — as liberal scholars would have us believe. Because God is infinitely great, no single name by itself can express or convey all that needs to be known about him. At the outset of God's special revelation, the name *'Elohim'* is used; it is a name which conveys the idea of power or might. An accurate concept of God begins with the knowledge and realization that God is almighty; he is infinitely great. He is big enough and powerful enough to create all things. God is *sovereign in his work of creation.*

On occasions, a naïve notion has emerged in which God has been depicted as having been lonely in eternity past; he created man, therefore, so the argument goes, to meet his need for fellowship and love. Aristotle, the ancient Greek philosopher, although a pagan, had greater insight; he recognized that if there were only an individual deity, the moment he created, he would have had a new experience — and could not, therefore, be eternally self-existent or self-sufficient. Without the information of God's Word, Aristotle had no answer. God has revealed himself, however, as triune: 'There are three persons in the Godhead, the Father, the Son and the Holy Spirit; these three are one God, the same in substance, equal in power and glory.'[5]

Because there are three persons in the Godhead, every possible relationship was known, experienced and enjoyed within the Godhead before creation. Because there are three persons in the Godhead, perfect fellowship, communion and love are a reality. God was, and still is, eternally self-sufficient. The creation of man, or anything else, was not necessary to meet any supposed need of God. He was, is, and always will be, 'infinite, eternal, and unchangeable in his being'. God is infinitely great. He is *Elohim* — the almighty Creator! Significantly, in other passages of Scripture, we learn that each of the persons in the Godhead had a distinct role in creation. Creation is attributed to the Godhead absolutely (Gen. 1:1,26), to the Father (1 Cor. 8:6), to the Son (John 1:3; Col. 1:16-17) and to the Holy Spirit (Gen. 1:2; Job 26:13; Ps.104:30).

When the Westminster divines framed the *Shorter Catechism*, they made a tremendous statement concerning God. (I shall refer to it frequently throughout this work). They stated that 'God is a Spirit, infinite, eternal, and unchangeable, in his being, wisdom, power, holiness, justice, goodness, and truth.'[6]

Consider the implications.

God's wisdom

Because God is 'infinite, eternal, and unchangeable in his ... wisdom', he has a great comprehensive plan which encompasses all things; he has overlooked no possibility, implication, or consequence. He knows all things comprehensively and exhaustively. He never needs to change his mind or alter his plan; if he were to do so, he would reveal that he is not infinite in wisdom.

God's power

God is 'infinite, eternal, and unchangeable in his ... power'. Whatever God plans, he is able to perform. Nothing can stop him from accomplishing his perfect plan.

God's moral attributes

God is also 'infinite, eternal, and unchangeable' in his moral attributes. All God's works are good because he is good; as the psalmist says, 'The LORD is righteous in all his ways' (Ps. 145:17). At the completion of the work of creation, God declared, 'It [is] very good' (Gen. 1:31). God does what is right because he is a moral God, perfect in himself and perfect in what he does. At the outset, it is important to understand that behind the creation there is a Creator who is:

- *wise* enough to plan all things;
- *powerful* enough to accomplish what he has planned;
- *righteous* enough to do everything properly.

When God created the world and all that it contains, he was not under any compulsion, coercion, or constraint. He created freely of his own will. As the eternally self-existent God, he was not playing or experimenting; he had a wonderful purpose and plan in view. God created because he willed to do so. The apostle John says, 'You are worthy, O LORD, to receive glory and honour and power; for you created all things, and *by your will* they exist, and were created' (Rev. 4:11, emphasis mine).

What is the work of creation?

'The work of creation is, God's making all things of nothing, by the word of his power, in the space of six days, and all very good.'[7] Consider this definition briefly.

'God made all things of nothing'

Throughout the creation account we are told that 'God said, "Let there be ..."; and it was so.' God called the creation into existence by his powerful word. There was, of course, one exception: 'The LORD God formed man of the dust of the ground, and breathed into his nostrils the breath of life; and man became a living being' (Gen. 2:7). By a very special act of creation, God made man in his own image. Critics have dismissed the biblical account of creation as unscientific mythology. To be sure, the account is quite simple, but how Godlike it is! In spite of all the learned attempts to explain the origin and meaning of the universe, no one has improved on God's own account, or offered a better explanation. God made all things out of nothing.

'By the word of his power'

The book of Hebrews says, 'By faith we understand that the worlds were framed by the word of God' (Heb. 11:3). The psalmist declares, God 'spoke, and it was done; he commanded, and it stood fast' (Ps. 33:9). When God speaks, his word is powerful; it accomplishes his purpose. Did not God himself say through his prophet, 'My word ... that goes forth from my mouth ... shall not return to me void, but it shall accomplish what I please, and it shall prosper in the thing for which I sent it'? (Isa. 55:11). God has spoken, not only to create; he speaks to redeem. He calls to life and liberty those whose lives are 'waste and void' and who are 'dead in trespasses and sins' (Eph. 2:1). The gospel 'is the power of God to salvation for everyone who believes' (Rom. 1:16). It must never be forgotten, however, that to create God simply spoke; to redeem, he sent his Son to die.

'In the space of six days'

Ever since the emergence of Darwin's theory of evolution, the question of the length of the days of creation has been argued passionately — often with more heat than light! Some take Peter's statement out of context to prove that one day with the Lord is as a thousand years (2 Peter 3:8). Having considered most of the arguments, I see sufficient reasons for literal days and no compelling reason for long periods of time — though I have many brethren whom I respect who believe otherwise. Actually, the length of the days is not really the primary issue; rather, it is the question of origins. If God is able to create, he can do it immediately.

'And all very good'

All of God's works are good; they are good in the moral sense and they are good because they are orderly, beneficial and beautiful. One of the most impressive testimonies to God's existence and power is the order and beauty of his creation. There is order, of course, in the progression of creation. Several years ago, at a student conference in Adelaide, a science student expressed her excitement to me when she discovered that the order of the creation in Genesis parallels the order of the so-called evolutionary process. It is truly amazing how a chance or random process can do things orderly and systematically! If everything originated by random selection and chance, we might expect to find living organisms emerge before there was food to feed them! While the evolutionary theory is based on chance, it cannot avoid orderly, sensible progression.

While I am not widely read in the theory of evolution, I have searched in vain for any explanation for the origin of the sexes. If there is one thing which defies the theory of evolution, surely it is the existence of the sexes. For the survival of each species, both sexes had to emerge immediately, simultaneously and fully mature. The existence of the sexes does not allow for long periods of development or intermediate stages; most species would be extinct if sexual maturity took more than a decade. The biblical explanation is much more realistic: God made the creatures male and female and they reproduced 'after their kind'.

Why the doctrine of creation is important

What is the importance of the biblical doctrine of creation and what are the implications for our lives? For life to be meaningful, two reference points are essential.

A meaningful origin

There must be, first of all, a meaningful origin. As creatures made in the image of God, we search for meaning because we know intuitively that we were made for a purpose. It is absurd, of course, to think that there can be meaning to our existence if we emerged from primordial slime by chance. No matter how clever the arguments, or how intense the search, meaning cannot be found in chance. When God created the universe, he was not playing, experimenting, or deciding what to do as he proceeded; God is never haphazard, disorderly, or aimless. When he created, he had a wonderful purpose in view. The biblical doctrine of creation provides the only adequate basis for a purposeful and meaningful origin.

Since God created all things, the whole creation owes its origin, its existence, its form and its substance to God. All creatures, not the least of which is man, are completely dependent upon the Creator. Having been made in God's image to exercise dominion over the creation, man is, of course, uniquely responsible to his Maker. The reality of sin in the human race presents a serious predicament, however; sinful man does not, and will not, acknowledge the existence of his Maker. In unrighteousness, he suppresses the truth and refuses to retain God in his thinking (Rom. 1:18,28). By foolish speculation, he invents incredible alternatives to explain his origin and to find a reason for his existence. Such explanations become imperative for him because, the moment he acknowledges the existence of his Maker, either he must bow before him and submit to his sovereign authority, or face his displeasure, condemnation and wrath. For sinners at enmity with their Maker, neither alternative is acceptable. Apart from a wise, powerful and righteous God, however, life must remain forever 'waste and void'. Life is meaningless, purposeless and empty without God. The search for meaning becomes increasingly futile as people experiment with anything which promises to bring them a new experience. Significantly, just about every pleasure sought by sinners in their desperate search for life is ultimately destructive; people fill their lungs with smoke, their stomachs with alcohol, their veins with drugs, their skins with tattoos and their minds with lust, violence and nonsense. As a converted alcoholic, drug addict and prostitute once told me, 'I spent twenty-five years killing myself just trying to live.'

Meaning in life depends on more than just knowing *about* our origin. We must know where we came from in order to know why we are here. As I have said, when God made us, he made us for a purpose. The only way to discover that purpose is to be reconciled to him through the Lord Jesus Christ. Life takes on meaning only when we are redeemed from sin and brought into fellowship with God. In glorifying him by doing his will, we find fulfilment and satisfaction. Meaning and purpose in life depend, therefore, on both creation and redemption. As implied earlier, creation and redemption are closely allied; the steps in the physical creation illustrate and parallel the work of redemption. To begin with, both creation and redemption are the work of God; both depend on the power of his word and are according to his will. Evangelist D. L. Moody noted several significant parallels in abbreviated form in his Bible: 'Stages of creation, illustrative of the stages in the new creation: chaos, brooding of the Spirit, light, life growth, fruit-bearing, dominion, God's image, rest, blessing. God creating, moving, speaking, observing, calling, dividing, blessing.'[8]

A meaningful destiny

Meaning and purpose in life necessitate, not only a meaningful origin, but also a meaningful destiny. We must know that we have a future; that we are going somewhere and moving towards an objective, goal and destiny. Not surprisingly, sinful men, in dismissing and denying their Maker, have destroyed the possibility of a meaningful destiny. For multitudes of people, there is no future — for them, this life is all that there is. On the other hand, those who believe that they have been made *by* God, *like* God and *for* God, and have been reconciled to God by the Lord Jesus Christ, have a glorious destiny and a wonderful hope. This applies, not only to human beings, but to the whole creation. Because of Adam's transgression, 'the whole creation was subjected to futility ... and groans' (Rom. 8:19-23); now it waits eagerly for redemption. As the creation was affected adversely by the Fall, it will be restored when Jesus Christ returns.

The hope for the Christian believer lies in the Second Coming of our Lord and Saviour Jesus Christ. When he returns, the dead in Christ will be raised incorruptible and those who are alive and remain will be caught up together with them in the air to meet the Lord (1 Thess. 4:14-17). At that climactic and glorious event, redemption will be complete, God's people will be delivered from the power and presence of sin and corruption, and ushered into the presence of the Lord whom they love and serve. At that point, they will realize fully the purpose for which they were made and fulfil their 'chief end' by 'glorifying God and enjoying him for ever'.[9] On what is that hope based? The Christian hope is based on the same powerful word that called all things into existence.

There is a problem, however. Christians have waited almost 2,000 years for the return of Christ and he still has not come. The clouds have not parted and the dead are still in their graves. The problem is exacerbated by ungodly men who mock our faith and challenge our hope. They ask sceptically, 'Where is the promise of his coming?' (2 Peter 3:4). To them, the delay in his coming proves that his promise is nothing more than religious talk. All this talk about the return of Christ is, to them, nonsense; it hasn't happened and it isn't going to happen! Undoubtedly, such mockery causes doubts in the minds of most Christians at times; cynical expressions like this do disturb our souls. But, when tempted to doubt, Christians are to remember something which unbelievers completely ignore. When they mock in unbelief, says the apostle Peter, 'they wilfully forget ... that by the word of God the heavens were of old [i.e., brought into existence]' (2 Peter 3:5). In other words, mockers forget about *creation*. How is the work of creation connected to the Second Coming of Jesus Christ? The answer is simply this: in creation, God said it and it was done! What God says, he always does! The return of Christ is absolutely certain because God said it will happen! God's righteous character guarantees it. The coming of Jesus Christ is based on the Word of God.

How does the doctrine of creation affect us?

We know where we came from and we know where we are going; we have a meaningful origin and we have a meaningful destiny. These are the two indispensable reference points for a meaningful and purposeful life — and the world has tried to destroy both! Life is somewhat like a journey; there is a starting point and a destination. Having considered those two reference points — the beginning and the end of our earthly existence — what about the journey? How does the doctrine of creation relate to the present?

While the book of Job is removed from Genesis so far as the order of biblical books is concerned, Job, the man, belonged to the patriarchal era and fits, therefore, into the time frame of Genesis. Through the loss of his wealth, health and friends, Job suffered greatly. He was in physical pain, emotional distress and spiritual conflict. His affliction and adversity generated many perplexing questions. During those agonizing months (perhaps years), he struggled with questions concerning the meaning and purpose of life. Significantly, when his trials were over, instead of giving him a lecture on ethics and explaining the mystery of suffering, God drew his attention to the creation – he took him on a tour of the universe. Why did God do that? Was it because there are no answers to life's deepest problems and most perplexing questions? Not at all! In showing Job his work of creation, God reminded him that he is absolute sovereign over all the creation. And, having observed God's handiwork, Job responded by saying, 'I know that you can do everything, and that no purpose of yours can be [thwarted]' (Job 42:2). Just a glimpse of God's sovereignty in creation enabled Job to get things into perspective. If God is able to create all things by the Word of his power, surely he is able to keep it all under control.

What does this mean for us? It means that God can be trusted at all times and under all circumstances; he can be trusted completely – even when things seem impossible. Job, having had a glimpse of creation, declared, 'He knows the way that I take; when he has tested me, I shall come forth as gold' (Job 23:10).

The biblical understanding of God's sovereignty over creation, therefore, is essential for a purposeful origin and a meaningful destiny, and it enables us to face and to make sense of the difficulties and problems of the present. The basis for a meaningful existence is a personal relationship to God our Maker. The first, and most foundational, aspect in our understanding of God's being and character is to know that he is absolutely sovereign in his wonderful work of creation. The creation reveals God's 'eternal power and Godhead' (Rom. 1:20). He is *Elohim*, the Almighty One. Creation reveals God's greatness. This is the starting point for our understanding of everything.

3.

The sovereignty of God in his works of providence

Some of the ancient Greek philosophers (notably, the Epicureans) acknowledged that there had to be a Creator of the universe — that fact was inescapable. They would not concede, however, the doctrine of providence. They could not tolerate a God who was actively involved in their lives and was cognizant of what they were doing. Similarly, some of the founding fathers of the United States were deists. That is, while they believed in God as Creator, they regarded him as an absentee landlord. They believed that when God made the world, he set it in motion, like winding a clock, and left it to run by itself. This notion was the outcome of the philosophy of such men as David Hume, who taught that human 'reason is the Divine Governor of Man's Life; it is the very Voice of God'.[1] (One can readily see why the deists were among the pioneers of radical criticism of the Bible; if human reason is the voice of God, it can stand in judgement on everything, including the Bible! 'It is an interesting fact,' says Warren Young, 'that any deism which refuses to be completely revelational theism, becomes more and more watered down ... until it ultimately culminates in the rejection of any real theism at all.'[2]) According to the deists, the creation functions on natural law and human reason; their philosophy is, in other words, a clever way to try to avoid the biblical doctrine of providence.

Not far removed from deism is theistic evolution — the naïve notion that God created the world and then let things evolve. Theistic evolution is a poor compromise between the claims of secular science and biblical truth. As Ranganathan points out in his booklet, *Origins*,[3] if God had created and left things to evolve, he would have had to begin with an incomplete and imperfect creation. If anything had been imperfect or incomplete, God could never have pronounced it all 'very good'. Theistic evolution is another attempt to evade the truth and implications of divine providence.

Many professing Christians seem to have difficulty with divine providence in practical matters. When problems arise, adversity strikes, or suffering is encountered, they respond by asking, 'Where is God when I need him?' The question implies either that God has forgotten, that he has taken a journey, or that he is incapable of helping. Rabbi Kushner's best-seller, *When Bad Things Happen to Good People*,[4] presents a God who is helpless to assist people in times of trouble or crisis. The proliferation of books addressing the issue in recent years suggests that this is a pressing problem for many people.

As far as secular thinking is concerned, there are only two possibilities or alternatives concerning our daily existence. On one hand, many events in life are attributed to *chance*. As R. C. Sproul points out so clearly in his book, *Not a Chance*, there is no such thing as chance. Nevertheless, lottery tickets are bought in the vain hope that 'luck' will bring up the right numbers. If enquiry is made concerning their relationship to God and where they will spend eternity, many people will respond by saying, 'I don't worry about that sort of thing; I'll just take my chances.' If we were nothing more than the product of a chance process, those who tried to live by chance would be consistent. The problem is that no one lives by chance; he wouldn't live long if he tried. Francis Schaeffer cites John Cage, who tried to write music by chance — the result was, of course, unmitigated noise.

Cage had a hobby of growing mushrooms; he acknowledged that if he ate mushrooms on the same principles as he wrote music, he would be dead within a very short period of time.[5] He could not live by chance — and neither can anyone else!

The second alternative is *fatalism*. The most popular expression of fatalism is, no doubt, the use of the daily horoscope. People read what the stars supposedly say to determine what each day will be like and anticipate what has been suggested. Some go much further and consult mediums and fortune-tellers. Fatalism is to be rejected because it destroys personal responsibility and freedom — it reduces human beings to cogs in a mechanistic universe. While fatalism is generally rejected in principle, ironically, it is constantly applied in practice. Fatalism tacitly acknowledges that something or someone is in control; there is something there which determines how and when things happen. While the rolling of the dice is seen as a matter of chance, those who gamble often recognize that something determines what happens. While they speak of 'luck' (whatever that is!), they recognize a certain determinism when they declare, 'My number must come up soon.' A fatalistic view of life is unsatisfactory because it destroys our 'humanness'; it leaves us without choice or responsibility.

Most people, it seems, try to steer a course somewhere between the extremes of chance and fatalism — they read their horoscope and then buy a lottery ticket! However, the Scriptures offer us a far better alternative than either extreme — and it is not somewhere between! It is not a little less chance and a bit more fatalism. These two alternatives are both wrong; any middle position between the two is equally wrong. The Bible teaches an entirely different system; it teaches the doctrine of divine providence. It teaches us that God is truly sovereign and man is fully responsible.

What are God's works of providence?

Having brought all things into being by his powerful word, what was, and is, God's relationship to his creation? The author of the Epistle to the Hebrews says that the Lord Jesus Christ upholds 'all things by the word of his power' (Heb. 1:3). Also, in writing to the Colossians, the apostle Paul says that in Christ 'all things consist [i.e., hold together]' (Col. 1:17). The powerful word of God which brought all things into existence continues to sustain and maintain the creation. The doctrine of God's providence may not be neglected or ignored without serious implications. The word 'providence' comes from *'pro'* (before) and *'vide'* (to see). God sees (or understands and knows) beforehand, and he *provides* accordingly. The *Shorter Catechism* summarizes the biblical teaching on providence by stating that 'God's works of providence are, his most holy, wise, and powerful preserving and governing all his creatures, and all their actions.'[6]

In the discussion of creation, I said that God is wise, power-ful and righteous; essentially, we find the same three words here. Consider the implications concerning providence.

God's wisdom

'God is infinite, eternal, and unchangeable in his ... wisdom.' God has a great comprehensive plan in which he has overlooked no possibility, forgotten nothing, nor omitted the slightest detail. In his infinite wisdom, God made the world; by his wisdom, he sustains and maintains it.

God's power

'God is infinite, eternal, and unchangeable in his ... power.' God has the power to accomplish what he has planned. He has power enough to create all things from nothing; he has the power to sustain his creation and to control everything within it.

God's holiness

'God is infinite, eternal, and unchangeable in his holiness.' God is morally perfect; whatever he does is good, right, just and true. All God's works are righteous; with him, there is no confusion, no mistake, no mismanagement, no oversight and no wrongdoing.

God's providence means that he is in control

Because the eternal God upholds all things by the word of his power, he is in complete control. Not a single atom goes astray or escapes his notice. He watches over the sparrows and has numbered the hairs of our heads! There is nothing like a biblical understanding of the doctrine of providence to relieve anxiety and bring peace and contentment.

When my youngest daughter was first married, she and her husband spent eight years on a farm growing grain. After four or five years of poor crops, they were forced off the farm. In the last harvest season, they had a bumper crop but, shortly before harvest, severe hail destroyed most of the crops in the area. What was God's purpose in allowing — indeed, in doing — that? Had he lost control? Had he forgotten their plight and that of their neighbours? Did God care? While I do not know the reasons behind God's providences, consider some of the possibilities:

- Some people in that community might have been un-believers who needed hardship and adversity to cause them to consider their ways and 'seek the Lord while he may be found'.
- Some possibly were professing Christians with materi-alistic values who needed to reassess their lives and get a biblical perspective on life.

- Some might have been disobedient and unfaithful believers who needed the chastening of the Lord.
- Some believers possibly needed to be uprooted from
their situation and placed in more fruitful fields of service
for the Lord.

There are numerous other possibilities; my point is that God
uses the same event to accomplish different purposes in different
lives. Elihu, that young man who entered into the dialogue with
Job and his three friends, understood God's providential works
when he said, 'Whether for correction, or for his land, or for
mercy,' God 'causes it to come' (Job 37:13). Truly, God 'governs
all his creatures and all their actions'.

God's providence illustrated in Genesis

I have used this illustration because of the way in which God
used droughts in the lives of the patriarchs in Genesis. Soon
after God called *Abraham*, we read that '... there was a famine in
the land, and [Abraham] went down to Egypt to dwell there, for
the famine was severe in the land' (Gen. 12:10). God used that
famine to test Abraham's faith — a test which he failed. 'Here
was a man who had journeyed all the way from Chaldea to
Canaan on the bare word of Jehovah,' says A. W. Pink, 'and yet
was now afraid to trust him in the time of famine.'[7] Abraham's
lack of faith caused problems for Pharaoh: '... the LORD plagued
[him] and his house ... because of [Sarah]' (Gen. 12:17). While
many details are not given, what is clear is that God was in
control. God used the famine to make Abraham move to Egypt
and he used Abraham's faithlessness to accomplish his purpose
in the life of Pharaoh. In other words, this incident reveals both
God's direct intervention and his use of secondary means to
accomplish his sovereign purpose. God did not forbid Abraham
to go to Egypt; on the contrary, he brought about conditions

which caused him to go. 'The Lord's commands are rarely accompanied with *reasons*,' says Pink, 'but they are always accompanied with *promises*.'[8]

A similar event took place in the life of *Isaac*. 'There was a famine in the land, besides the first famine that was in the days of Abraham. And Isaac went to Abimelech king of the Philistines, in Gerar' (Gen. 26:1). This fact is recorded without any indication as to whether or not Isaac was right in going to the Philistines; it was an act of God's providential ordering of events. We do not know 'whether he had consulted God about it, whether it was undertaken by the will of God, or prompted by his own unaided wisdom. In any case the Lord appeared to him and prevented him from going further southward into Egypt as his father had done under similar circumstances.'[9]

Isaac was informed concerning God's covenantal promise to his father Abraham. He knew that the land of Canaan had been deeded to him and his descendants by God, but now a famine rested on that very land. What was he to think of God's promise when God's providence was adverse? His reaction appears to have been to turn to Egypt for help and sustenance. God appeared to Isaac, however, and expressly commanded him not to go to Egypt but to remain where he was. He believed God and did not proceed.

One of the greatest passages of Scripture concerning the providential works of God is the last quarter of the book of Genesis, covering the events in the life of *Joseph*. (Another great passage, incidentally, is the book of Esther — a book in which God is not mentioned but where his governing hand is clearly evident.)

Immediately after informing us that Joseph was loved by his father and despised by his brothers, the Scriptures recount how Jacob sent him to enquire concerning the welfare of his brothers (Gen. 37:14). They seized the opportunity to vent their anger and express their hatred of him. They took Joseph and threw him into a pit with the intention of killing him later. Why didn't they kill him immediately? Before they carried out their dastardly intent, a caravan of Ishmaelites appeared on the horizon who happened to be going to Egypt. Those traders were interested in making a few shekels so, rather than murder him, Joseph's brothers sold him for twenty pieces of silver.

When Joseph was offered in the slave market, Potiphar, the captain of Pharaoh's guard, happened to be present. He decided to buy Joseph. Potiphar's wife became infatuated with the young slave and sought to seduce him; because of his integrity and virtue, Joseph refused her advances only to have her turn against him. As a result, Joseph was incarcerated in the royal prison. While he was there, two fellow prisoners had troubled dreams which, after being interpreted by Joseph, came to pass. The king's butler forgot his promise to Joseph for two years; it came to mind when the king himself had a troubled dream. When Joseph interpreted the king's dream, he was delivered from prison and elevated to second in command in the kingdom. In due course, the famine announced by Joseph came to pass and began to take its toll. Jacob and his other sons, who lived in Canaan, began to feel the effects of the drought. The hardship caused by the famine forced Joseph's brothers to go to Egypt for food. While the whole narrative reads as though these things just happened, nothing was coincidental. The subsequent events, in which Joseph tested his brothers and brought guilt and repentance to their hearts and salvation to the family, make fascinating reading.

In all those adverse experiences of rejection, betrayal, slavery, false accusation, imprisonment and waiting, there is no suggestion that Joseph wavered in his faith towards God. There must have been many occasions when he could have thought that God had forgotten and forsaken him; so far as we can determine, his confidence in God's sovereign control does not appear to have been shaken at any stage.

Some time after Joseph's brothers and their families had migrated to Egypt, Jacob died. The brothers were afraid that since their father was dead, Joseph would seek revenge. Instead, they found mercy and forgiveness. Joseph knew that every step of the way God was in complete control and would not fail him. What a great declaration of confidence in God's providential and sovereign control Joseph makes when he says, 'Do not be afraid, for am I in the place of God? But as for you, you meant evil against me; but God meant it for good, in order to bring about as it is this day, to save many people alive'! (Gen. 50:19-20). Though there was no question about the evil intent of his brothers, Joseph knew that God was accomplishing his purpose. Joseph was content to leave everything in the hands of God, who would, in his own time and way, vindicate and use him to accomplish that purpose. He understood that 'God's works of providence are his most holy, wise, and powerful preserving and governing all his creatures and all their actions.' Similarly, the apostle Paul declared that the adverse things which had happened to him had turned out for the furtherance of the gospel (Phil. 1:12) — and that was cause to rejoice.

Significantly, God does not deal with his people in set patterns or identical ways. There are some paths in which he has forbidden all his children to walk, of course; he never leads his people in the paths of unrighteousness; he never leads contrary to his revealed will. Other issues concerning guidance are not so clear. Sometimes in his providence, God directs one servant to stay and another to go. God guides personally and individually; all must learn to trust him in all circumstances — even in famine! What a striking contrast there is between the patriarchs! Abraham went to Egypt; in his case, there does not appear to have been any particular guidance involved. Isaac, on the other hand, was specifically forbidden to go to Egypt. To Jacob, however, God appeared and said, 'I am God, the God of your father; do not fear to go down to Egypt, for I will make of you a great nation there. I will go down with you to Egypt, and I will also surely bring you up again [to Canaan]' (Gen. 46:3-4).

Numerous other examples of God's sovereign works of providence are to be found in Genesis.

Concerning *the longevity of people before the Flood*, Matthew Henry says that '... it must chiefly be resolved into the power and providence of God. He prolonged their lives, both for the more speedy replenishing of the earth and for the more effectual preservation of the knowledge of God and religion.'[10]

In describing the receding waters of *the Flood*, Henry comments, 'The work of creation being finished, this work of providence was effected by the concurring influence of second causes, yet thus enforced by the almighty power of God.'[11] Noah's ark 'rested upon a mountain, whither it was directed, not by Noah's prudence (he did not steer it), but by the wise and gracious providence of God'.[12]

In the departure of *Hagar* from the family of Abraham, the Angel of the LORD met her to provide for her and to direct her. Again, Matthew Henry comments, 'Many that are much exposed by their own imprudence are yet strangely preserved by the divine Providence, so much better is God to them than they deserve, when they not only forfeit their lives, but hazard them.'[13]

When *Abraham* found the ram caught in the bushes on Mount Moriah, that did not happen by chance.

When *Abraham's servant* was sent to find a wife for Isaac, he declared, 'Blessed be the LORD God of my master Abraham, who has not forsaken his mercy and his truth toward my master. As for me, being on the way, the LORD led me' (Gen. 24:27). In negotiating with Laban and Bethuel, he said, 'I bowed my head and worshipped the LORD, and blessed the LORD God of my master Abraham, who had led me in the way of truth to take [Rebekah]' (Gen. 24:48).

God's providence illustrated in the life of Job

Since Job belongs to the patriarchal period, it is appropriate to comment on him also. He is a classical example of one who trusted in God's providence and found strength in God's sovereign control. Naturally, Job had deep questions about the adversity and suffering which had befallen him, but he never seems to have doubted that God was in control, or that he knew what he was doing. On the contrary, he cried out from the depths of despair, 'Though he slay me, yet will I trust him' (Job 13:15). While he did not understand what God was doing, he knew that he could trust God's judgement. He declared, 'He knows the way that I take; when he has tested me, I shall come forth as gold' (Job 23:10). He knew that he could trust God's judgement in all matters and understood that God was at work accomplishing his gracious purpose and fulfilling his wonderful plan. At the end of the book, God not only showed him the creation, but also took him on a tour of the animal kingdom to show him that he cares for his creatures.

God is faithful

When times are difficult and circumstances are adverse, we are tempted to ask what has happened to God and where he is when we need him most. The psalmist answers:

> Your faithfulness endures to all generations;
> You established the earth, and it abides.
> They continue this day according to your ordinances,
> For all are your servants
>
> (Ps. 119: 90-91).

> Where can I go from your Spirit?
> Or where can I flee from your presence?
> If I ascend into heaven, you are there;
> If I make my bed in hell, behold, you are there.
> If I take the wings of the morning,
> And dwell in the uttermost parts of the sea,
> Even there your hand shall lead me,
> And your right hand shall hold me
>
> (Ps. 139: 7-9).

God is there, but what is he doing? He is holding all things together even when it seems to us that they are falling apart! God is there and he is actively involved in his creation and with his creatures. One reason why we have problems with God's works of providence is that we, unlike Job, fail to trust his promises. Thomas Watson said, 'Men murmur at God's providences because they distrust his promises.'[14]

What this means in practice for God's people

In his classical work, *The Mystery of Providence*,[15] John Flavel presents some of the practical implications of divine providence; I shall simply note some of his major points:

1. If God performs all things for you, God is to be owned by you in all that befalls you in this world, whether it is in the way of success or comfort, or of trouble and affliction. Paul tells us that 'all things work together for good to those who love God, to those who are the called according to his purpose' (Rom. 8:28).

2. If God performs all things for you, how great is his condescension to, and care over, his people! Flavel says, 'You are too dear to him to be trusted in any hand but his own.'[16]

3. If God performs all things for you, see how obliged you are to perform all duties and services for God. 'Is Providence every moment at work for you, and will you be idle? To what purpose then is all that God has done for you?'

4. Does God perform all things for his people? Do not distrust him, then, when new or great difficulties arise. If anything puts a stop to his mercy, it is your iniquities, your distrust and infidelity.

5. Does God perform all things for you? Then seek for all by prayer, and never undertake any design without

him. That which begins not with prayer seldom ends with comfort.

6. If God performs all things for us, then it is our great interest and concern in all things to study to please him, upon whom we depend for all things. Luther said, 'I had utterly despaired had not Christ been the head of the church.' When one told Borromeus that there were some that laid wait for his life, his answer was: 'What! Is God in this world for nothing?'

Because God is wise enough to plan all things, powerful enough to carry out what he has planned and righteous enough to do everything properly, we can entrust our lives into his hands with complete confidence. Because he preserves and governs all his creatures and all their actions, nothing can touch us without his gracious permission. When adversity, affliction and suffering come, we can be assured, like Job, that 'He knows the way that I take; when he has tested me, I shall come forth as gold' (Job 23:10). May God enable us, his people, to 'trust in the LORD with all [our] heart, and lean not on [our] own understanding; in all [our] ways acknowledge him, and he shall direct [our] paths' (Prov. 3:5-6).

When we understand that God is sovereign in all things; that he 'preserves and governs all his creatures and all their actions,' we can declare with Moses:

Ascribe greatness to our God.
He is the Rock, his work is perfect;
For all his ways are justice,
A God of truth and without injustice;
Righteous and upright is he

(Deut. 32:3-4).

God's sovereignty in his work of creation reveals his *greatness*. His sovereignty in his works of providence, as he 'preserves and governs all his creatures', reveals his *goodness*.

4.

The sovereignty of God in choosing his people

While basic teaching on the doctrine of God is possibly the most urgent need within the contemporary church, another area of great need is for biblical instruction on the doctrine of sin. The two doctrines are closely tied together, of course. Many professing Christians, it seems, have an inadequate concept of sin because they have an inadequate concept of God. Sin is generally not taken too seriously these days because people do not realize *who* has been offended. And, if these great biblical doctrines are not understood, the doctrine of salvation will not be understood or appreciated either.

Following creation, the first recorded event in human history is the fall of our first parents, Adam and Eve. As we saw in chapter 1, Man was made:

- *by God* — in a special creative act;
- *like God* — in God's image; and
- *for God* — 'to glorify God and enjoy him for ever'.

The effects of the Fall

Man is wonderful but because of Adam's first transgression, he is now in a state of defiance, rebellion and disobedience towards his Maker. The Fall had a *total* effect on man and as a result he was, and is, alienated from God. The effects of the Fall are both objective (outward) and subjective (inward):

• Adam rejected the *Word of God* (objective) as his authority, and *his mind* (subjective) became prejudiced against, and antagonistic to, the truth. As we have seen previously, men do not like to retain God in their thinking and they suppress the truth in unrighteousness (Rom. 1:28,18).

• Adam rejected the *character of God* (objective) as the standard by which to measure morality, and *his heart* (subjective) became opposed to true goodness and righteousness. That is, he set up his own criteria and standards for righteousness. When God is rejected as the standard, all moral issues become relative, and truth, goodness, justice and righteousness become purely subjective. Because the standard has been set aside, 'There is none righteous, no, not one... There is none who does good, no, not one' (Rom. 3:10,12).

• Adam rejected the *will of God* (objective) as his purpose for life, and *his will* (subjective) became set against God's purpose and will. 'The carnal mind is enmity against God; for it is not subject to the law of God, nor indeed can be. So then, those who are in the flesh cannot please God' (Rom. 8:7-8).

In one sense, these objective and subjective aspects cannot be separated. Rejection of God's Word as the truth inevitably means prejudice against the truth — because God's Word is truth! Rejection of God's perfect moral character as the standard for righteous conduct inevitably means the rejection of right-eousness — for God is perfectly righteous! And the rejection of God's will as one's purpose in life inevitably means the loss of meaning and fulfilment in life. Life becomes empty and futile when the purpose for which we were created is removed. Because of sin, man's rejection of God is total — he has rejected God's Word, his character and his will. Man has been totally affected also; he loves darkness (falsehood) rather than light (truth) because his deeds are evil (John 3:19). Instead of measuring himself against God, man measures himself by himself and compares himself with himself (2 Cor. 10:12). Instead of doing the will of God and thereby fulfilling the purpose for which he was made, he follows the 'way that seems right to a man, but its end is the way of death' (Prov. 14:12; 16:25). Since Adam's fall, man is an enemy of God; he is 'not subject to the law of God, nor indeed can be' (Rom. 8:7).

Man's rejection of God's sovereignty

Because of the effects of sin, man's rejection of, and opposition to, God is evident in three fundamental areas: he objects to God's sovereignty in creation, providence and election.

God's sovereignty in creation

Sinful man will not admit that God is his Maker; to do so makes him dependent upon God and morally accountable to him. He will not have God rule over him; indeed, he '[takes] counsel [with others] against the LORD and against his Anointed' (Ps. 2:2), seeking ways to cast off his restraints. In rejecting God as Creator, man rejects the *greatness* of God.

God's sovereignty in providence

Sinful man will not tolerate the idea of God watching over him; to acknowledge God's providence is a tacit admission of one's need for, and dependence on, God. He thinks that he does not need God watching over him or caring for him; he thinks that he is able to provide for his own needs and take care of himself. He imagines that he is in complete control. He rejects the *goodness* of God.

The sovereignty of God in election

In this chapter, we will discuss the sovereignty of God in election. There are many differences over this important doctrine; we cannot ignore it for that reason — nor would we want to! It is far too important to treat lightly. What is often forgotten is that God's sovereign election depends on who and what God is. God's greatness in creation and his goodness in providence must be understood before his sovereign election can be appreciated. In the previous chapter on providence, I pointed out the two alternatives which the world has:

Chance —————————————————— Fatalism

Some people equate the doctrine of election with fatalism. And, as I pointed out, the answer is not somewhere between those two extremes. It is not a little less fatalism and a bit more chance. God's Word reveals an entirely different system in which God is truly sovereign and man is fully responsible. Ultimately, those two matters cannot be reconciled this side of heaven, but the Bible teaches both and holds them together.

Because sinful man has established his own moral standards and principles of conduct, he does not see himself as a sinner. He claims, therefore, that he is innately morally good and he considers himself to be righteous. He does not recognize that his rejection of, and rebellion against, God is wrong. Man imagines that he is able to shape and enact his own destiny. When sinful man gets himself into too much trouble, he thinks that he can come to God whenever he pleases and that he can do so on his own terms. Consequently, all religions (apart from true and undefiled religion) have a common denominator; all religions delineate what sinful man must *do* to get to God. Often, pilgrimages, penances and prayers are costly and demand great sacrifice but, given enough effort, sincerity and persistence, God's wrath can be appeased and his favour secured — so people are told! That one's salvation is dependent entirely on God is offensive to proud, self-sufficient man. The nature of sin is such that man imagines that he is still in control — even when everything seems out of control. Sinners will not admit that the potter, to use Paul's metaphor, has any power over the clay. He rejects the *grace* of God.

Man's rejection of God is total

Because of his sinful condition, man refuses to acknowledge the sovereign God as his Maker, Sustainer and Redeemer. I repeat, his rejection of God is total. An important comparison appears in Psalms 1 and 2. In Psalm 1, the focus is on the man who *meditates* on the law of God — he will, says the psalmist, be blessed and fruitful like a tree planted by streams of water. Psalm 2, on the other hand, speaks of people 'devising a vain thing' (NASB). In Hebrew the word for 'devise' is actually the same one that is used in Psalm 1 for 'meditate'. The man of God meditates on the law of God; the wicked, by comparison, meditate on a vain thing. What is that vain object of meditation? They meditate and take counsel together, says the psalmist, 'against the Lord and against his Anointed [Messiah]' — the

wicked seek ways to break God's control over them and cast
away his restraint. Sinners object to God's sovereignty, because
they refuse to have God rule over them. Professing Christians
are not immune; while they generally acknowledge God as their
Maker and Sustainer, many object to his sovereignty when it
comes to salvation. They will not allow God to choose his own
people. Undoubtedly, they do so because they have not understood the righteous character of God or the magnitude of sin
and its serious effects on the mind, the heart and the will.

Man's lost condition and God's eternal plan

The biblical truth concerning the effects of sin is summarized in
the *Shorter Catechism*: it says, 'All mankind by their fall lost
communion with God, are under his wrath and curse, and so
made liable to all miseries in this life, to death itself, and to the
pains of hell for ever.'[1]

This is the pitiable condition of all men. God could have
destroyed Adam and Eve for their disobedience immediately, or
he could have left all men to wallow in their sin and misery and
eventually to perish in hell — and would have been perfectly just
in doing so! The fall of Adam did not catch God by surprise,
however; it did not happen by chance! It did not mean that God
was unaware of the consequences, nor did it mean that God had
to scrap his original plan and move to 'Plan B'. God was fully
aware of the effects and consequences of sin. His sovereignty
over all things was not suspended or overruled by man's sin.

God had a wonderful plan and purpose in view — a plan
which he devised and established *before the foundation of the
world* (Eph. 1:4). Though God's plan included the problem of
sin, he is not the author of sin, nor is he responsible for it in any
way. God does not approve, condone, or excuse sin; on the
contrary, he hates sin, he condemns sin, he judges sin and he
works to destroy sin. Ultimately, when his great comprehensive

plan is consummated and complete, sin will be destroyed; God will vindicate his righteousness and maintain his infinite justice.

Praise God, he has not left all mankind to perish in their sin and misery; rather, as the catechism says, 'God having, out of his mere good pleasure, from all eternity, elected some to everlasting life, did enter into a covenant of grace, to deliver them out of the estate of sin and misery, and to bring them into an estate of salvation by a Redeemer.'[2]

Each phrase in that statement is important and worthy of consideration.

'Out of his mere good pleasure'

God was under no obligation, compulsion, or constraint to save anyone from the effects or consequences of sin; he did not act out of necessity. Twice in Ephesians 1:3-14 (the longest sentence in the Greek New Testament) the apostle says that our salvation is 'according to the good pleasure of his will' (Eph. 1:5,9).

'From all eternity'

The redemption of sinners was not an afterthought; it was planned before God made the world. Again, the apostle, under the inspiration of God's Spirit, says that believers have been chosen in Christ 'before the foundation of the world' (Eph. 1:4).

'Elected some to everlasting life'

God has not left all men to perish in their sin and misery. He has chosen some, who, along with all the others, deserve his wrath and judgement, and has given, or will yet give, them everlasting life. Why has God chosen some and not others? That is a question which only he, in his sovereignty, can answer. God's sovereignty in 'electing some to everlasting life' demonstrates his mercy and grace; on the other hand, those who are lost will vindicate his righteousness and justice.

'Did enter into a covenant of grace'

That was, and is, a unilateral covenant. God himself took the initiative. Under no circumstances is he subject to the whims or dictates of sinners. As I have already said, he did not act out of necessity or under coercion; he has covenanted freely. Because of his matchless grace, he has covenanted to save his people from their sins. When God made that covenant, he swore by himself because there was no one greater by whom he could swear (Heb. 6:13); that means, of course, that its fulfilment is certain – his word is immutable because it depends solely upon his righteous character.

'To deliver them out of the estate of sin and misery'

God's covenant of grace concerns deliverance from sin and its awful consequences. The alternative to deliverance is, of course, destruction.

'To bring them into an estate of salvation'

God's plan of redemption concerns deliverance *from* sin; it concerns also deliverance *to* the state of salvation. In other words, salvation is not merely receiving forgiveness for sins; it is also a matter in which sinners are progressively transformed into the likeness of God – and one day will be perfected.

'By a Redeemer'

To fulfil all the moral requirements of God's law and to satisfy the demands of God's infinite justice, God sent his Son into the world. The Lord Jesus Christ lived a sinless life (and thereby kept all the requirements of the law) and, on the other hand, he died to pay the penalty of sin (and, hence, satisfied the demands of divine justice on behalf of sinners). Both the life and the death of Jesus Christ were *substitutionary* – that is, he lived and died on behalf of those whom God has chosen. As sinners, we are utterly helpless; indeed, we are incapable of doing anything to save ourselves; we are already 'dead in trespasses and sins' (Eph. 2:1). We must have a Redeemer who is qualified, willing and able to save by imparting new life. In his sovereignty, God has a great eternal purpose and plan for the redemption of sinners.

God's sovereign election demonstrated in Genesis

In chapter 1, I pointed out that the first eleven chapters of Genesis are a unique section of God's Word; they are, I believe, God's own introduction to his Word. They reveal the uniqueness of man, the entry of sin and both its immediate and continuing consequences, as well as the extent and ultimate consequences of sin. They also show man's solution to the sin problem. The importance of these events cannot be over-emphasized and they must not be ignored if we are to understand and appreciate fully what God says in the rest of his Word. In other words, the magnitude of the problem of sin must be understood before the significance and wonder of the solution in Jesus Christ can be appreciated.

In Genesis 12, when God gave his covenantal promise to Abraham, he 'preached the gospel to him' (Gal. 3:8). In revealing his great plan of redemption to Abraham two thousand years before the coming of Christ, God showed that his plan was no afterthought — it was in operation from the very beginning. He knew exactly what he would do. Under that covenant, God promised to bless all the nations of the earth through Abraham. Significantly, the book of Revelation states that some from 'every tribe and tongue and people and nation' (Rev. 5:9; 7:9) are among the redeemed. At the culmination of history, God will have accomplished exactly what he planned to do; he is sovereign in his great work of redemption. No one can prevent or hinder him from what he is doing.

From Adam to Noah

While God's covenant was formally initiated with the call of
Abraham, there are indications and evidences that the covenant
was in effect from the very beginning (see Gen. 6:18; 9:9-17).
Immediately after the Fall, God declared that 'the Seed' of the
woman would bruise the head of the serpent (Gen. 3:15). God's
promised deliverer would be 'born of a woman' and he would
destroy the works of the devil. Further, the essence of the gospel
is portrayed at the Garden of Eden when God made clothing for
Adam and Eve from the skins of animals. Certainly, the covenant of God's grace is evident in the preservation of Noah and his
family at the time of the Flood. The actual initiation or implementation of the covenant began, however, with the call of
Abraham, even though it was already in effect before that time.

The call of Abraham

Who was Abraham? As we have seen previously, Abraham was
a pagan when God called him (Josh. 24:2). With his fathers, he
served other gods in the land of Chaldea. Since he was a pagan,
why did God choose him? God's choice was 'according to the
good pleasure of his will'. Abraham is declared to be the father
of the faithful; 'with respect to the promise of God,' the apostle
says, 'he did not ... waver through unbelief' (Rom. 4:20). Yet
God did not choose him because of his faith. Indeed, in several
trials, he proved weak; on occasions, he faltered and failed. In
many respects, he was just like us; he was merely a sinner saved
by God's grace — and by God's grace alone!

God's promise to Abraham and the birth of Isaac

God informed Abraham that he would make of him a great
nation. The making of a nation does not happen overnight —
especially when it begins with *one* man. Abraham did not see the
promise fulfilled; he died believing that God would accomplish

what he had promised (Heb. 11:13; Rom. 4:21). Abraham realized that if he was going to be the father of a nation, he needed an heir. That presented a significant problem to him. When God gave his covenantal promise, Abraham was seventy-five years of age (Gen. 12:4). Sarah, his wife, was ten years younger (Gen. 17:17). The Scripture states that Sarah was childless and past the age of bearing children (Gen. 11:30; 16:1). God had declared that through Abraham's seed the promise would be fulfilled; humanly speaking, however, it was impossible. Rather than trusting God to accomplish his plan, Abraham tried to work it out in his own wisdom and strength. Recognizing the sheer impossibility of the situation, he sought an alternative solution.

Though God had instructed him to leave his relatives behind, Abraham took his nephew, Lot, along with him. Undoubtedly, he did so because he considered Lot to be the most likely candidate to be his heir. As Abraham's nephew, Lot was the nearest person to a son. In the course of time, God blessed both Abraham and Lot to such an extent that their herdsmen began to argue over grazing rights for the livestock. To settle the dispute, Abraham gave Lot the choice of selecting the rugged hills of Canaan or the well-watered plain of Jordan. I have been to the plain of Jordan and, had I been Lot, I believe that I would have made the same choice; from all appearances, the hills of Judea are not very attractive for grazing purposes. He chose the well-watered plain of Jordan and pitched his tent towards Sodom. Abraham, on the other hand, believed God; he realized that he could commit the matter to him with confidence. In his sovereignty, God providentially forced the separation; he did so because although Lot was chosen by Abraham, he was not chosen by God. Significantly, after the separation, God reiterated his promise to Abraham (Gen. 13:14-16). God is sovereign; he will keep his word and he will accomplish his purpose in his time — even if it is impossible with men!

With Lot out of the picture, Abraham went back to the drawing board, as it were. '[Abraham] said, "Lord GOD, what will you give me, seeing I go childless, and the heir of my house is Eliezer of Damascus?" Then [Abraham] said, "Look, you have given me no offspring; indeed one born in my house is my heir!" ' (Gen. 15:2). Abraham was growing desperate; one can almost detect a note of reproof towards God in his remarks. In essence, he says, 'Look, you made this promise but you haven't done anything!' Time was running out and there was no sign of an heir. God responded by informing him that 'This one shall not be your heir, but one who will come from your own body shall be your heir' (Gen. 15:4). Eliezer was set aside because he had not been chosen by God; God's promise would not be fulfilled by a servant. Why? Because God is sovereign; he works his purpose according to his sovereign will.

When God informed Abraham that the promise would be fulfilled through a son, Abraham and Sarah discussed the problem. Sarah was barren and too old to bear children so, in their minds, she was ruled out as the mother. They thought that an alternative was needed: 'Now [Sarah], [Abraham's] wife, had borne him no children. And she had an Egyptian maidservant whose name was Hagar. So [Sarah] said to [Abraham], "See now, the LORD has restrained me from bearing children. Please, go in to my maid; perhaps I shall obtain children by her." And [Abraham] heeded the voice of [Sarah]' (Gen. 16:1).

Hagar bore a son to Abraham but, in the course of time, that generated terrible jealousy and conflict — and continues to create problems today! The tensions in the home resulted in separation. Why? Because God had not chosen Ishmael. Significantly, immediately after the separation, God graciously reiterated his covenantal promise to Abraham (Gen. 17:1-7). God declared specifically that Abraham *and Sarah* would have a son (Gen. 18:10). Sarah laughed at such a prospect. She could not believe it possible; she doubted God's sovereignty. If necessary, God performs miracles to accomplish his purpose. Indeed, in giving Abraham and Sarah a son when, humanly speaking, it was impossible, God showed that another miracle child — one born of a virgin — would be given in the fulness of time in order to accomplish that covenantal promise and bring blessing to the nations. Isaac was God's chosen instrument; no alternative or substitute would do. Isaac was born when Abraham was one hundred years old and Sarah was ninety — that was twenty-five years after the promise had been given. God was in no great hurry; his purpose will be accomplished because he is sovereign.

Jacob and Esau

Isaac was forty years of age when he married Rebekah (Gen. 25:20) and, again in God's providence, she too was barren. Isaac, however, wisely took the matter to the Lord (Gen. 25:21). After twenty years, God gave them twins, Jacob and Esau (Gen. 25:24). Esau was the firstborn but God, in his sovereign wisdom, chose Jacob. In Old Testament times, children were often named in keeping with their character; the name 'Jacob' means 'deceiver' (or 'supplanter' — literally, 'one who holds the heel' — as happened at his birth). If God had consulted us, we would have objected, no doubt. We would have informed the Lord that he had made a very poor choice!

God chose Jacob over Esau; in both the Old and New Testaments, God actually says that he loved Jacob and hated Esau (Mal. 1:2-3; Rom. 9:13). Some commentators have tried to explain that statement to avoid the implications; others ignore it completely. Regardless of what one might do with it and how it might be explained, God himself said it. Further, God explains that his choice of Jacob had nothing to do with either Jacob or Esau or anything they might have done. He says, '... though the twins were not yet born and had not done anything good or bad, so that God's purpose according to his choice would stand, not because of works but because of him who calls...' (Rom. 9:11, NASB). ' "I will have mercy on whom I have mercy, and I will have compassion on whom I have compassion." So then it does not depend on the man who wills or the man who runs, but on God who has mercy ... he has mercy on whom he desires, and he hardens whom he desires' (Rom. 9:15,18, NASB).

We cannot comprehend how this relates to human freedom and responsibility, of course, but we must recognize that God is sovereign and in complete control. God warns us against arguing with him about the matter (Rom. 9:20-21). Because he is sovereign, God chooses his people, 'not by works of righteousness which we have done, but according to his mercy' (Titus 3:5).

God's choice is often contrary to our expectations

Similarly, just after our Lord delivered his Sermon on the Mount, a scribe made a fine-sounding statement of commitment and voluntarily offered to follow him. As a scribe, he was well acquainted with the Old Testament, was respected by the people and was probably wealthy. Jesus turned the man away, however (Matt. 8:19-20). Instead, he called Matthew, who, as a tax collector, would have been regarded as a cheat and traitor to his people. In our judgement, the scribe would have made a far better disciple than all the tax collectors and fishermen of Galilee. We would have judged Matthew to have been a very poor choice. God is sovereign; he chooses people in his wisdom without respect for their antecedents or character traits.

As with Jacob and Matthew, and many others, God often chooses contrary to our expectations or preferences: '... not many wise according to the flesh, not many mighty, not many noble, are called. But God has chosen the foolish things of the world to put to shame the wise, and God has chosen the weak things of the world to put to shame the things which are mighty; and the base things of the world and the things which are despised God has chosen' (1 Cor. 1:26-27).

It is noteworthy that, contrary to the custom of the times, God often chose the younger before the elder. He chose:

Abel (and later Seth) over Cain.	The sons of Adam.
Shem over Japheth.	The sons of Noah.
Isaac over Ishmael.	The sons of Abraham.
Jacob over Esau.	The sons of Isaac.

Though Judah was not the eldest son of Jacob, he was chosen over Reuben to be the one through whom God's Redeemer would come (Gen. 49:10). Who was Judah? In Genesis 38, he is portrayed as an unethical and immoral man — he forced his daughter-in-law into prostitution and he himself committed adultery with her. We might ask how the Lord could possibly choose someone like that. Why not choose Joseph, of whom nothing negative or sinful is recorded? The life story of Joseph occupies about one quarter of the book of Genesis and, in many respects, he reflects the life of the Lord Jesus. Even though God delighted in Joseph, accorded him honour by devoting a large portion of Scripture to his life, and by giving him a double inheritance in Israel, he was not the chosen line for the Redeemer. Why not? Because God is sovereign and he chooses whomsoever he wills to accomplish his great and glorious purpose.

Undoubtedly, the most perplexing question which I face and to which I have no answer, other than the sovereignty of God, is: 'Why did God choose me?' Certainly, not because of who or what I am! When we get to heaven, I am quite sure that no one will declare that he or she is there because they happened to be at the right place at the right time and made the right decision. We shall all have to acknowledge that we have been redeemed by God's mercy and grace alone.

Objections to the doctrine considered

As I said at the outset, many people have problems with the doctrine of election; admittedly, it is a difficult doctrine. Many of the difficulties arise, however, from one of the following causes:

1. The nature of sin

As sinners, we imagine ourselves to be in complete control of our lives and of our destiny. Because we are sinners, we have an inflated concept of ourselves (self-esteem is alive and well!) and, conversely, we have a deflated concept of God. We would usurp sovereignty from God if we could. We imagine that we are wiser than he is. God's sovereignty is unacceptable to us because it casts us entirely upon his mercy.

2. A wrong approach to Scripture

Some people, it seems to me, begin their consideration of the doctrine of election at the wrong end of the Bible, with the wrong passages and isolated verses. These matters need to be seen as God has disclosed them to us. To understand what God has done in 'electing some to everlasting life',[3] we must begin in Genesis. That great New Testament passage on election, Romans 9-11, depends on what God has revealed in Genesis.

3. The belief that it gives rise to presumption

Some sincere believers object to the doctrine of election because they believe that it engenders carelessness and presumption. Examples of presumption are not difficult to find; some, by their lifestyle, have brought dishonour to this doctrine, but truth is not determined by what people believe or do. The doctrines of grace never lead to presumption or carelessness — on the contrary, the apostle Paul refutes that notion when he asks, 'Shall we

continue in sin that grace may abound?' and replies, 'Certainly
not!' (Rom. 6:1-2).

4. The belief that it denies human responsibility

Some object to the doctrine of election because they think that it
conflicts with, and relieves man of, all responsibility. As I have
pointed out, the sovereignty of God in choosing his people must
never be equated with fatalism. While God is sovereign and has
chosen us from before the foundation of the world, he nevertheless deals with us in such a way that we are fully responsible.
While we cannot finally resolve those two aspects, the Word of
God is clear: God is sovereign and man is responsible. We are
responsible to 'be even more diligent to make [our] call and
election sure' (2 Peter 1:10).

5. The place of prayer

Another problem concerns prayer. If God orders all things
according to his will, what is the point of prayer? In his sovereignty, God has not only ordained the *effect*, he has ordained the
cause or the *means*. Obviously, God could save the heathen
without our help; for some reason, however, in his sovereignty,
he has chosen to use people. Similarly, he has chosen to work in
response to the prayers of his people. He has chosen us, not
only that we might have everlasting life — that is wonderful and
glorious — but also to be instruments, or vessels, for his use.
While we cannot comprehend these things fully, we know that
this is the way God works — he has told us so! It is our responsibility to be obedient and faithful in both worship and service.
Significantly, the apostle concludes his discussion on the doctrine of election in Romans 9-11 with an amazing statement; he
says, 'I do not desire, brethren, that you should be ignorant of
this mystery, lest you should be wise in your own opinion... Oh,
the depth of the riches both of the wisdom and knowledge of

God! How unsearchable are his judgements and his ways past finding out!' (Rom. 11:25,33).

The benefits of understanding this doctrine

A biblical understanding of the sovereignty of God in election gives meaning, direction and purpose to life and ministry as does nothing else. If I were to go to Australia, my homeland, without the knowledge that some people there are chosen by God, I would be disheartened, discouraged and pessimistic; Australia is a very difficult land for the preaching of the gospel. If the salvation of souls were up to me, I could have no basis for optimism or hope. Knowing that God has chosen his people and that he has called me, a weak and insignificant vessel, to reach some of them gives me hope and makes me optimistic and dependent on him to 'give the increase'. This knowledge gives me a sense of purpose, expectation and hope; it motivates me in prayer and work. I know that I am not there by chance and that the success of my ministry does not rest on my ability; it rests upon the sovereignty of God.

At the outset of Scripture, God has revealed himself as sovereign in creation, in his works of providence, and in choosing his people. For an accurate understanding of the being, nature and works of God, we must begin in Genesis. The sovereignty of God is only the beginning, however; the following four books reveal other important attributes and characteristics of God. As I said at the outset, the being and nature of God are expressed in his work. In our redemption, Genesis shows God initiating his great eternal plan; in his sovereign wisdom and power he has chosen a people for his name. That is only the beginning; in the books that follow, redemption is accomplished and applied to sinful people.

Part II
Exodus — the power of God

5.
The power of God in judgement

Popular Australian radio and television personality Caroline Jones declared a few years ago that 'We cannot expect vision for the future from the religious fundamentalists [a category into which I believe she would place those who take the Bible seriously] who have a vested interest in Armageddon,' and therefore cannot 'light the way forward'.[1] (Armageddon is, of course, the prelude to judgement!) Her comment is intended to be derogatory but it is true. Obviously, she does not like the concept of judgement. She is right, however, in believing that religious fundamentalists have a vested interest in judgement — in fact, everyone does, including Caroline Jones!

No doubt, the moment I mention my intention to discuss the power of God in judgement, some people, at least, will groan inwardly and think to themselves, 'Not that! I want to be encouraged. Judgement is negative; it is too unpleasant to contemplate.' If that was your reaction, I have news for you. Of course, the world has a totally negative attitude towards judgement — and not without reason! It rejects the concept of judgement because of the guilt of sin and the subconscious realization that when sinners stand before God and face judgement, they will not fare too well. 'The ungodly shall not stand in the judgement, nor sinners in the congregation of the righteous' (Ps. 1:5).

Sinners do not like to be reminded of judgement; perhaps there is the vain hope that, if it is not mentioned, God might forget and that it might never happen.

Another reason that the world rejects the concept of judgement is because it has no understanding or appreciation of the character of God. Sinners are enemies of God; they readily accuse him of unrighteousness and injustice. Ironically, in spite of the ever-increasing miscarriages of justice in law courts these days, the world is quite vocal in demanding political correctness, religious tolerance, social justice, personal rights, redistribution of wealth, racial equality and affirmative action. While some of these concepts are based on contemporary philosophy, political agendas and social prejudices, the demand for them is a tacit acknowledgement that justice is needed. The demand for these things is actually an appeal for righteous and just judgement. When the judgement of God comes, all those issues of equality, rights and fairness will be settled once for all because the character of God guarantees that his judgement is always righteous and just.

Praise to God for his righteous judgement

While we take no delight in the death of the wicked, nevertheless, the judgement of God is wonderful — we can sing about it because it is righteous. Judgement is, in fact, the subject of many of the psalms and of the great hymns of the church. When God told Abraham of his plan to judge Sodom, the patriarch pleaded with God to spare the city for the sake of the righteous; in his request Abraham said, 'Shall not the Judge of all the earth do right?' (Gen. 18:25).

When my youngest son, Daniel, was a member of the Seattle Symphony Chorale, our family attended the Christmas presentation of Handel's magnificent oratorio *Messiah*. It was the first performance of *Messiah* I had ever attended at which the audience was given a copy of the words. As the chorale sang those wonderful biblical passages so magnificently, I was in the seventh heaven. For the first time, however, I realized where Handel placed his famous 'Hallelujah Chorus'. He could have placed it almost anywhere, of course; it would have made a wonderful refrain to be sung periodically throughout the entire oratorio. Handel could have made it the grand finale; what a fantastic conclusion it would have made! Where did he place it? He placed it immediately after Psalm 2. And what is the message of Psalm 2? It is the message of judgement: 'You shall dash them in pieces like a potter's vessel.' 'Hallelujah!' (See also Rev. 11:15 and 19:6 in which the word 'Hallelujah' is used in the context of judgement.) That is radical!

Maurice Roberts says, 'The angels rejoice to do the will of God even though at times it requires them to blow trumpets of judgement against mankind and to empty vials of wrath upon the world.'[2]

In Revelation 19 a great multitude is depicted in heaven, saying, ' "Allelujah! Salvation and glory and honour and power to the Lord our God! For true and righteous are his judgements, because he has judged the great harlot who corrupted the earth with her fornication; and he has avenged on her the blood of his servants shed by her." Again they said, "Allelujah!" ' (Rev. 19:1-3, emphasis mine).

Though God judges the wicked, is that a reason for the righteous to sing 'Hallelujah'? Often in the psalms, God's people rejoice in God's judgement; the reason we can, and should, rejoice in judgement is grounded in the knowledge that God does it — and whatever God does is right, just and glorious.

After God had judged ancient Egypt, and Israel had been delivered from bondage, God's people assembled and sang the song of redemption; the words of which are recorded in Exodus 15:

I will sing to the LORD,
For he has triumphed gloriously!
The horse and its rider

He has thrown into the sea!
The LORD is my strength and song,
And he has become my salvation;
He is my God, and I will praise him;
My father's God, and I will exalt him...

Who is like you, O LORD, among the gods?
Who is like you, glorious in holiness,
Fearful in praises, doing wonders?
You stretched out your right hand;
The earth swallowed them.
You in your mercy have led forth
The people whom you have redeemed;
You have guided them in your strength
To your holy habitation

                                        (Exod. 15:1-2,11-13).

The plagues of Egypt

In the only Bible class offered at the liberal Methodist college in
Melbourne which I attended, we were taught that the plagues
which came on ancient Egypt, recorded in Exodus 7-12, were
just natural events. Egypt frequently suffered plagues, we were
told, but as the tribal elders related stories to their grandchildren
around ancient campfires, they naturally embellished and
exaggerated the accounts of them. The river being turned into
blood, for example, was nothing more than the muddy waters of
the Nile in flood, which, with the sun setting, looked like blood.
It was a serious flood in which the fish were killed and the frogs
were driven out. They died and that brought flies, and the flies
brought disease — and so forth. Every semblance of the miraculous hand of God's judgement was casually and subtly denied
and dismissed. To our teacher there was nothing supernatural
about the plagues of Egypt at all — they were just natural and
coincidental events. So much for modern scholarship — so

called! A serious study of these chapters reveals that those
plagues were no mere bedtime stories; they were brought about
by the powerful hand of Almighty God.

List of the plagues

The ten plagues were as follows:

1. The waters turned into blood (Exod. 7:14-25).
2. The plague of frogs (Exod. 8:1-15).
3. The plague of lice (Exod. 8:16-19).

4. The plague of flies (Exod. 8:20-30).
5. The plague on the cattle (Exod. 9:1-7).
6. The plague of boils (Exod. 9:8-12).

7. The devastating lightning and hail (Exod. 9:13-35).
8. The plague of locusts (Exod. 10:1-20).
9. The three days of darkness (Exod. 10:21-29).

10. Death of the firstborn (Exod. 11:1 – 12:30).

I have listed the plagues in groups of three to show how systematically and progressively God dealt with the Egyptians. The first
plague in each group (nos. 1, 4, 7) was announced by the
riverside in the morning. The second plague in each group (nos.
2, 5, 8) was announced in Pharaoh's palace. God was gracious
in his dealing with those people; he gave them fair warning. One
would have thought that after the first couple of plagues, at least,
the Egyptians would have realized that God always keeps his
word. If his warnings are not heeded, however, suddenly
judgement comes without warning. Hence, the third plague in
each group (nos. 3, 6, 9) was sent *without warning*. Did Solomon
have this in mind when he wrote, 'He who is often reproved,
and hardens his neck, will suddenly be destroyed, and that
without remedy'? (Prov. 29:1).

As the plagues progressed, a new level of severity and gravity was reached:

- The first three plagues affected the *comfort* of the people.
- The second group affected their *health* and that of their cattle.
- The third group brought *devastation* and *death.*
- The tenth plague stands by itself; it was *the culmination* of judgement.

The plagues displayed God's power over every realm; they touched the creation, the creatures and man himself — even Pharaoh!

The miraculous nature of the plagues

These plagues were miraculous in at least five ways:

1. They were given by the command of Moses.
2. They were of much greater intensity than anything previously known.
3. They were given for specific periods.
4. They were given in progressive sequence.
5. They were discriminatory in their application (the latter ones affected the Egyptians but not the Israelites).

Significantly, in the plague of frogs, Moses allowed Pharaoh to choose the time when the plague should cease in order to convince him that it did not depend on astrology or magical arts. Matthew Henry comments: 'This was designed for Pharaoh's conviction, that, if his eyes were not opened by the plague, they might be by the removal of it... Pharaoh sets the time for *tomorrow* (v. 10). And why not immediately? Was he so fond of his guests that he would have them stay another night with him?'[3]

The order in which the plagues were sent

A remarkable introversion occurs in the order in which the plagues were given. By that, I mean that there is a similarity or correspondence between:

the first plague, the turning of water into blood,	and	the tenth plague, the death of the firstborn;
the second, the plague of frogs (creatures of the night),	and	the ninth, the three days of darkness;
the third, the plague of lice, which caused the magicians to declare, 'This is the finger of God' (Exod. 8:19),	and	the eighth, the plague of locusts, which caused Pharaoh to say, 'I have sinned against the LORD your God' (Exod. 10:16);
the fourth, in which the swarm of flies was not on the land of Goshen (Exod. 8:22),	and	the seventh, in which there was no hail in the land of Goshen (Exod. 9:26);
the *fifth*, in which domestic animals of the Egyptians were diseased (Exod. 9:6),	and	the *sixth*, in which the animals were again afflicted (Exod. 9:9).

I do not know the significance of this introversion; it is, however, too remarkable to be coincidental. Perhaps it is to impress upon the people that the judgements of God are never fortuitous, capricious, or arbitrary. In all of God's works — even in judgement — there is order, design, purpose and plan.

The hardening of Pharaoh's heart

Significantly, as the judgements intensified and progressed in severity, Pharaoh's heart was progressively hardened. He began by declaring, 'Who is the LORD, that I should obey his voice to let Israel go? I do not know the LORD, nor will I let Israel go' (Exod. 5:2).

'Israel was now a despised oppressed people, looked on as the tail of the nation, and, by the character they bore, Pharaoh makes his estimate of their God, and concludes that he made no better figure among the gods than his people did among the nations... Ignorance and contempt of God are at the bottom of all wickedness that is in the world. Men know not the Lord, or have very low and mean thoughts of him, and therefore they obey not his voice.'[4]

Grace in the midst of judgement

In the midst of God's judgement, there are evidences of God's grace. Before God hardened Pharaoh's heart as a judicial measure, he had been warned six times. God sent Moses to inform him that God would send plagues upon his heart (Exod. 9:14) — that he was marked for ruin. 'Now that no place is found for repentance in Pharaoh, nothing can prevent his utter destruction. God promises to send, not only temporal plagues upon [his] body, but spiritual plagues upon [his] soul.'[5] Moses was obliged to tell Pharaoh that he must go down in history as a standing monument to the justice and power of God's wrath (Exod. 9:16). (Significantly, this passage is quoted by the apostle Paul in his treatment of the doctrine of election in Romans 9:17.)

God revealed his grace not only in warning Pharaoh, but also in advising him to prepare. When Moses predicted the plague of hail, he encouraged Pharaoh to bring his servants and cattle under shelter (Exod. 9:19). 'When God threatens ruin,' says Matthew Henry, 'his mercy, at the same time, shows a way of

The power of God in judgement   97

escape ... so unwilling is he that any should perish.'[6] Sin grows
like a plant; there is first the blade, then the ear, and finally the
mature head of grain. If sin is not dealt with and rooted out, it
matures and hardens the heart. All along the way, God graciously warns the wicked to cease from their wicked ways and
escape the tragic and awful consequences of their sin. It was true
for Pharaoh as an individual and it was true for the nation.

When a nation turns its back upon God and refuses to heed
his Word, he uses other means to secure the attention of the
people. He is a God of mercy and compassion; he does not
delight in the death of the wicked — he warns them to 'flee from
the wrath to come'. Tragically, many, like Pharaoh, ignore and
resist God's gracious dealings and continue to harden their
hearts against him. They continue to do so until they pass the
point of no return where God hardens their hearts as a judicial
measure. When a person or nation passes the point of no
return, they can no longer repent and return. To reject God's
gracious dealings is a very serious matter.

The purpose of the plagues

The Egyptian plagues were far more than demonstrations of
God's mighty power; God was not showing off — if I may
express it in those terms. God was accomplishing four things, at
least, through the plagues on Egypt.

1. In his mighty acts of judgement, God revealed his righteous character

When God called Moses to lead the Israelites out of Egypt, he
reminded him of his covenant with Israel. He said, 'I have
remembered my covenant. Therefore say to the children of
Israel: I am the LORD; I will bring you out from under the
burdens of the Egyptians, I will rescue you from their bondage,

and I will redeem you with an outstretched arm and with great judgements. I will take you as my people, and I will be your God. *Then you shall know that I am the* LORD *your God'* (Exod. 6:5-7, emphasis mine).

Similar statements about God making himself known to Pharaoh, to the Egyptians and to the Israelites appear about a dozen times in these chapters:

- to Pharaoh (Exod. 7:17; 8:10,22; 9:14,29);
- to Egypt (Exod. 7:5; 14:4,18);
- to Israel (Exod. 6:7; 10:2; 16:6,12).

In sending these judgements, God was making himself known to his people and to the wicked. Significantly, Pharaoh acknowledged his wickedness and God's righteousness in dealing with him (Exod. 9:27). 'The great design both of judgements and mercies is to convince us that there is none like the Lord our God, none so wise, so mighty, so good, no enemy so formidable, no friend so desirable, so valuable.'[7]

When God began to make himself known, however, the enemy of men's souls endeavoured to subvert and confuse the issue. As God manifested himself in power, Satan contested it. The magicians of Egypt duplicated three miracles which God did at the hand of Moses (the first was turning their rods into serpents). Their duplication of those miracles was not merely a contest of power; they were an open expression of hostility and opposition to God. Satan is a master of counterfeit miracles; he imitates and duplicates the works of Almighty God – but he does so *to deceive*.

When Satan motivates and empowers people to do signs and wonders, however, his power is limited. We find, for example, that when the plague of lice came upon Egypt, the magicians were forced to admit that this was nothing less than the finger of God.

Also, Satan's works are destructive; when God sent the first plague, water was scarce. Therefore, 'To turn more of it into blood, only to show their art, plainly intimates that the design of the devil is only to delude his devotees and amuse them, not to do them any real kindness, but to keep them from doing a real kindness to themselves by repenting and returning to their God.'[8]

In Moses' farewell message to Israel (the book of Deuteronomy), he warned Israel against falsehood and deception. He said that false prophets would perform signs and wonders in order to deceive God's people. If a prophet caused the people to deviate from following the Lord, they were not to listen to him; on the contrary, they were to put him to death. False prophets not only did signs and wonders back in ancient times; they do them today. In fact, in the book of Revelation, God says that the spirits of demons will do signs again (Rev. 13:13; 16:14; 19:20).

God does not deceive; he uses his power to make himself known. Actually, no one needs any demonstration of power to convince them of God's existence; such a demonstration already exists in the creation. God's eternal power and deity are clearly seen, says the apostle, so that all men are without excuse (Rom. 1:20). When the evidence of God's existence and power, which confronts us at every turn, is ignored and the special revelation which he has given of himself in his Word is rejected, in his mercy, he sends temporal judgements to remind us that he is still there and that he is still in control. God never uses his power arbitrarily, fortuitously, capriciously, or indiscriminately; when he judges, he uses his power righteously, purposefully and justly. In sending temporal judgements, God makes himself known. In making himself known, he vindicates his righteousness and justice; he preserves his moral integrity and credibility.

Further, as a God of mercy and grace, he always has the welfare of his creatures in view. Significantly, in speaking of the future, the prophet Isaiah says, 'The LORD will be known to Egypt, and the Egyptians will know the LORD in that day... And the LORD will strike Egypt, he will strike and heal it; they will return to the LORD, and he will be entreated by them and heal them' (Isa. 19:21-22).

In the words of Matthew Henry, 'Every thing concurred to signalize this, that God's name (that is, his incontestable sovereignty, his irresistible power, and his inflexible justice) might be declared throughout all the earth.'[9]

2. God sent temporal judgements to awaken the Egyptians to the folly and futility of trusting in idols

The plagues were designed to discredit the gods of Egypt and to show how worthless they were before the living God. This point is noted several times. For example, God says, 'Against all the gods of Egypt I will execute judgement: I am the LORD' (Exod. 12:12). In the song of redemption, God's people sang, 'Who is like you, O LORD, among the gods? Who is like you, glorious in holiness, fearful in praises, doing wonders?' (Exod. 15:11).

The first plague, for example, was the turning of the water into blood — that included the River Nile. The Nile was, and still is, the stream which makes an otherwise barren and desolate land fertile and fruitful. When God turned it into blood, instead of it being a stream of life, it became a channel of death. The river Nile was worshipped because it was the life supply of the nation. Pharaoh, it will be remembered, had ordered the Israelites to cast their baby boys into the river (Exod. 1:22). When he saw that river turned into blood, there should have been conviction, remorse and repentance for the blood which was upon his hands.

The fourth plague was that of flies. Egyptians worshipped Beelzebub; the lord of the flies. They wanted flies; God gave them flies! What a pest their god proved to be!

The fifth plague brought disease on the cattle; cattle were particularly sacred to the Egyptians. At the Oriental Institute at the University of Chicago, there is a massive Egyptian statue of a bull. I have forgotten the actual dimensions but it is so immense that an additional room had to be built to house it. When the

Israelites foolishly thought that Moses and God had forsaken them at Mt Sinai, Aaron constructed a golden calf and declared it to have been responsible for their deliverance from the land of bondage.

The tenth plague was the death of the firstborn in every household. Not even Pharaoh could save the life of his own son. Many of the drawings of the Egyptian pharaohs on the throne have lines radiating from the king; at the end of those lines there is a little hand. This was to depict the idea that Pharaoh was the giver of life. Though he was supposed to be the giver of life, he could not stop the angel of death in his own palace. 'Those that are not bettered by judgements and mercies are commonly made worse.'[10]

3. God sends temporal judgements to remind people of their moral duty

People cannot live reckless, indulgent lives in defiance of God's law and still expect God to smile on them. Temporal judgements, as a means of God's grace, are sent to remind us, as the Israelites were reminded, that our moral duty is 'to do justly, to love mercy, and to walk humbly with [our] God' (Micah 6:8). Or, as Moses expressed it: 'And now, Israel, what does the LORD your God require of you, but to fear the LORD your God, to walk in all his ways and to love him, to serve the LORD your God with all your heart and with all your soul, and to keep the commandments of the LORD and his statutes which I command you today for your good?' (Deut. 10:12-13). Failure in moral duty has serious consequences.

4. God sends temporal judgements to warn people of judgement to come

Though the judgements on Egypt were temporal in nature, they had a certain eschatological prolepsis — that is, though they happened away back there in ancient Egypt, they reflect and anticipate what is yet to come. There are striking parallels between the plagues of Egypt and those described in the book of Revelation. This merits further serious study; I will simply list some of them:

- The enemies of God will again perform miracles (Rev. 13:13-15).
- Water will again be turned into blood (Rev. 8:8; 16:4-6). Significantly, the reason given for this is that the blood of the prophets has been shed.
- Unclean spirits like frogs will appear (Rev. 16:13).
- A severe plague of creatures described as locusts will appear to torment men (Rev. 9:2-11).
- Men will again be smitten with loathsome boils (Rev. 16:2).
- There will again be destruction by hail and fire (Rev. 8:7; 16:21).
- Intense darkness will cover the kingdom of the beast (Rev. 16:10).
- Many people will seek death; they will harden their hearts against the works of the Lord (Rev. 9:20-21).
- Death will consume multitudes — one third of mankind (Rev. 9:15).

As has already been mentioned, after their deliverance from Egypt, God's people sang the song of redemption recorded in Exodus 15. In Revelation, when the wrath and judgement of God have been completed, the redeemed will 'sing *the song of Moses* ... and the song of the Lamb' (Rev. 15:3, emphasis mine).

In spite of all the terrible things described in the book of Revelation (the pouring out of vials of wrath, plagues, demonic activity, destruction and death) God's people will be spared and delivered. The ancient Israelites were affected by some of the early plagues in Egypt with good reason. God often allows his

people to taste of temporal judgements; the reality and strength
of genuine religion is not in happy-go-lucky, back-slapping, foot-
stomping, carefree, fun-packed meetings and activities. Genuine
religion is demonstrated under stress and difficulty. Although
God keeps his people through the most troubled times, there is a
vast difference between the response of God's people and the
wicked.

I readily admit that I do not have all the answers concerning
eschatology; in fact, I probably have more questions than
answers. I used to know all about the end times; I grew up
espousing the Dispensational scheme of events. Like many, I
had all the details mapped out; I believed that the church would
experience a secret rapture before the tribulation and hence
escape that perilous time. When a teenager challenged me to
prove my position from the Scripture, I found myself in real
trouble. More importantly, I discovered that a primary reason for
holding to a secret rapture was due to the fact that I did not
believe that God would — or that he could — keep his people
through times of tribulation. I discovered that I was fearful of
perilous times. I thought that my survival was dependent on me
and I was afraid that I would not be able to take care of myself.
Simply, I lacked confidence in the power of God. Possibly, many
of the details of my eschatology might be wrong — please don't
be offended if you disagree.

The tribulation period, I believe, will be God's final warning
to a corrupt and wicked world; it will be the last opportunity for
the wicked to repent before they are turned into hell. No matter
what form tribulation might take or when it might come, the
principle still stands; temporal judgements are designed to warn
us of judgement to come. In times of trouble, God's power is
manifest in two ways: he drives the wicked to their knees, and, at
the same time, he keeps his people through those same adverse
circumstances.

In Revelation, the announcement of judgement is described
and God reveals that his design in sending plagues upon men is
to bring them to repentance. 'The rest of mankind, who were

not killed by these plagues, *did not repent* of the works of their
hands ... and they *did not repent* of their murders or their sorcer-
ies or their sexual immorality or their thefts' (Rev. 9:20-21,
emphasis mine). In that final manifestation of God's power, he
will act righteously and justly — the wicked will be destroyed and
the righteous will be redeemed.

As temporal judgements have come to various regions of the
world in recent years — the earthquakes, floods, fires, famines,
tornadoes and other calamities and disasters, including the
scourge of AIDS and other fatal diseases — we must ask what
more does God need to do to get our attention and cause us to
return to him with all our hearts? Yet we, as sinful people,
continue to ignore God, defy his Word and pursue wickedness.
Do we really expect God to ignore sin and to condone wickedness? Are not God's temporal judgements designed to cause 'the
wicked [to] forsake his way, and the unrighteous man his
thoughts', and to cause him to 'return to the LORD'? (Isa. 55:7).
Surely, his temporal judgements are designed to cause us to 'seek
the LORD while he may be found, [and] call upon him while he
is near' (Isa. 55:6).

The implications for us of God's righteous judgements

God has not only declared that he is righteous in his judgements; he has demonstrated and proved it by sending his Son to
this world. When the Lord Jesus came into this world, he did
not come to judge but to save. He came to bear the wrath and
judgement of God so that we might escape the wrath to come.
Because he bore the judgement which we deserve, 'There is ...
now no condemnation to those who are in Christ Jesus' (Rom.
8:1). If we know him as our personal Saviour, we can declare
with the apostle, 'I know whom I have believed and am persuaded that he is able to keep what I have committed to him
until that Day' (2 Tim. 1:12). Before we rejoice and sing the
'Hallelujah Chorus', however, we had better make sure that we

truly belong to the company of the redeemed and that we stand under his powerful hand of protection and not under his hand of judgement. When our Lord comes the second time, he will come in power and great glory — and he will come to judge!

As I have said, God never uses his power arbitrarily, fortuitously, capriciously, or indiscriminately; when he judges, he uses his power righteously, justly and purposefully. That means, of course, that those who know him can trust him to keep them to the end. Because he is righteous, he never will deceive us.

6.
The power of God in redemption

When God made his covenant with Abraham, he promised that his descendants would occupy the land of Canaan. In the light of that promise, why didn't God establish him in the land from the outset? Instead, through providential circumstances, God took Jacob and his family to Egypt for four centuries. (That is the period between the events at the end of Genesis and those at the beginning of Exodus.) In giving his defence before the Sanhedrin, Stephen said that Israel experienced affliction in Egypt for 400 years (Acts 7:6). Immediately, the question arises: 'Why did God keep his people waiting so long, and why did he take them through such a long period of adversity?' There are several reasons.

Firstly, God informed Abraham that 'the iniquity of the Amorites [was] not yet complete' (Gen. 15:16). That is, the wickedness of the Canaanites had not yet run its full course, or reached the point where it was ripe for judgement. Had God judged them prematurely, he might have been accused of injustice; he does not judge the wicked before their time. Significantly, God revealed to Abraham that the fourth generation of his descendants (a generation being more or less a century) would be his instrument to execute judgement upon the wicked Amorites.

Secondly, that long period of adversity concerns the justice of God. Joseph's brothers sought to destroy him by selling him as a slave into Egypt (Gen. 37). God never ignores such wicked actions; what those brothers sowed, they reaped. The sins of the fathers were visited upon the children to the fourth generation. Because Joseph was sold into slavery in Egypt, the children of Israel experienced, as a just and appropriate punishment, the grief and hardship of Egyptian slavery for 400 years.

Similarly, the Jews handed Jesus over to the Romans to be crucified; within a few short years, God delivered them into the hands of the Romans. In A.D. 70, imperial Rome marched against Jerusalem and destroyed it. Or, viewed from another angle, the Jews delivered the Lord Jesus Christ into the hands of Gentiles; for almost 2,000 years, the Jews have suffered at the hands of Gentiles. God's justice is exact and appropriate. Let no one think that any sin goes unnoticed or unpunished by God.

Thirdly, why do the wicked seem to prosper while the righteous are made to wait and to suffer affliction? We are told, for example, that God gave the mountains of Seir to Esau to possess but Jacob and his family went down to Egypt (Josh. 24:4). Esau received his inheritance immediately; Jacob and his family had to wait almost 500 years for theirs. God was making his people acutely aware of their need for redemption, of their inability to deliver themselves, and to prepare them for their inheritance. God was working to make his mercy and grace known. The wicked receive their reward now; God's people have a future ahead of them.

When the Israelites went down to Egypt, they occupied the land of Goshen — the most fertile part of the Nile delta. They had the most productive land available. Egypt was an attractive place; it offered all kinds of treasures and pleasures. Had the Israelites been allowed to settle there peacefully and undisturbed, undoubtedly they would have forgotten God's purpose for them as a nation — they would have forgotten their higher calling and they would have seen no good reason to leave. For God's people, however, Egypt was not their home.

The plight of man

Consider, first of all, how the Israelites happened to be in Egypt
in the first place. The first verse of Exodus says that 'Each man
and his household came with Jacob.' Significantly, the name
'Jacob' is used. 'Jacob', as we have seen, means 'deceiver' (or
'supplanter'). His name described his character; before his
encounter with God at Bethel, Jacob had deceived his twin
brother, Esau, and his father, Isaac, in obtaining the birthright.
At Bethel, his name was changed by God to 'Israel', meaning
'Prince with God'. Why is the earlier name, 'Jacob', used here? It
was not chosen arbitrarily or carelessly. Jacob brought all his
descendants into the land of bondage.

Important spiritual lessons are to be derived and learned
from this historical narrative. The land of Egypt is typical of the
world system with which all God's people have to contend and
struggle in their spiritual lives. Adam, through his disobedience
and rebellion, brought his descendants into an attractive place
where all kinds of treasures and pleasures have a powerful
attraction. It is, however, ruled by a powerful monarch who
enslaves his subjects and treats them mercilessly. Before the
power of God can be known in redemption, God allows his
people to experience adversity and affliction to make them aware
of their helpless condition and of their need of his deliverance.

After the Israelites had lived in Egypt for a time, a new king
came to power who 'did not know Joseph' — as the text expresses it. The evidence suggests that he was not just a different
king with new policies, but that he was a king of a different kind.
(In his defence before the Jewish elders, Stephen rehearsed the
history of Israel; in his reference to the Egyptian pharaoh he
used the Greek word 'heteros' (Acts 7:18), meaning 'another of a
different kind'). Our knowledge of Egyptian dynasties is far from
complete, but evidently Assyria, the rival power, took control of
Egypt and placed one of their own on the throne. Apparently,
this was the king who 'did not know [or "recognize"] Joseph'. Is
this not typical of Satan, who has usurped control over this

world? He is, as the Scripture says, 'the ruler of this world' (John 16:11).

This pharaoh said to his people, ' "The people of the children of Israel are more and mightier than we; come, let us deal shrewdly with them, lest they multiply, and it happen, in the event of war, that they also join our enemies and fight against us, and so go up out of the land." Therefore they set taskmasters over them to afflict them with their burdens' (Exod. 1:9-11).

Pharaoh's concern that Israel might not be loyal — even after four centuries of living there — indicates that he recognized their uniqueness as a nation. Further, his reference to their going 'up out of the land' suggests that he might have known something of God's purpose for them. At any rate, he was not about to jeopardize security or lose his workforce; he sought, therefore, to control Israel by force and thereby frustrate the plan of God. The more he afflicted them, however, the more they multiplied and grew. 'And they were in dread of the children of Israel' (Exod. 1:12). When Pharaoh's plan failed, he resorted to the destruction of all the baby boys at birth by commanding that they be cast into the river. This pharaoh was utterly ruthless; he would stop at nothing — including infanticide. Israel was afflicted with unreasonable work demands and physical suffering.

When God called Moses, he said, 'I have surely seen the oppression of my people who are in Egypt, and have heard their cry because of their taskmasters, for I know their sorrows [or pain]' (Exod. 3:7). God had not forgotten his people, though at times they must have wondered where he was and what had become of his covenantal promise to their father Abraham. Even after Moses appeared on the scene, their burdens were increased and their suffering intensified.

Why all that suffering, heartache and pain? No doubt the purpose of God is far more complex than we can comprehend or understand, but one thing is clear: God was making them acutely aware of their need for deliverance and of their own utter helplessness to do anything about it. It would have been no act of kindness for God to have made his people comfortable in

Egypt; they were called to more important, more permanent and much better things. Ironically, even after they were delivered, many of them did not appreciate what God had done; frequently they longed to return to Egypt.

Self-confidence is one of the primary characteristics of sin; sinners imagine that they are in charge of their lives and can handle anything. Young people are confident that they are invincible — they think that they don't need parents, or anyone else, telling them what to do or warning them against the pitfalls and dangers of life. No one, I suppose, deliberately sets out to be an alcoholic derelict or a drug addict but, alas, how frequently it happens! In many ways, many persist in that attitude throughout life. While self-confidence exists, however, there will be no realization of the need for deliverance. Often God, in his mercy, allows a person to come to the point of desperation in order to force him to acknowledge that he is not in control — that sin has complete mastery over him. In his excellent little book, *The Thought of God*, Maurice Roberts says that we 'have an urgent need to study the theme of sin again in biblical light. Sin is arguably the greatest power in existence but for the power of God himself.'[1]

Before a sinner can experience the power of God in redemption, he must recognize the power of sin over his life. He must, says Matthew Henry, recognize the *fact* of sin, the *fault* of sin, the *fountain* of sin, the *folly* of sin, the *filth* of sin and the *fruit* of sin.[2] He needs to realize also that, no matter what he might do, he cannot deliver himself; there is no help apart from God. Before sinners can experience the power of God, they must first realize their predicament. While God's great power was expressed in his judgement of the Egyptians, he displayed his power in redeeming his people. Judgement and redemption are closely allied, of course; they are, in fact, two sides of the same coin. When God redeemed his people from Egypt, he delivered them from the sphere and effects of judgement.

The provision of redemption

Identification

Just before the final plague on Egypt, God instituted the Pass-over. He informed Moses and Aaron that 'This month shall be your beginning of months; it shall be the first month of the year to you.' On the tenth day of that month, every man was to take a lamb without blemish and keep it at his house; it was to be identified with the family. On the fourteenth day, the lamb was killed and its blood applied to the doorposts of the house. Members of the family were to remain in the house, dressed ready to leave Egypt and feast upon the lamb.

God said, 'When I see the blood, I will pass over you' (Exod. 12:13). The instructions were to be followed carefully because this important event concerned both judgement and redemp-tion: 'For the protection of Israel from this plague they were ordered to sprinkle the blood of the lamb on the doorposts, their doing which would be accepted as an instance of their faith in the divine warnings and their obedience to the divine precepts.'[3] 'Not but that the destroying angel could have known an Israelite from an Egyptian in the street; but God would intimate to them that their safety was owing to the *blood of sprinkling*.'[4]

Substitution

The application of the blood to the doorpost signified that a death had already occurred — that judgement had already fallen on a substitute. There had to be substitution. A simple but quite remarkable progression appears in this passage; it moves from '*a* lamb' in verse 3, to '*the* lamb' in verse 4 and to '*your* lamb' in verse 5. Before anyone can be redeemed, he must recognize the need for a substitute to bear the penalty for his sin. That is not sufficient, however; he must understand also that there is *only one* acceptable substitute — the Lamb of God who is without spot

and blemish. Finally, he must identify with that Lamb and
embrace him as his *personal* substitute.

The Passover is one of the outstanding pictures of redemption in the Old Testament; the apostle directly identifies the
Passover with Christ when he says, 'Christ, our Passover, was
sacrificed for us' (1 Cor. 5:7). Every detail parallels the redemptive work of Jesus Christ on the cross. Matthew Henry points
out that 'As Christ was crucified at the Passover, so he solemnly
entered into Jerusalem four days before, the very day the paschal
lamb was set apart.'[5]

Participation

When a person embraces the Lord Jesus Christ by faith, '[His]
blood ... cleanses us from all sin' (1 John 1:7) and the one who
is cleansed begins a new life. 'If anyone is in Christ, *he* is a new
creation' (2 Cor. 5:17). The application of the blood of the lamb
was just the first step. Every member of the family was required
to remain in the house and feast on the lamb with bitter herbs.
The lamb was their nourishment and sustenance; the family was
their fellowship and support. Bitter herbs were to remind them
of the bitterness of sin and of the sorrow it has caused. 'This will
give an admirable relish to the paschal lamb. Christ will be sweet
to us if sin be bitter.'[6] Redemption concerns, not only reconciliation to God, but also reconciliation to God's people. The
church is the family of God in which true believers find support
and fellowship as they feast together on the Lamb. The communion of the saints is much more than a phrase in the
Apostles' Creed; it concerns that which believers hold in common and share. The life of the family is expressed in mutual
concern, interaction and love. The Scripture nowhere endorses
or encourages the notion that all a person has to do is 'accept
Jesus' and then he is free to do as he pleases. 'Those whom God
has marked for himself must not mingle with evil-doers.'[7] There
had to be participation.

Anticipation

Participants in the Passover feast were to be dressed ready for departure from the land of bondage; they were to eat the meal with their robes girded around their waist and their staff in their hand. The Israelites were to be ready for departure from Egypt at a moment's notice. What was the significance of this? 'Shortly there will be an alarming cry at midnight, "Behold, the bridegroom cometh." '[8] When believers participate in the Christian Passover — the Lord's Supper — they are to do so with an eye to the future. As often as we partake, says the Scripture, we 'proclaim the Lord's death *until he comes*.' In other words, the Lord's Supper is an anticipation.

Many years ago, I knew a delightful teenager in Adelaide who was radiant when she talked about her Lord. In due course, she completed training as a nurse and began studies at Adelaide Bible Institute (as it was then known). There she met a fine young man and they became engaged to be married; they planned to serve the Lord on the mission field. Before Vicki had completed her course or was married, she was diagnosed with cancer and a few months later she died. At her funeral, the principal of the Bible institute said that Vicki had packed her bags and was ready to go. Believers should be prepared and ready to go at a moment's notice — or without any notice! The wicked, by way of contrast, invest everything in this life because that is all that they have. The psalmist says that the 'inner thought [of the wicked] is that their houses will last for ever' (Ps. 49:11). For God's people, 'This world is not our home, we're just a-passing through.'

The accomplishment of redemption

The pillar of cloud and fire

The Israelites began their departure from the land of bondage on the night of the Passover. They journeyed to a place called Etham — 'the edge of the unknown'. At that point, '... the LORD went before them by day in a pillar of cloud to lead the way, and by night in a pillar of fire to give them light, so as to go by day and night' (Exod. 13:21). God personally led his people forth from the land of bondage.

Significantly, the visible presence of God brought light to the Israelites but it kept the Egyptians in darkness (Exod. 14:19-20). The visible presence of God (the Shekinah glory) went before and continued with Israel for centuries — the prophet Ezekiel describes the presence of God leaving the temple at the time of the Babylonian Captivity. The Shekinah glory is typical of the work of God's Holy Spirit in illuminating the path of the righteous and guiding his people. It is the Spirit of God who applies the redemption purchased by Christ. The apostle says that the gospel is the fragrance of life to those who are being saved and the aroma of death to those who are perishing (2 Cor. 2:15-16). It is amazing, is it not, that the presence of God and the message of the gospel produce such opposite reactions and responses in people?

'By coming under this cloud, they signified their putting themselves under the divine guidance and command by the ministry of Moses. Protection draws allegiance; this cloud was the badge of God's protection, and so became the bond of their allegiance.'[9]

The Red Sea

In this great work, God first made his people acutely aware of their need for redemption. He then took the initiative in calling

Moses and manifested his great power in delivering them from the land of bondage.

As the children of Israel began to move out of the land, Pharaoh realized that he was about to lose his workforce. 'It is easy to imagine what a rage Pharaoh was now in, roaring like a lion disappointed of his prey, how his proud heart aggravated the affront, swelled with indignation, scorned to be baffled, longed to be revenged: and now all the plagues are as if they had never been. He has quite forgotten the sorrowful funerals of his firstborn, and can think of nothing but making Israel feel his resentments; now he thinks he can be too hard for God himself; for, otherwise, could he have hoped to conquer a people so dear to him?'[10]

Pharaoh knew that the Israelites could not escape; he could easily overtake them and he knew, no doubt, that he had them trapped. He could readily recapture them and bring them back into slavery. Quite literally, God's people were caught 'between the devil and the deep blue sea'. For the Israelites, of course, their impossible situation was a trial of their faith. But had not God acted in power on their behalf already? Surely they had reason enough to trust him now! If they were to die at the hands of the Egyptians, why had God spared them from the plagues and the angel of death? God brought them to this impossible situation that they might discover the wonder and greatness of their redemption and learn that they could trust him fully and completely. They needed to know that 'If God is for us, who can be against us?' (Rom. 8:31).

Humanly speaking, their situation was utterly impossible; they were helpless. There was nothing they could do to defend themselves against Pharaoh's military might, they could not escape across the rugged terrain on either side, and they could not cross the Red Sea. But when their redemption seemed impossible, it was time for God to act. Moses said, 'Do not be afraid. Stand still and see the salvation of the LORD, which he will accomplish for you today' (Exod. 14:13). God rebuked him for this remark and told him to go forward.

Salvation is all of God; nothing can be contributed by sinners towards it. Significantly, the sea which the Israelites faced and feared was the way of deliverance; for the Egyptians, however, it was the means of destruction. God did not take his people to the Red Sea, open it up and tell them, 'It's up to you; you can go through if you want.' In his book, *Redemption, Accomplished and Applied*, Professor John Murray shows that God did not merely make redemption *possible*; he made it *actual*. Salvation is not an arbitrary matter, nor is it dependent on the whims of men. When redemption is complete, God will have accomplished exactly what he has purposed and planned. He will have redeemed his people for the glory of his name.

In commenting on the crossing of the Jordan river, Matthew Henry observes: 'By the dividing of the waters from the waters, and the making of the dry land to appear which had been covered, God would remind them of that in which Moses by revelation had instructed them concerning the work of creation ... and that they might know that the God whom they worshipped was the same God that made the world and that it was the same power that was engaged and employed for them.'[11]

In recounting this great event, Moses declared, 'They are your people and your inheritance, whom you brought out by your mighty power and by your outstretched arm' (Deut. 9:29). Forty years later in the city of Jericho, Rahab said to the two spies, 'We have heard how the LORD dried up the water of the Red Sea for you when you came out of Egypt' (Josh. 2:10). The redemption of God's people was a mighty display of his great power. Is it not still true? What but the power of God can deliver a person from the bondage of sin and make him a new creature in Christ?

Moses and his people from Egypt's land did flee;
The enemy behind them and in front of them the sea.
God raised the waters like a wall and opened up the way;
And the God who lived in Moses' time is just the same today.[12]

The Exodus as a picture of the work of Christ

In one sense, the Passover and the Exodus must be kept to-gether; they are not really two separate events but different aspects in the redemption of God's people. Indeed, they bear the same relationship to one another as the death of Christ does to his resurrection. God raised his Son from the dead to accomplish what he planned. A. W. Pink states that 'The miracle of the Red Sea occupies a similar place in the Old Testament scriptures as the resurrection of the Lord Jesus does in the New; it is appealed to as the standard of measurement, as the supreme demonstration of God's power.'[13]

Having been delivered from bondage, they did not find that everything was smooth sailing after that. Their deliverance was followed by times of testing.

- First, they needed *food*; God displayed his power in sending them manna (Exod. 16). As Matthew Henry puts it, 'God would have them to depend upon him for their daily bread, and not to take thought for tomorrow. He that led them forth would feed them.'[14]
- Also, they needed *water*. God instructed Moses to smite the rock at Rephidim and, by his great power, he provided water for their need (Exod. 17).
- Also, the Israelites were ruthlessly attacked by the Amalekites; after Moses interceded, the children of Israel accomplished a great *victory*. When the battle was over, Moses erected an altar and named it *'Jehovah-Nissi'* — 'the Lord our banner', or 'victory'.

These events relate to our Lord.

- In John 6, Jesus directly identifies himself with the manna given in the wilderness.

• In 1 Corinthians 10, Paul says that the smitten rock was Christ.

• And one cannot miss the significance of the name of the altar; through the sacrifice of our Lord there is victory over the enemies of God's people.

The power of God displayed in redemption today

The power of God is seen, not only in the initial work of redemption, but also in the daily provision for the needs of his people in the wilderness. While many within Christendom today seem to think that an unbelieving world will be impressed by, and convinced of, Christianity by physical signs and wonders, the greatest manifestation of God's power is in the redemption of sinners from spiritual bondage. Nothing is more convincing than a transformed life.

While sinners are redeemed individually, there is more to God's redemptive work than saving a mass of people. His purpose is, as the apostle affirms, to save individuals, cement them together as bricks in a building in order to build a spiritual building in which he himself dwells (Eph. 2). He takes each brick, as it were, and cements it into the wall to create his glorious temple. By his abundant grace, God enables his people to live in unity and love. Redemption, then, is not simply an individual matter; it has this wonderful corporate dimension. The unity and love expressed and enjoyed by God's people cause the angels to look in awe at the wisdom of God (Eph. 3:10). The unity and love among God's people are the envy of the world — though, unfortunately, these things are not always evident in the church today. 'By this all will know that you are my disciples,' said Jesus, 'if you have love for one another' (John 13:35). When redemption is complete, God's infinite power and abundant mercy will be evident to all. He will have redeemed a people for the glory of his name.

7.

The power of God in revelation

God's covenant promise to Abraham

When God called Abraham from Ur of the Chaldees, he said, 'I will make you a great nation ... and in you all the families of the earth shall be blessed' (Gen. 12:1-3). That covenantal promise contains three important facts which need to be kept in mind as one reads the entire Bible.

> 1. God has a great and glorious plan and purpose for this world: 'All the families of the earth shall be blessed.'
> 2. The 'seed of Abraham', the Messiah, is the means by which the world will be blessed.
> 3. The church is the instrument, or channel, through which his blessing comes; God will bless all the families of the earth through a specially chosen people.

Abraham did not live to see that promise fulfilled. A period of about 200 years elapsed from the time God gave his covenantal promise to the end of the book of Genesis. When Jacob, Abraham's grandson, went down to Egypt he took his extended family consisting of seventy people. That is not a nation!

A nation consists of four major things, at least.

1. There must be people

As I mentioned in the previous chapter, an interval of about 400 years occurred between the end of Genesis and the beginning of Exodus. In the opening chapter of Exodus, we read that, in spite of great adversity and affliction, the children of Israel had multiplied exceedingly. Literally, the land swarmed with them. In keeping with his promise, God made the children of Israel numerous.

2. There must be a code of law

No nation can exist for long if it has no law and everyone does what is right in his own eyes (Judg. 17:6). People must have a clear understanding of their mutual relationships and of their common responsibilities. This is the aspect which we shall cover in this chapter.

3. There must be a place for the people to live

After Mt Sinai and the forty years of wilderness wanderings, Joshua led the children of Israel in the conquest of the land of Canaan, the land that had been deeded to them by God. The account of that is in the book of Joshua.

4. There must be a king

There must be someone who oversees and is responsible for the welfare of the people; he must possess authority to enforce the law, to protect the people and to maintain harmony and peace. Some people believe that it was not God's intention for Israel to have a king, but that God himself should rule over them directly. There are several problems with that idea; if that were the case, the laws regulating the life and behaviour of a king in Deuteronomy 17 would be superfluous. Later, when Saul became king, he was chosen for the wrong reasons.

Israel was unique among the nations; no other nation can claim to be a people in covenant relationship to God, to have a code of law revealed by God, or possess a land deeded to them by God. No nation owes its origin to God as Israel does. Exodus begins by showing that God multiplied the family of Jacob greatly during their bondage in Egypt. By the time of the Exodus, Israel had become a host of more than two million. Having delivered them by his mighty power, God took them to Mt Sinai where he gave them his law. At Mt Sinai, his power was displayed as he revealed his holy will.

Because God is the Creator, he is in a position to dictate what he requires of his creatures. It ought not to be forgotten, however, that when he made his covenant with Abraham, he placed himself under solemn obligation. In other words, God is not a dictator who simply orders people what to do. 'He had laid himself under obligations to them by promise, and therefore might justly lay his obligations on them by precept.'[1]

The setting and preparation for the giving of the law

'In the third month after the children of Israel had gone out of the land of Egypt, on the same day, they came to the wilderness of Sinai' (Exod. 19:1). God records the exact day. Jewish tradition says that the giving of the law on Mt Sinai was fifty days after the observance of the Passover. When it is remembered that the Jews used a lunar calendar and that the Passover was observed on the fourteenth day of the first month, the fifty-day interval is entirely possible – even probable. If so, the giving of the law on Mt Sinai corresponds with Pentecost – which took place fifty days after Passover. When the Feast of Pentecost was completed and fulfilled with the coming of the Holy Spirit in the New Testament, God again manifested his power in ways which made people amazed as they heard the word of the Lord in their own tongue.

When Israel arrived at Mt Sinai, Moses went up the mountain to speak with God. They had seen the judgements of God on Egypt; they had experienced his great power at the Red Sea; they had witnessed his guiding presence in the pillar of cloud and fire; they had gained victory over the Amalekites at Rephidim in answer to the intercession of Moses; and they had enjoyed the mercies of the Lord in providing daily manna and refreshing water from the smitten rock — all these things, and more besides, were demonstrations of God's great power and expressions of his love for his people. These tremendous manifestations of God's power were indicative of the fact that he intended to fulfil his covenantal promise to Abraham.

On their arrival at Mt Sinai, God reminded his people that, having destroyed the Egyptians, he had borne them on eagles' wings and brought them to himself (Exod. 19:4). That is a most graphic picture. During the forty years he spent in the wilderness, Moses had plenty of opportunities to observe eagles, no doubt. Later, in the book of Deuteronomy, he elaborates when he says:

> As an eagle stirs up its nest,
> Hovers over its young,
> Spreading out its wings, taking them up,
> Carrying them on its wings,
> So the LORD alone led [Jacob]
>
> (Deut. 32:11).

Eagles build their nests on lofty heights. After the fledglings have matured, at the appropriate time, I understand that the parent bird pushes the young bird out of the nest. The young eagle falters and flutters as it tumbles earthward. When it appears as though the young bird must surely perish, the parent bird swoops underneath and bears the fledgling back to the lofty heights for the next lesson. God disturbed the nest of his people, as it were, and cast them out into the wilderness where they faltered and fluttered. He had now borne them as on eagles' wings and had brought them to the lofty heights of Mt Sinai. They were a special people called to a unique purpose; they were, as he says in Exodus 19:6, 'a kingdom of priests and a holy nation' — a designation which the apostle Peter applies to believers in Christ (1 Peter 2:9). They were, therefore, to be governed by special laws. What a momentous occasion this was as the people assembled at the foot of the mount to receive the moral law from the living God!

To impress on the people the solemnity and seriousness of the occasion, God instructed the people to prepare themselves in the following ways:

1. By sanctifying themselves by washing their clothes

The word 'sanctify' means 'to set apart'. A. W. Pink says, 'How plainly this intimated that God would draw nigh only to a people who were clean.'[2] If 'Man looks at the outward appearance, but the LORD looks at the heart' (1 Sam. 16:7), why did God require external cleanliness? Many times, of course, one's outward appearance is indicative of the inner condition and state of the heart. (In the light of this, I must confess that I have real difficulties when I see people attend the worship of God wearing a tee-shirt advertising 'Budweiser', 'Victorian Bitter', some godless rock group, or something equally incongruous with the occasion.) Be that as it may, the purpose of washing their clothes was to impress on them, and us, the fact that 'We are all like an unclean thing, and all our righteousnesses are like filthy rags' (Isa. 64:6). In the presence of God and in the hearing of his Word, we need to be cleansed and clothed in righteousness.

2. By abstaining from sexual relations

This was not because such relationships are wrong within the bond of marriage, but because of the importance and significance of the occasion. This was particularly important in the light of the sensuous and orgiastic rites which characterized the religious rituals of the pagan nations which surrounded them. Nothing, not even the most intimate relationship between a man and his wife, was to detract their attention from this momentous occasion. In the New Testament, Christian husbands and wives are encouraged to abstain from sexual relations on occasions in order to give themselves to fasting and prayer (1 Cor. 7:5). There are occasions when God's people should devote their attention entirely to the Lord.

When the people had prepared themselves, a line was drawn around the base of the mountain beyond which no one was permitted to go on pain of death (Exod. 19:12). They needed to understand that coming into the presence of the living God is an awesome experience; they must not come carelessly or presumptuously. A. W. Pink says, 'Such a view of God's majesty as Israel were favoured with at Mt Sinai is the crying need of our day.'[3] A. W. Tozer says, 'No religion has ever been greater than its idea of God. Worship is pure or base as the worshipper entertains high or low thoughts of God.'[4] We have lost sight of the majesty of God. Tozer continues: 'So necessary to the Church is a lofty concept of God that when that concept in any measure declines, the Church with her worship and her moral standards declines along with it. The first step down for any church is taken when it surrenders its high opinion of God.'[5]

That briefly is the setting and preparation at Mt Sinai. There is much more to be learned from this momentous event; not the least of which is, of course, the fundamental fact that God is to be approached in reverence and godly fear. What a privilege we have in Christ in being able to come 'boldly to the throne of grace'! (Heb. 4:16).

The manner in which the law was given

God's revelation of his character and requirements before Sinai

It is important to understand that the law of God did not originate at Mt Sinai. It was, and it continues to be, the eternal 'word of God which lives and abides for ever' (1 Peter 1:23). When God gave the moral law, he did not sit in heaven, as it were, thinking up various restrictions to keep his creatures under control and to inhibit their freedom. The moral law originates in God's character; he requires his people to be true, for example, because *he* is true. He requires us to be just and righteous because *he* is just and righteous. He demands that we be perfect as *he* is perfect. Since the moral law is an expression of God's righteous character, it has always been in effect — and it always will be! (In the light of the events surrounding the Clinton White House scandal, someone asked, 'Aren't you glad that God didn't commit the task of writing the moral law to the United States Congress?' — or any other human government, for that matter!)

There is sufficient evidence in Scripture to show that those who lived prior to Mt Sinai were acquainted with the law of God. Matthew Henry says, 'This law God had given to man before (it was written in his heart by nature); but sin had so defaced that writing that it was necessary, in this manner, to revive the knowledge of it.'[6]

Before Israel reached Sinai, God said to his people, 'If you diligently heed the voice of the LORD your God and do what is right in his sight, *give ear to his commandments and keep all his statutes*, I will put none of the diseases on you which I have brought on the Egyptians. For I am the LORD who heals you' (Exod. 15:26, emphasis mine).

Abraham offered sacrifices in keeping with the Levitical law long before it was formally given. Also, the Israelites were required to keep the Sabbath day before they arrived at Sinai

(Exod. 16:26). This suggests that the people were acquainted with the law and were responsible to keep it *before* the commandments were formally given. Obviously, it cannot be otherwise; the moral law is derived from the character of God. It has always been in force and always will be; there never has been a time when God did not require his creatures to be moral.

The awesome nature of the revelation

The children of Israel had three days of preparation for hearing and receiving God's law. (Oh that God's people today would prepare themselves for the hearing of the Word of God! How casually we enter his glorious presence!) After their preparation, '... there were thunderings and lightnings, and a thick cloud on the mountain; and the sound of the trumpet was very loud, so that all the people who were in the camp trembled' (Exod. 19:16). The trumpet blast, we are told, grew louder and louder, the earth quaked and God himself descended in fire (Exod. 19:19). Only a few weeks before, Israel had witnessed the devastating thunder and lightning which God had sent as judgement on Egypt. This display of God's great power, however, was to impress on them the importance of his law and how seriously they must regard it.

Truly, this was an awesome experience. Why did God speak in this manner? Matthew Henry cites several reasons:

1. It was designed (once for all) to give a sensible discovery of the glorious majesty of God, for the assistance of our faith concerning it, that, *knowing the terror of the Lord,* we may be persuaded to live in his fear.

2. It was a specimen of the terrors of the general judgement, in which sinners will be called to an account of the breach of this law: the archangel's trumpet will then sound an alarm, to give notice of the Judge's coming, and a *fire shall devour before him.*

3. It was an indication of the terror of those convictions which the law brings into conscience, to prepare the soul for the comforts of the gospel. Thus was the law given by Moses in such a way as might startle, affright, and humble men, that the *grace and truth which came by Jesus Christ* might be the more welcome.[7]

Moses encouraged the people with that same great exclamation he used at the Red Sea: 'Fear not.' On this occasion, it almost sounds like a contradiction; in essence, he said, 'Do not fear ... that his fear may be before you' (Exod. 20:20). He explained that God's purpose in revealing his power in this way was 'to prove them, to try how they would like dealing with God immediately, without a mediator, and so to convince them how admirably well God had chosen for them, in putting Moses into that office. Ever since Adam fled, upon hearing God's voice in the garden, sinful man could not bear either to speak to God or hear from him immediately.'[8]

When Moses rehearsed all that God did at Mt Sinai forty years later, he asked, 'Did any people ever hear the voice of God speaking out of the midst of the fire, as you have heard, and live?' (Deut. 4:33). After experiencing the power of God as he gave his Word, '... all the people witnessed the thunderings, the lightning flashes, the sound of the trumpet, and the mountain smoking; and when the people saw it, they trembled and stood afar off. Then they said to Moses, "You speak with us, and we will hear; but let not God speak with us, lest we die"' (Exod. 20:18-19).

No doubt, this seems rather remote to us; we tend to take the Word of God for granted and handle it casually. Something of the awesome nature of the occasion needs to be recaptured in our day when we attend to the hearing of God's holy Word. In the final chapter of his great book, the prophet Isaiah says, 'Hear the word of the LORD, you who *tremble* at his Word' (Isa. 66:5, emphasis mine). Ezra also declared to the people of his day (and to us), 'Let us make a covenant with our God ... according to the

advice of my master and of those who *tremble* at the commandment of our God; and let it be done according to the law' (Ezra
10:3, emphasis mine). If we realized that the living God is
speaking to us, we too would tremble! Too often little preparation is done and what God says is not taken too seriously.

How did God communicate the revelation?

Before leaving this aspect, I want to comment briefly on the
question of *how* God spoke to his people; we have read of
thunder, lightning and the sound of a trumpet — in all this, how
did God speak? This is an important question in the light of
some contemporary theological ideas; Karl Barth has informed
us that God is *totaliter aliter* (totally other); it is impossible,
therefore, for him/her/it to communicate in human language.
Instead, we are now told that we must *feel* God speaking. It is
exceedingly difficult to understand how God gave his promise to
Abraham in such detail if he didn't use words. And one wonders how the moral law could be so explicit if Moses had
nothing more than a fuzzy feeling. Well, I am thankful to say
that God has not left us to foolish speculation; in verse 19, we
read, 'And when the blast of the trumpet sounded long and
became louder and louder, Moses spoke, and God answered
him *by voice*' (emphasis added). In other words, there was direct
verbal communication. It is rather absurd to think that the God
who made our vocal cords and gave us language for communication wouldn't know how to express himself to men. Similarly,
when the apostle Paul gave his personal testimony before King
Agrippa and recounted his conversion experience on the road to
Damascus, he says that the Lord spoke to him 'in the Hebrew
language' (Acts 26:14). God speaks Hebrew! At Mt Sinai, God
spoke in verbal propositions which can be understood by men
and which must be obeyed.

The content of the law

The law which God gave at Mt Sinai covered three major areas:

The civil law

This aspect of the law concerned judicial and civil matters which pertained to, and specifically applied to, the state of Israel when the land was occupied and settled. Those laws can and do have application to civil matters in any society and we would do well to discern the principles involved and apply them. Some within the church today believe that the civil law is actually part of the moral law and should be rigidly applied in society today. The *Westminster Confession of Faith* is correct, however, when it says, 'To [Israel] also, as a body politick, he gave sundry judicial laws, which expired together with the state of that people, not obliging any other now, further than the general equity thereof may require.'[9]

The moral law

The moral law is summarily comprehended in the Ten Commandments. In one of his letters, John Newton wrote, 'Ignorance of the design and nature of the law is at the bottom of most religious mistakes.'[10] Throughout church history, men and movements have gone from one extreme to the other concerning God's law. Periodically, *antinomianism* (that is, being 'against the law') has appeared in various forms. Sinners will do everything possible to avoid God's law. Some denigrate the law and ignore its requirements; they quote the verse, 'You are not under law but under grace' (Rom. 6:14), without understanding what is intended. On the other hand, all kinds of expressions of *legalism* appear periodically. Some insist on the law to such an extent that it becomes the means of salvation and grace is forgotten. Both extremes exist in the church today and both have a destructive influence.

The moral law cannot be separated from the Lawgiver; it reveals his righteous character. One of the Puritans said somewhere that 'God's righteousness is that righteousness which God's righteousness requires him to require.' Further, the dramatic way in which God gave the law points to its tremendous importance. The law is fundamental to the justification of sinners before God. Justification relates to, and depends upon, justice; there can be no justification if justice is not done. Justice, in turn, is abstract and meaningless if it is not rooted in, and based on, law. Similarly, for sanctification to be meaningful, it must be determined according to the 'righteousness of the law'.

The Ten Commandments were given on two tablets of stone. No doubt, stone was used to convey the permanence of the law. The first four commandments concern man's relationship to God; in order to live, man must have a right relationship to his Maker. Man must love the Lord God with all his heart, soul and mind (Matt. 22:37). As we observed earlier, the word 'worship' comes from an old Anglo-Saxon root and originally it meant 'to recognize the *worth*-ship'. The extent to which one loves God depends, of course, on how much one values God — how much is God worth? The first four commandments concern worship:

1. 'You shall have no other gods before me.' This command concerns the *object* of worship and answers the question, 'What?' What, or who, is considered to be of the most worth?

2. 'You shall not make for yourself a carved image ... you shall not bow down to them nor serve them.' This command concerns the *method* of worship and answers the question, 'How?' Because God is a Spirit, he is to be worshipped in spirit and truth (John 4:24). How God is approached is exceedingly important.

3. 'You shall not take the name of the LORD your God in vain.' God's name expresses who and what he is. Implied in this command is the *reason* for worship and it answers the question, 'Why?'

4. 'Remember the Sabbath day, to keep it holy.' This command concerns the *place* or *priority* of worship and answers the question, 'When?' When a person engages in business activities in a money-hungry, pleasure-crazy, self-seeking world, he can readily forget the principles of righteousness, justice, goodness and truth. Regular, consistent worship is essential if one is to maintain a proper scale of values and keep one's priorities right.

These first four commandments teach us the importance of a proper relationship to God. If these commandments are understood and applied correctly, the remaining six will flow naturally from them. If a person's relationship to God is right, he will love his neighbour as himself (Matt. 22:39). The commandments concerning our relationship to one another require respect, concern, purity, honesty, truth and integrity. The reason God requires these things is because of who he is. God's Word is essential for life; it converts the soul, makes wise the simple, rejoices the heart and enlightens the eyes (Ps. 19:7-8).

The ceremonial law

A significant part of the book of Exodus is devoted to a detailed description of the tabernacle — the structure in which the priests offered the sacrifices and ministered before the Lord. The tabernacle will be discussed in a little more detail in the next chapter; here, I want to point out that the book of Hebrews says that the tabernacle, and all that pertained to it, was a shadow of things to come (Heb. 8:5; 9:23). Everything, from the ark of the covenant to the altar of sacrifice, foreshadowed and typified the person and work of Christ. The Lord Jesus Christ, as our great High Priest, offered a better sacrifice and now mediates between God and sinful men at the throne of divine justice. Because his sacrifice and mediation are perfect, no other sacrifice or mediator is needed. When he died on the cross, the veil of the temple was torn from top to bottom, depicting that he had opened a new and living way into the presence of God. Now his people may draw near with confidence to the throne of grace to receive mercy and to find grace to help in time of need (Heb. 4:16). In other words, the ceremonial law was fulfilled completely in Christ; when Jesus cried from the cross, 'It is finished!' all that had been pictured in the ceremonies was complete.

The purpose of the law

As already stated, the law is an expression of the character of God. It shows what righteousness is and provides an objective standard for morality. When sinners measure themselves by themselves, and compare themselves among themselves (2 Cor. 10:12), they will appear comparatively good, but they are unwise because they are using the wrong standard. When measured by the perfect standard, they discover how far short of the glory of God they come (Rom. 3:23). The enormity and heinousness of sin are realized when one is confronted with the requirements and demands of the law. Through 'the law [comes] the knowledge of sin' (Rom. 3:20). When the nature of the offence and its awful consequences are understood, there is really no option but to appeal to God for mercy. The law then becomes 'our tutor to bring us to Christ' (Gal. 3:24). When the Lord Jesus came to this world, he was born under the law, he fulfilled all the requirements of the law, he upheld the law and he died under the law. No aspect of his ministry or work contradicted or nullified the law. He fulfilled the law on our behalf and he paid the penalty for our transgression of the law. He did so, in order that 'the righteous requirement of the law might be fulfilled in us' (Rom. 8:4).

The moral law teaches us our duty towards God and towards our fellow man. When the Israelites arrived at Mt Sinai to receive the law, they declared, 'All that the LORD has spoken we will do' (Exod. 19:8). What a tremendous resolution that was! They committed themselves to doing the will of God — fully and completely. Alas, how soon their resolve lay broken in ruins — a fact symbolized so clearly by Moses as he dashed the tablets of law to the ground when he saw the people worshipping the golden calf! How often we resolve to do what is right, only to find that that we lack the power to do it! When God resolves, however, he never breaks his Word; what he has said, he will do.

As awesome as the experience at Sinai was, it was only the beginning. In chapter 24, God's covenant with his people was ratified. Moses built an altar and offered burnt and peace offerings on it. The blood of the sacrifice was taken — half was sprinkled on the altar and the other half sprinkled on the people. This is a dramatic picture of the work of Christ in making atonement for his people; by his blood, the wrath of God is appeased, the curse of sin is removed, sinners are forgiven and cleansed, and have peace with God. Following that solemn and momentous event, Moses, Aaron, Nadab, Abihu and seventy of the elders went up the mountain. All the previous thundering, lightning, earthquakes and fire seem to fade into insignificance in comparison to what they experienced. Picture it if you can! The Scripture says that '... they saw the God of Israel. And there was under his feet as it were a paved work of sapphire stone, and it was like the very heavens in its clarity' (Exod. 24:10). And what did those seventy-four men do? Verse 11 says, 'They saw God, and they ate and drank.' What is this? Here are sinful men, who a short time before stood at the foot of the mount trembling, now eating and drinking in the presence of God. Fear has been dispelled now that a sacrifice has been offered and the blood applied. Those elders now have fellowship together in the presence of God. Only God's mercy and grace could make this possible. Oh that we could recapture something of the wonder and awesome nature of this!

God has spoken

God has spoken, not only at Mt Sinai, but also through his prophets and apostles. He has given us *his written Word*. That Word is 'powerful, and sharper than any two-edged sword' (Heb. 4:12). Because it is God's Word, it is *authoritative*; it is reliable and trustworthy in all its parts. The Scriptures are the 'only infallible rule of faith and practice'. The Scriptures are not only authoritative, they are *sufficient*. Nothing additional is needed to show us the path of life; the Bible tells us what we need to know. 'The Scriptures principally teach what man is to believe concerning God, and what duty God requires of man.'[11] Extra or additional revelation is not necessary; mystical experiences are inadequate because they lack objectivity and cannot stand scrutiny or investigation. God has spoken powerfully in his Word. What God has said is powerful – powerful enough to break the most hardened heart, powerful enough to quicken the guilty conscience and powerful enough to set the most imprisoned spirit free. 'The gospel of Christ ... is the power of God to salvation for everyone who believes' (Rom. 1:16).

God has not only spoken to us in his Word; he has spoken to us *'in his Son'*. 'For the law was given through Moses, but grace and truth came through Jesus Christ' (John 1:17). The Lord Jesus is the living Word; he is the full, final and complete revelation of God. What a powerful testimony he gave, and still gives, to the mercy and grace of God! Of him, God the Father declared, 'This is my beloved Son, in whom I am well pleased. Hear him!' (Matt. 17:5). God has spoken in him; we must give heed to what he has said.

'We must pay much closer attention to what we have heard, so that we do not drift away from it. For if the word spoken through angels proved unalterable, and every transgression and disobedience received a just penalty, how will we escape if we neglect so great a salvation? After it was at the first spoken through the Lord, it was confirmed to us by those who heard' (Heb. 2:1-3, NASB).

8.

The power of God's presence

Theologians who ignore or abandon divine revelation as the authoritative source of information concerning God inevitably find themselves in difficulty. They must, of necessity, resort to and depend on human imagination and speculation in formulating their ideas. No matter how brilliant or ingenious a person might be, however, he cannot comprehend God by his own unaided wisdom or understanding. Concepts of God formed in the imagination result in idolatry; images are always the product of the imagination.

Three essential aspects of God's being must be understood and kept in balance if one is to have a satisfactory and biblical view. First, God is *transcendent* — that is, he is above and beyond human understanding; he is incomprehensibly great. If God could be comprehended, he would, of course, be much too small. He is also *immanent*; this is a theological word (not to be confused with 'imminent'), meaning 'to remain near, operating within'. God is close at hand; he is involved with his people. And God is a *personal* being — not some impersonal force or idea.

As theologians have departed from the Scriptures, they have vacillated from one extreme to the other. Beginning with Friedrich Schleiermacher, who taught that God is perceived by the senses rather than comprehended by the mind, the modernists, or 'Higher Critics', as they were known, emphasized the immanence of God. He is, they claimed, the Father of all, and all men are brothers. At the height of this theological emphasis in Europe, World War I broke out and, not surprisingly, many people became disillusioned with the church. If all men were brothers, why were they killing one another? Further, a sentimental God who loves everybody and acts as a celestial Santa Claus is of little or no value in such times of crisis. The modernists made God so immanent that they lost sight of his transcendence.

At the end of the war, Swiss theologian Karl Barth recognized the paucity of modernism and dropped what was described as a theological bombshell by calling for a return to the sovereignty of God. That sounded good, of course, but, unfortunately, he gave new meaning to the term. Barth taught that God is 'totaliter aliter' — 'totally other'. God is, therefore, beyond man's comprehension; he can be known only in an existential moment. That is, one is suddenly overwhelmed with the realization of existence. According to Barth, God is not a person among persons or an object among objects — he is 'totally other'. Personal or indefinite pronouns ('him' or 'it') cannot properly be used, therefore, to describe him.

It is true, of course, that sin has brought separation between God and man, but the separation is *moral* — not in essence! In other words, man still bears God's image in that he is a rational being, a moral being and a being with purpose. If God were 'totally other', the image of God in man would be meaningless and reconciliation to God an impossibility. Barth made God so transcendent, he lost sight of his immanence. According to Barth's system, there are two kinds of truth — scientific and religious. Religious truth is supposedly subjective and mystical; it is irrational and absurd. If this were so, all communication with God would be pointless nonsense.

Subsequently, Paul Tillich regarded God as the 'Ground of Being'. Everything, from sticks and stones to people and ideas, has being. When the entire creation is taken into consideration, it is completely beyond us — it is incomprehensible. It transcends us. On the other hand, we are part of the creation; it is near to us. It is immanent. In this pantheistic speculation, Tillich brought transcendence and immanence together but lost sight of God as a personal being. God became an abstract and intangible notion.

God's self-revelation, the Bible, offers a far better alternative than such speculative ideas. God has revealed himself as a personal being who transcends human comprehension but who, at the same time, condescends to dwell among his people. He is transcendent, immanent and personal. Because God is a personal being, he has communicated with his creatures in reasonable and practical propositions which can be understood. '"Come now, and let us reason together," says the LORD' (Isa. 1:18). The transcendent God, who inhabits eternity and dwells above the circle of the earth, has not only condescended to speak to sinful men, but also to dwell among them and care for them. He has done so in order to bring sinners into communion with himself.

Exodus is one of several books in the Bible in which these three essential aspects of God's being are clearly revealed. In sending the plagues on Egypt, in the deliverance of his people at the Red Sea and in revealing his Word at Mt Sinai, God manifested his *transcendent* power and greatness. In leading his people forth from bondage by the Shekinah glory, the pillar of cloud, and in establishing his residence among them in the Holy of Holies in the tabernacle, he revealed his *immanence*. And, in giving the moral law at Mt Sinai and in establishing a special personal relationship with Moses, God demonstrated and proved that he is a *personal* being. God is a personal being who dwells among his people and communes with them. He is Immanuel — God with us!

The tabernacle

When God demonstrated his great power in giving the law at Mt Sinai, he instructed Moses also concerning the building of the tabernacle. Since both were given at the same place and at the same time, they need to be seen, not as separate matters, but as complementary – they belong together. When the law was given, the people were forbidden to approach the mountain out of curiosity; they could not go into God's presence as they were. In the tabernacle, on the other hand, God condescended to come into *their* presence and dwell among them.

As we saw previously, the law shows 'what duty God requires of man'.[1] The law was weak, however, in that it could not provide the motivation for people to fulfil the requirements, or give them the power to do genuine works of righteousness. Though the tabernacle was a simple physical structure, it expressed and typified the means by which the law is upheld and fulfilled. As a great object lesson, it was designed to teach God's people essential truth concerning reconciliation to God. On Mt Sinai, the people were confronted with, and were terrified at, the awesome, transcendent majesty of God's presence. At the tabernacle, that same glorious presence was in their midst; God was with them. While they could not approach God, he approached them and dwelt with them!

The amount of space devoted to the tabernacle in the Scriptures, the detail with which it is described and the repetition of the details when it was constructed, suggest its tremendous importance. Without an understanding of the structure and function of the tabernacle, many aspects of our eternal salvation are difficult to comprehend. Pink writes, 'More space is devoted to an account of the Tabernacle than to any other single object or subject treated of in Holy Writ. Its courts, its furniture, and its ritual are described with a surprising particularity of detail. Two chapters suffice for a record of God's work in creating and fitting this earth for human habitation, whereas ten chapters are needed to tell us about the tabernacle.'[2] And Matthew Henry comments, 'He that gave us no account of the lines and circles of the globe, the diameter of the earth, or the height and magnitude of the stars, has told us particularly the measure of every board and curtain of the tabernacle; for God's church and instituted religion are more precious to him and more considerable than all the rest of the world.'[3]

Simply, the floor plan of the tabernacle was as follows:

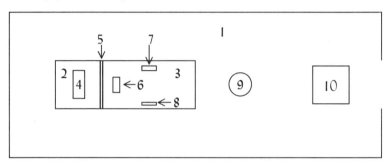

1. Outer court
2. Holy of Holies
3. Holy Place
4. Ark of the covenant
5. Veil
6. Altar of incense
7. Table of shewbread
8. Lampstand
9. Laver
10. Altar of sacrifice

Floor plan of the tabernacle

Several excellent studies on the tabernacle are available in which the furnishings and function are discussed in detail and the significance of each aspect is explained;[4] it is beyond my purpose to duplicate that material. Nevertheless, comments on certain aspects are appropriate.

God gave specific instructions concerning every detail

First, the emphasis which God gave to the careful construction of the tabernacle shows something of its tremendous importance and significance. 'No less than seven times are we informed that Moses was commanded to make the Sanctuary after the pattern of it which was shown to him in the Mount — see Exodus 25:9; 25:40; 26:30; 27:8; Numbers 8:4; Acts 7:44; Hebrews 8:5. Nothing was left to man's wisdom, still less to "chance"; everything was to be in exact accordance with the divine model.'[5]

The structure and contents of the tabernacle

The tabernacle proper consisted of two rooms separated by a veil. The Holy of Holies, the smaller of the two, was, as it were, the throne room of God. Not even the high priest was permitted to enter the Holy of Holies except on the Day of Atonement — and then only after certain elaborate preparations had been made, including the offering of appropriate sacrifices. Within it were two items of furniture: the ark of the covenant and the mercy seat. The pillar of cloud and fire, the Shekinah glory, the visible presence of God, rested on the tabernacle (Exodus 40:34-35 indicates that the cloud rested on the whole tabernacle; the Shekinah glory filled the temple according to 1 Kings 8:10-11, and Leviticus 16:2 shows that God appeared in the cloud in the Holy of Holies on the Day of Atonement). To enter the presence of God was, and is, a solemn matter. The Holy Place contained the golden altar, the table of shewbread and the seven-branched candlestick. Just inside the entrance to the outer court was the altar of sacrifice; no one could approach God carelessly or presumptuously; there had to be an appropriate sacrifice offered by a qualified priest. In front of the tabernacle was the laver where the priests were to wash; they were not permitted to enter the Holy Place unclean.

Only the best was good enough for the worship of God

The description of the tabernacle begins with the Israelites bringing costly materials to offer to the Lord (Exod. 25:2). Those items had been given to them by the Egyptians prior to their departure from the land of bondage (Exod. 11:2). As a redeemed people, the Israelites were called to worship the living and true God. They gave the best materials, employed the most skilled craftsmen and women and, when the tabernacle was complete, they brought the best of their animals for sacrifice. They did not withhold anything from the Lord God on the grounds that it was too valuable or precious. Because God

redeemed his people from destruction, he was worthy to receive
the best and most valuable gifts they had to offer.

The sacrificial system

Some studies on the tabernacle begin with man coming to God.
It is true that the believing Israelite brought his sacrificial lamb,
slaughtered it and engaged the priest to offer it and to present the
blood in the Holy Place. All of that was to show that sin was
taken seriously and that atonement needed to be made for
reconciliation to God. If it is understood that we are talking
about believers, this approach is valid enough, no doubt. While
there is only one way to God, sinners do not approach God on
their own terms or initiative. The Israelites came to the tabernacle because they were a redeemed people; their presentation
and offering of sacrifices constituted an expression of faith in
which they anticipated that, in the fulness of time, God would
send forth his Son (Gal. 4:4), 'the Lamb of God who takes away
the sin of the world' (John 1:29). Incidentally, there was only
one entrance to the tabernacle; there is only one way to God.
Jesus Christ is 'the way... No one comes to the Father except
through [him]' (John 14:6).

The ark of the covenant and the mercy seat

The description of the tabernacle itself begins with the ark of the
covenant (Exod. 25:10). The ark depicted, and was representative of, the throne of God. By starting with the ark and moving
outwards, God shows that he takes the initiative in approaching
man. As the Scripture says, 'There is none who seeks after God'
(Ps. 14:2-3; 53:1-3; Rom. 3:11) God moves towards man – and
man must respond appropriately.

As I have said, the Holy of Holies contained both the ark of
the covenant and the mercy seat. While these two items were
separate, they fitted together; the ark supported the mercy seat.
The mercy seat was fashioned as an ancient king's footstool with

two cherubim gazing intently upon it — it was all made from one piece of solid gold. (Cherubim were also embroidered on the veils which covered the entrances into both the Holy Place and the Holy of Holies.) What were the cherubim? The first appearance of cherubim in Scripture was at the gate to the Garden of Eden; they were sent to prevent Adam and Eve from returning to the garden to partake of the tree of life. Throughout Scripture these heavenly beings are responsible to execute divine justice. Hence, while the throne of God is the seat of *mercy*, it is also the place where divine *justice* is administered. God is abundant in mercy; he is also 'infinite, eternal and unchangeable in his ... justice'. Justice and mercy are blended together perfectly at the throne of God.

The ark of the covenant, on which the mercy seat rested, was a box constructed of acacia wood overlaid with gold. Eventually, three items were placed in the ark: the tablets of law, the rod of Aaron and a golden pot containing manna (Heb. 9:4). Those items were kept in the ark, not merely for safe keeping or sentimental value, but because they were significant. *The law* testified to the fact that God is true. *The rod* was placed there after the role of Aaron as high priest was challenged and contested by Korah. God instructed Aaron to place his rod along with twelve other rods in front of the ark; Aaron's rod budded, blossomed and bore ripe almonds all at once. Through that miracle, God's righteous leaders were vindicated. The constancy with which God provided *the manna* was adequate testimony to his faithfulness. In other words, the mercy and justice of God were not arbitrary or whimsical; they are perfectly blended together because they are based upon, and undergirded by, truth, righteousness and faithfulness. I have shown elsewhere that these three objects speak of, and relate to, the offices of Christ as Prophet, Priest and King.[6]

The tabernacle was at the centre of the camp

Although the tabernacle was filled with costly furnishings, it was covered with animal skins — its outward appearance was actually no different from the tents of the Israelites with which it was surrounded. As we shall see in our studies on the book of Numbers, one of the families of Levites was camped on each side of the tabernacle — with the family of Aaron immediately outside the entrance. Beyond the Levites, three tribes were camped on each side. The tabernacle was, therefore, at the very centre of the entire encampment. Even when the Israelites journeyed across the wilderness, the ark of the covenant remained at the centre of the procession. This was not because God's throne needed protection from marauding bands of thieves — any more than it needed the supporting hand of Uzzah! (1 Chr. 13:9-10). It was central because the High and Holy One whose throne is in the heavens condescended to dwell among his people. He was their God and they were his people.

The presence of God among his people

What difference did the presence of God make? (As one reads the sacred record, one sometimes wonders if it made any difference to them at all! The Israelites always seemed to be murmuring and complaining about their circumstances and blaming God for their conditions.) The divine commentary on the power of God's presence in the midst of his people is Psalm 46:

> God is our refuge and strength,
> A very present help in trouble.
> Therefore we will not fear,
> Even though the earth be removed,
> And though the mountains be carried into the midst of
>   the sea...

God is in the midst of her, she shall not be moved;
God shall help her...

The LORD of hosts is with us;
The God of Jacob is our refuge.

In commenting on this psalm, Matthew Henry asks, 'Are we pursued? God is our refuge to whom we may flee... Are we oppressed by troubles? ... God is our strength, to bear up under our burdens... Are we in distress? He is a help ... *a present help...* Or, a help at hand, one that never is to seek for, but that is always near.'[7] God did not remain aloof from his people or place himself at a distance from them. He was there for their benefit, encouragement, security and protection. He was their source of blessing, their object of worship and the basis for their unity.

A reminder of all God had done for them

God's presence was a powerful and constant reminder of their preservation during the plagues in Egypt, of their miraculous deliverance from Egyptian slavery, of the daily provision of manna and water in the desert, and of the giving of the law at Mt Sinai. The presence of God should have brought to their re-membrance that fearful night when they reached Etham (Exod. 13:20) — the edge of the unknown — and did not know where to turn. There the Shekinah glory met them and shed light on their path while keeping the Egyptians in darkness. Also, having experienced victory over the Amalekites at Rephidim (Exod. 17:8-16), Israel had reason to recognize God as 'Jehovah-Nissi' — 'the Lord our banner' or 'victory'. 'How well-grounded the defiance of danger is,' says Matthew Henry, 'considering how well guarded the church is.'[8]

The basis of unity

The presence of God was also the basis for unity. By way of
contrast, those who tried to construct the Tower of Babel sought
to find unity and security in a common project. Any effort to
achieve unity apart from God is doomed to failure because the
seeds of disintegration are inherent in the nature and effects of
sin. The intention of bringing people together might be well-
meaning, of course, but sooner or later, evil desires and corrupt
motives will emerge and prove its undoing. For unity to be true
and lasting it must be rooted in, and based on, a person. When
a body of redeemed people look to God for wisdom, depend on
him for provision, wait on him for direction and endeavour to
glorify him together, the basis exists for genuine unity, peace,
security and joy. As the apostle makes clear in Ephesians chapter
2, what the world can never achieve through its ingenious
schemes, God has accomplished through the cross of Christ.
Christian unity is not automatic, however; God's people are
exhorted 'to keep the unity of the Spirit in the bond of peace'.
They must 'put off [their] former conduct', 'be renewed in the
spirit of [their] mind' and 'put on the new man' (Eph.
4:3,22,23,24).

A motive for worship

With the presence of the living God in her midst, Israel had a
powerful motive to worship — God's people were to recognize
the worth of their God consistently and constantly. Their 'chief
end [was] to glorify and enjoy God for ever'.[9] They were to trust
in the Lord with all their hearts and acknowledge him in all their
ways (Prov. 3:5-6). Detailed instructions were given, not only
concerning the construction of the tabernacle, but also concerning the work of the priests — the ministration of their office. The
method of worship was not a matter of personal preference or
subject to popular demand; it was to be carried out precisely as
God had prescribed. The moral law stipulated the proper *object*

of worship (the First Commandment) and the proper *method* of worship (the Second Commandment). *How* people worship is as important as, and indicative of, *what* they worship. Sinners are averse to proper, acceptable worship of the true God, of course, and are, therefore, apt to follow 'the way of Cain' (Jude 11) by trying to approach God on their own terms. Worship of the living God must be in accordance with his instructions. God's people have good reason to worship him acceptably!

With the visible presence of the living God in their midst, one wonders why ancient Israel ever doubted God's protection and provision. Surely, the Shekinah glory over the tabernacle day and night should have been a constant reminder to them to trust the Lord at all times and to worship him constantly. Instead of glorifying God and enjoying his presence, they doubted his covenantal promise, questioned his motives, murmured and complained about his goodness and were disobedient and rebellious. Though God did not withdraw his presence from ancient Israel immediately, he 'swore in [his] wrath [that they would] not enter [his] rest' (Ps. 95:11). Because of continued disobedience and rebellion over a period of several centuries, God threatened to withdraw his presence. Through his prophet, he declared, 'I will return again to my place till they acknowledge their offence' (Hosea 5:15). If they really are God's people, eventually they will acknowledge their offence and return to him. 'In their affliction they will earnestly seek me' (Hosea 5:15). The worst possible judgement any people can experience is for God to withdraw his gracious presence and give them up. The prophet Ezekiel describes how Israel had taken all kinds of abominable practices into the temple and he records the actual departure of God's glorious presence without anyone noticing (Ezek. 8-10).

A shadow of things to come

The tabernacle and its function were, we are told, a 'copy and shadow of heavenly things' (Heb. 8:5). 'The Tabernacle was mean, humble, and unattractive in outward appearance. Altogether unlike the costly and magnificent temple of Solomon there was nothing in the externals of the Tabernacle to please the carnal eye... So it was in the Incarnation. The Divine majesty of our Lord was hidden behind a veil of flesh... To the unbelieving gaze of Israel He has no form or comeliness; and when they beheld Him their unanointed eyes saw in Him no beauty that they should desire Him.'[10]

'The Old Testament tabernacle is full of meaning because it is a symbol of the Messiah and His salvation.'[11] When the Lord Jesus came to this world, many people wondered at the power of his presence, but they did not recognize him as God. 'He came to his own, and his own did not receive him' (John 1:11). Though he came in the likeness of sinful flesh, he was 'full of grace and truth' (John 1:14). In the introduction to his Gospel, the apostle John says that 'The Word became flesh and dwelt among us' (John 1:14). The word 'dwelt' is literally 'tabernacled'. There are many indications that John had the Old Testament tabernacle in mind as he wrote of Christ. He speaks of the 'Lamb of God', 'the Bread of Life' and 'the Light of the world'. And, in chapter 17, he takes his reader right into the Holy of Holies as he records the high-priestly prayer of the Lord.

After our Lord ascended to heaven, he sent the Holy Spirit into the lives of believers to comfort, teach and guide them. His presence was signified by tongues of fire — and was thereby identified with the pillar of fire. At the Tower of Babel, tongues were confused to break up the consolidation of sinful men; at Pentecost, tongues were loosed to proclaim the gospel and thereby bring sinners into a true relationship with God and his people. The presence of God is still powerful; his power is seen at its greatest when he takes a rebellious, disobedient sinner and transforms him by his grace and makes him a child of God. By bringing such into the body of Christ, the Holy Spirit is building a magnificent temple in which he dwells. In Christ, 'the whole building, being fitted together, grows into a holy temple in the Lord, in whom you also are being built together for a dwelling place of God in the Spirit' (Eph. 2:21-22).

The greatest evidence of the powerful presence of God is where a sinner is declared righteous (justification), is being made righteous (sanctification) and is enabled, by God's grace, to 'dwell together in unity' (Ps. 133:1) with other believers. Significantly, when the tabernacle was constructed, God was pleased and 'the glory of the LORD filled the tabernacle' (Exod. 40:34).

When God gave instructions concerning the ark of the covenant, he told Moses, 'You shall put the mercy seat on top of the ark... And there I will meet with you, and I will speak with you from above the mercy seat, from between the two cherubim which are on the ark of the Testimony, about everything which I will give you in commandment to the children of Israel' (Exod. 25:21-22).

What it means to know the presence of God

From the occasion of the burning bush, Moses stood in awe at God's majestic presence and power; he understood that any undertaking is futile without the presence of God. After all his personal communion with God, all the spectacular signs and wonders he had performed at the hand of God, and all that he had witnessed of the presence of God, Moses still desired to know God more intimately. 'Moses had lately been on the mount with God, had continued there a great while, and had enjoyed as intimate a communion with God as ever any man had on this side of heaven; and yet he is still desiring further acquaintance. Moses had wonderfully prevailed with God for one favour after another, and the success of his prayers emboldened him to go on still to seek God.'[12]

The conversation between Moses and God is recorded for us. Moses requested, ' "Please, show me your glory." Then he said, "I will make all my goodness pass before you, and I will proclaim the name of the LORD before you. I will be gracious to whom I will be gracious, and I will have compassion on whom I will have compassion." But he said, "You cannot see my face; for no man shall see me, and live." And the LORD said, "Here is a place by me, and you shall stand on the rock. So it shall be, while my glory passes by, that I will put you in the cleft of the rock, and will cover you with my hand while I pass by. Then I will take away my hand, and you shall see my back; but my face shall not be seen" ' (Exod. 33:18-23).

After he had communed with God, 'Moses came down from Mount Sinai ... [but] Moses did not know that the skin of his face shone while he talked with him' (Exod. 34:29).

Back in the days of the corner grocery store, there was a grocer in the city of Melbourne who had been gloriously converted to Christ. His favourite expression was 'Hallelujah!' On one occasion, someone addressed a letter to 'The Hallelujah Grocer, Melbourne', and he received it. Such was his testimony, the radiance of the Lord Jesus was on his countenance. I was only a child when I met him but his face is one that I have never forgotten. Evidently, he spent a great deal of time in the presence of his Lord and he knew and experienced the power of God's presence. Was that not the request of the apostle? He prayed 'that I may know him and the power of his resurrection' (Phil. 3:10).

Knowledge of the presence of God satisfies the human spirit as does nothing else because we were made 'to glorify and enjoy God'. The knowledge and power of God's presence are essential in all undertakings in life. We need his wisdom, direction, strength, power and grace. Following the episode with the golden calf, Moses was somewhat apprehensive, it seems, to press on towards the promised land. Moses understood the importance and power of the presence of God; he was not about to undertake the mission without the knowledge that God himself would go with him. 'Then Moses said to the LORD, "See, you say to me, 'Bring up this people.' But you have not let me know whom you will send with me... Now therefore, I pray, if I have found grace in your sight, show me now your way, that I may know you and that I may find grace in your sight. And consider that this nation is your people." And he said, "My Presence will go with you, and I will give you rest" ' (Exod. 33:12-16).

Has our Lord not promised his disciples, 'Lo, I am with you always, even to the end of the age'? (Matt. 28:20).

Part III
Leviticus — The holiness of God

9.
The barrier to communion with God

While ministering in Australia a few years ago, I heard a radio broadcast in which a Roman Catholic priest from South America was interviewed. At one point, the reporter asked him why sin is rarely mentioned in the Roman church these days and if he believed that this is the reason why the confessional has fallen into misuse. The priest expressed his shock and dismay to learn that the reporter, at least, believed that sin is being ignored within his church. He proceeded to comment that the reality of sin is the reason for the existence of the church. Historically, the Roman Catholic Church has kept tight control over its people by emphasizing sin and its fearful consequences; it has used this doctrine as a manipulative tool to keep its people fearful of purgatory and dependent on the church. With the emergence of liberation theology and its intrusion into the church, the emphasis has shifted to sinful social structures rather than the moral condition of the human heart. Hence, in addressing an estimated 500,000 people in St Louis in February 1999, the pope spoke about abortion, capital punishment and other social ills.

The Roman Catholic Church abandoned the biblical view of sin (which had been articulated clearly by Augustine in the third century) when it embraced the teaching of Thomas Aquinas at the time of the so-called Enlightenment. The Roman church is not the only religious body within Christendom to hold a defective and unbiblical view of sin, of course. There are, in fact, half a dozen different views on this important question. The question is not a matter of indifference; what one believes about sin affects everything. As might be expected, since the Roman Catholic Church has a distorted and false view of sin, it also has a defective and unbiblical view of salvation. It is imperative, therefore, that the nature and magnitude of the problem be understood clearly. Failure to do so will inevitably lead to a defective view of salvation.

Several years ago, I was invited to speak at a major Bible conference in Australia; I was specifically asked to address the question of sin. Believing the *Westminster Shorter Catechism* to be an accurate statement of biblical truth, I used Question 14 as the outline for my message. When I had finished speaking, the chairman of the meeting stood up and said, 'This has been a difficult message; I know that the young people have not understood what has been said.' He then proceeded to preach another message for more than twenty minutes to assure the audience that sin was not nearly as serious as I had portrayed. He wanted everyone to know that we are *not* inwardly corrupt; sin, according to him, is nothing more than doing bad things. In making that assertion, he was, of course, contradicting clear biblical teaching and denying the historical position of the church. My message, incidentally, was not really difficult at all; the manner in which he objected and the response of the young people afterwards showed that it had been understood.

I relate that incident to make the point that even within so-called evangelical circles there are many who object to what God says about the biblical doctrine of sin. Almost all the criticism which I have received over a lifetime of ministry has come as a result of my preaching on this doctrine. Possibly such criticism is warranted and deserved; I try never to dismiss it lightly. I believe, however, that the gravity of the problem must be understood before the wonder of the solution can be known. Usually, I have been told that people want to go away from church feeling good about themselves, not being reminded of their sin and guilt. I regret to say that the most vocal critics have been school teachers. (I am thankful to say that many teachers agree with the biblical truth concerning sin.) I suspect that teachers object most strongly because they have been trained by secular humanists and, in many cases, have embraced the secular view of human nature. With our sinful propensity to evade, avoid and minimize the truth about ourselves, it is most important that we understand and believe what God says. He alone is able to speak with authority; he knows us far better than we know ourselves. 'The heart is deceitful above all things, and desperately wicked; who can know it?' (Jer. 17:9). In other words, sin is so deceitful that we really do not know ourselves. It is never pleasant or popular to talk about the corruption of human nature, of course, but unless we do so, we shall never see our true need of the Saviour. When the issue is addressed, however, it must be done out of genuine concern and with true compassion.

God's holiness and man's sin

A significant portion of Exodus and Leviticus is devoted to God's law. The nature, purpose and content of the law needs to be understood clearly because, as the apostle says, 'By the law *is* the knowledge of sin' (Rom. 3:20). John Newton said, 'Ignorance of the design and nature of the law is at the bottom of most religious mistakes.'[1] In other words, a biblical understanding of sin is essential if the message of the book of Leviticus is to be appreciated. Without the knowledge of sin, Leviticus will prove to be uninteresting and unprofitable. On the other hand, when we grasp the magnitude and heinousness of sin, this wonderful book comes alive. The law, by which the knowledge of sin is gained, reveals three foundational matters:

1. The law shows the moral perfection (holiness) of God

God did not sit up there in heaven and formulate a moral code
to inhibit his creatures and restrict their freedom. He gave the
moral law because he is a moral God. The law originates and
has its roots in God's righteous character and being; therefore,
God's law will never pass away while God exists. In other words,
the law cannot be separated from the Lawgiver. The law requires
perfection and purity because God is absolutely perfect and pure.

2. The law shows the moral standard that God requires of all his creatures

Usually, people claim to be good because they compare themselves with other people. Such a claim is ill-founded, however,
because other people, no matter how good or bad they might be,
are not the standard by which character and conduct are to be
measured. How are goodness, righteousness and justice determined and judged? The only absolute, objective standard by
which we must measure ourselves is the law of God, which, as
we have seen, is the expression of God's righteous character.
God requires us to be holy because he is holy. Three times in
Leviticus, God says, 'Be holy; for I am holy' (Lev. 11:44,45;
19:2). God requires us to be just because he is just. He requires
us to be good because he is good. He requires us to be true
because he is true.

3. The moral law shows where we come short of the standard

When Adam disobeyed the command of God, he asserted his
independence from God. He thought that he was free to set his
own standards and do as he pleased. Hence, sinful man is an
enemy of God; he is not subject to the law of God, neither can
he be (Rom. 8:7). When the only true, objective, absolute
standard for morality is ignored and rejected, every aspect of
morality becomes relative and loses all meaning. Apart from

God's law, sinful man sets his own standards and does what is right in his own eyes (Judg. 17:6; 21:25). When we measure ourselves by the law of God, however, we discover that we 'have sinned and fall short of the glory of God' (Rom. 3:23). In other words, the law of God gives meaning to the doctrine of sin.

The matter of sin is, of course, a very serious problem. 'The reason why the Puritans magnified the quickening power of God,' says J. I. Packer, 'is because they took so seriously the Bible teaching that man is *dead* in sin (Eph. 2:1,5; Col 2:13), spiritually impotent (John 3:3,5; 6:[44]; Rom 8:7; 1 Cor. 2:14), radically depraved, sin's helpless slave (Rom 3:9; 6:20-22). Sin has such strength, they held, that only omnipotence can break its bond; only the author of life can raise the dead. Total inability requires total sovereignty for its overcoming.'[2]

The doctrine of sin

The theme of Leviticus is the holiness of God. Because God is morally perfect, sinners cannot enter his presence. If God were to tolerate sin and admit sinners into his presence, he would no longer be morally perfect. Our eternal existence depends upon communion and fellowship with our Maker. We must, therefore, answer the question: 'How can a man be righteous before God?' (Job 9:2). How can we, as sinful creatures, come into his presence and have communion with him? In the following chapters, we shall discuss the *basis* and the *blessing* of communion with God. Before we consider those aspects, we need to consider the doctrine of sin. Sin is the *barrier* to communion with God; it hinders and destroys communion with God.

Significantly, only two historical events are recorded in Leviticus — the rest is instruction. Both events concern serious transgression of God's law; they are:

- The sin of Nadab and Abihu, priests who ignored God's instructions and tried to do things their own way (Lev. 10).
- The sin of a half-Israelite who blasphemed God (Lev. 24:10-16).

Having introduced the subject of sin, it is necessary to define it. Though many people seem to suppose that there is a common or general understanding of the meaning of sin, there are, as I have said, several different, conflicting views within the church. So then, What is sin? The *Westminster Shorter Catechism* gives the answer: 'Sin is any want of conformity unto, or transgression of, the law of God.'[3]

The two key words, 'conformity' and 'transgression', are important. '*Conformity*' means 'complying with' — doing what is required. The law of God carries moral obligations; morality is not neutral or passive — there are requirements which must be fulfilled. '*Transgression*', on the other hand, means 'crossing over'. The law has limits and carries prohibitions; it can be broken. We have all failed on both counts; no one (other than the Lord Jesus Christ) has kept the righteous requirements of the moral law, and we have all broken the law by constant disobedience and rebellion. There are always two aspects to our sin; while we do those things that we ought not to do, we leave undone the things which we ought to do.

Both conformity to and transgression of the law, in one sense, concern what we do — they relate to conduct and behaviour. Sin goes much deeper and is far more serious than actions and deeds, however. The *Shorter Catechism* spells out clearly the biblical teaching on the nature of sin; it asks, 'Wherein consists the sinfulness of that estate whereinto man fell?' and gives the answer:

The sinfulness of that estate whereinto man fell, consists in:

- the guilt of Adam's first sin,
- the want of original righteousness, and
- the corruption of our whole nature, which is commonly called Original Sin;
- together with all actual transgressions which proceed from it.[4]

To help in our understanding, I have set the answer out systematically; I want to comment briefly on each of the phrases.

1. The guilt of Adam's first transgression

Adam, as the father of the human race, acted as our representative. When he disobeyed the command of God, he incurred guilt, not only for himself, but also for all his posterity. Sometimes people claim that it is not fair that we should be held responsible for what Adam did so long ago. We accept the principle in other areas of life, however; my children and grandchildren are US citizens because of a choice I made before they were born. Similarly, our political leaders make decisions which affect us and future generations. Because of Adam's wilful transgression, his guilt is imputed and imparted to us. As a result, we are all born with the same disobedient and rebellious sinful nature as Adam. We are guilty because of Adam's transgression.

2. The want of original righteousness

Contrary to popular opinion, babies are not born into this world as innocent little creatures. No one begins life morally neutral with a clean moral slate. From the outset, we lack original righteousness; that is why a child never needs to be taught to lie or blame others for his or her disobedience and sin. 'There is none righteous, no, not one' (Rom. 3:10). 'We are all like an unclean thing, and all our righteousnesses are like filthy rags'

(Isa. 64:6). Even the best that we do is corrupted by ulterior motives, selfish interests and personal desires. We are destitute of righteousness.

3. The corruption of our whole nature

We are not sinners simply by what we *do*; we are sinners by what we *are*. We are not sinners because we sin; we sin because we are sinners. In other words, our minds, desires, attitudes and wills have been adversely affected by sin. We are antagonistic to righteousness, prejudiced against truth and opposed to goodness; we are incapable of doing anything to impress God or win his approval or favour. As the apostle says, 'In me ... nothing good dwells' (Rom. 7:18). We are corrupt by nature.

4. Actual transgressions which proceed from our corrupt nature

Since we are corrupt in nature, it is not surprising that this is expressed in our conduct. We transgress the law of God continually in thought, word and deed because our nature is corrupt. As Jesus said, 'A bad tree [cannot] bear good fruit' (Matt. 7:18). Further, sinners transgress the law of God without any pangs of conscience, sense of guilt, or remorse.

Sin is the root cause of all problems: personal, family, social, national and international. We, as sinners, are corrupt in nature and we are, therefore, totally depraved. In speaking of 'total depravity' we do not mean that people are as wicked as they might be — thank God, he restrains us and inhibits us from doing exactly as we please. It means that we are incapable of pleasing God; that we are in rebellion against God, destitute of righteousness, corrupt in nature, and we transgress his law continually. Consequently, there is nothing within us, and nothing that we can do to cause God to look upon us with favour; we cannot bring ourselves into communion and fellowship with him. Because of our sinful condition, we are enemies of God; we would not come to him even if we could. 'There is none who seeks after God' (Rom. 3:11). What an awful condition we are in!

Are all sins equally heinous?

Since this chapter is actually an introduction to the book of Leviticus, I want to consider another question relating to this matter of sin. Occasionally, people say that all sin is bad and that there is no real difference — sin is sin! It is true, of course, that all sin deserves God's wrath and judgement. God never excuses, condones, or ignores any form or expression of sin. The *Larger Catechism* asks the question: 'Are all transgressions of the law of God equally heinous in themselves, and in the sight of God?'[5] To put it simply, the answer is: 'No!' Some sins are more heinous or serious than others. This is borne out in the book of Leviticus.

The next question in the *Larger Catechism* is, 'What are those aggravations that make some sins more heinous than others?'[6] The lengthy answer is given under four headings. Some sins are more heinous than others because of the following factors:

1. The persons offending

God records ten occasions when the children of Israel sinned before he judged them and forbade them from entering the promised land. Moses, on the other hand, was forbidden to enter the land for just one act of rebellion. Why did God judge him so harshly? Moses was the prophet sent by God; he was the leader. Some people have greater influence and hold positions of leadership; when someone has a place of responsibility, his example is very important.

It is always bad for a child to lie to his parent; it is much more serious if the parent lies to the child. Some forms of behaviour are bad for unbelievers; the same conduct is disgraceful within the church. What is bad for Sodom is abominable for Jerusalem (or Capernaum — Matt. 10:15). Homosexuality is vile and wicked at any time, but when it is accepted, condoned and endorsed by the church, it is an abomination before God. (That is not to say that homosexuals are to be despised or hated, of course; they are to be shown the love of God, and every effort should be made to help them find deliverance from their bondage. As sinners, they need to be reconciled to God. Yes, there is forgiveness for the most heinous and disgraceful sin.)

In his epistle, James says, 'My brethren, let not many of you become teachers, knowing that we shall receive a stricter judgement' (James 3:1). That applies, not only to Sunday School teachers, but to any teacher. Teachers are influential; they can impart ideas and lifestyles which are false, misleading and destructive. If anyone does offend, it would be better, according to our Lord, that 'a millstone [be] hung around his neck, and [if] he were drowned in the depth of the sea' (Matt. 18:6). Some sins, then, are more heinous than others because of the persons offending.

2. The parties offended

It is bad to tell lies at any time; to lie to God is terrible. In confronting Ananias with his sin, Peter declared, 'You have not lied to men but to God' (Acts 5:4). Stealing from a neighbour is a serious offence; to rob God is an affront to his goodness and providential care. The prophet Malachi accused the people of robbing God of their tithes and offerings. Is it not true that often the last obligation that concerns Christian people is their duty towards God? It is bad to offend men, but to offend God is much worse. One might speak evil against one's neighbour — that is awful under any circumstance — to speak evil against the one whom God sends to bring his Word, as the Israelites did against Moses, is an affront to God himself. To lift up one's hand against the Lord's anointed is to lift it up against the God who sent him. Some sins are therefore more heinous than others because of the persons offended.

3. The nature and quality of the offence

One might think evil thoughts — that is a serious sin — but if those thoughts are expressed in actions, the sin is compounded. It is awful to allow hatred to occupy one's thoughts and to burn in one's heart. If, however, that hatred is expressed in murder, the action can never be undone or reversed. Similarly, it is a serious sin to steal from one's neighbour — in contemporary society, that is about the worst thing one can do. (That reveals contemporary values!) If someone steals his property, however, restitution can be made. If someone gossips about him, on the other hand, those words can never be recalled or undone. So we see that some sins are more heinous than others by the nature and quality of the offence.

4. The circumstances of time and place

It is bad to think evil thoughts at any time; how much worse to entertain those same thoughts when the mind should be occupied with the worship of God! To my shame, I can recall more than one occasion when my mind was occupied with thoughts far removed from the things of God while I was supposedly engaged in prayer or participating in the Lord's Supper. The circumstances and time make some sins more heinous than others.

The consequences of sin

Because God is morally perfect, how awful and offensive our sin must be to him! He cannot, and indeed he does not, condone, excuse, or ignore sin. So then, what are the consequences of sin?

Or, as the catechism expresses it, 'What is the misery of that estate whereinto man fell?' In view of the message of the book of Leviticus, the answer is most important. The catechism says, 'All mankind by their fall lost communion with God, are under his wrath and curse, and so made liable to all miseries in this life, to death itself, and to the pains of hell for ever.'[7]

Each of these phrases is important; again, I will comment on them briefly.

1. All mankind by their fall lost communion with God

The loss of communion with God is not, I suppose, of any great interest or concern to multitudes of people; indeed, without understanding the consequences of sin, they prefer to be without contact with God. To understand the significance of the loss of communion with him, we must remember that man was made in the image of God. I have outlined this in some detail in my book, *Let Us Make Man;*[8] at this point, let me say simply that:

- Being made in God's image as *rational beings*, we were made to reason together with God. We were made to be one in *mind* with him.
- Being made in God's image as *moral beings*, we were made to be righteous as he is righteous. We were made so that the desires of our *hearts* should be one with God.
- Being made in God's image as *beings with purpose*, we were made to fulfil the role for which God made us. We were made to obey his perfect *will*; his will was to be our will.

God made us like himself so that communion with him would be a wonderful reality. Indeed, we *must* have communion with him if we are to live. As Campbell Morgan says, 'No man can truly live who does not have conscious dealings with God.'[9]

The word 'communion', incidentally, concerns that which is held in common. We were made to walk with God and talk with him — to be one with him in mind, heart and will. We were made to delight in the joy, comfort and security of his presence. Because of the Fall, however, we have lost communion with him. We are now separated from the Source and Giver of life and lost in subjectivism and corruption. Having lost communion with God, we are 'dead in trespasses and sins' (Eph. 2:1). But that is not all. We have not only lost communion with God.

2. We stand 'under his wrath and curse'

Today, we are told that God loves everybody and that he is patiently waiting for them to invite Jesus into their hearts. Somewhere we have forgotten that we are 'sinners in the hands of an angry God'.[10] While John 3:16 tells about God's love for the world, John 3:36 is often ignored; it states that 'He who does not believe the Son shall not see life, but *the wrath of God* abides on him' (John 3:36, emphasis mine). Sin is offensive to God; it is destructive of that which God made in his own image and which he pronounced 'very good'. God cannot ignore, tolerate, or act indifferently towards that which is contrary to his holy and righteous nature and is destructive of his creatures.

3. Sin has made us 'liable to all the miseries of this life, to death itself, and to the pains of hell for ever'

The one consequence of sin to which people object, and about which they complain the most, is actually the least important. When the miseries of this life are experienced — whether in sickness, accident, material loss, or hardship — people often blame God for not making them healthy and happy. It is as though God were under some sort of obligation to pamper those who live for themselves and who ignore and defy him. In mercy, however, God brings miseries in this life to remind us of worse things to come. And the adversities of the present are designed to cause us to turn to him. The miseries of this life, death and the pains of hell are a reality for the wicked — and it is not God's fault! Briefly, these are the effects, or consequences, of sin. All of this is portrayed graphically in Leviticus.

Sinners declare themselves independent of God and try to avoid the issue of sin by affirming their belief in the goodness of man, by using the wrong standard and by telling themselves that all their problems are simply due to a lack of 'self-esteem'. The ways in which we try to evade, avoid, minimize and deny the issue of sin show something of the magnitude and power it has over us. We are not only skilful in avoiding and excusing sin in our lives, but we are equally ingenious at avoiding the solution and inventing alternatives in the form of religion. The truth is that we are sinners: we are guilty of Adam's first transgression, we lack original righteousness, we have a corrupt nature and we continually transgress the law of our Maker. Sin is the barrier that separates us from God and prevents us from enjoying communion with him. Jesus Christ, the Son of God, came into this world, not to judge sinners but to save them. He is the only means by which sinners may be reconciled to God and brought into communion with him. He declared, 'I am the way... No one comes to the Father except through me' (John 14:6).

10.
The basis for communion with God

Because of its importance, I want to repeat the *Shorter Catechism's* statement concerning our spiritual condition. It says, 'All mankind by their fall lost communion with God, are under his wrath and curse, and so made liable to all miseries in this life, to death itself, and to the pains of hell for ever.'[1]

While we, as sinful human beings, usually bemoan the miseries of this life and abhor the reality of death, the more serious aspect of our condition is that we have 'lost communion with God and are under his wrath and curse'. The miseries of this life and death are the consequences of our having lost communion with God.

Since we stand under the wrath and curse of God, we dare not presume to come into his presence. It is a fearful thing for sinners to fall into the hands of an angry God; for God is a consuming fire (Heb. 12:29). Before we are able to stand in his presence, his wrath must be appeased and the curse of sin removed; otherwise, we stand condemned and have cause to fear and tremble. God could have left us in our sin and misery to perish in hell for ever — and would have been perfectly just in doing so!

Thank God, he did not 'leave all mankind to perish in the state of sin and misery'! 'God having, out of his mere good

pleasure, from all eternity, elected some to everlasting life, did
enter into a covenant of grace, to deliver them out of the estate of
sin and misery, and to bring them into an estate of salvation by a
Redeemer.'[2]

The catechism proceeds to identify the Redeemer and explain
how he fulfils the offices of Prophet, Priest and King. Thus,
biblical truths are systematically brought together to show how
God's people are delivered from the consequences of sin and
brought into communion with their Maker.

The most important question for every person in the entire
world is: 'How can I, a sinner, come into God's presence
without being condemned?' How is the wrath of God appeased
and the curse of sin removed? How are sinners justified before
God? How can I have peace with God and enjoy communion
with my Maker? No one can afford to be careless, ignorant,
misinformed, or presumptuous on this issue; there is no margin
for error; to be wrong is to 'suffer the pains of hell for ever'.
Tragically, because many people have a false view of God, they
assume that he will look upon them with favour and receive
them into heavenly bliss. Many assume that they are right with
God, but they know nothing of communion with him. The
words of Jesus concerning the Day of Judgement are a most
solemn warning against presumption. He said, 'Not everyone
who says to me, "Lord, Lord," shall enter the kingdom of
heaven, but he who does the will of my Father in heaven. Many
will say to me in that day, "Lord, Lord, have we not prophesied
in your name, cast out demons in your name, and done many
wonders in your name?" And then I will declare to them, "I
never knew you; depart from me, you who practise lawless-
ness!"' (Matt. 7:21-23).

Many people apparently think that their relationship to God
is fine, but they are not right with God at all. I believe that it was
Bishop Ryle who said that many people hope to go to heaven
but if they were admitted, they would be entirely out of place. If
they have not known or enjoyed communion with God here on
earth, what makes them think that they will seek and enjoy it

then? Anyone who has no desire for, or enjoyment of, the presence of God needs to do some serious self-examination. How is reconciliation to God and communion with him possible? The book of Leviticus provides the answer.

There are two major parts to this wonderful book:

1. The means of approach to God (Lev. 1-16).
2. Continuance in communion with God (Lev. 17-27).

In this chapter, we shall consider the first section. Four important matters are covered in these chapters — all of which relate to communion with God. Further, this section progresses systematically from the state of sin and misery to the consummation, or completion, of redemption. The four major subjects covered are:

1. The laws of sacrifice (Lev. 1-7).
2. The office of the priest (Lev. 8 -10).
3. The laws of purity (Lev. 11- 15).
4. The Day of Atonement (Lev. 16).

Leviticus begins with the declaration: 'The LORD called to Moses, and spoke to him from the tabernacle of meeting' (Lev. 1:1). Throughout the book, we are told frequently that 'The LORD spoke to Moses.' Even in that simple statement there are overtones of the gospel; Matthew Henry says, 'The moral law was given with terror from a burning mountain in thunder and lightning; but the remedial law of sacrifice was given more gently from a mercy seat, because that was typical of the grace of the gospel, which is the ministration of life and peace.'[3]

1. The laws of sacrifice (Lev. 1 - 7)

The first seven chapters give explicit instructions concerning five separate sacrifices. Since this is not an exposition of Leviticus, a detailed discussion of the sacrifices is beyond our purpose;

anyone familiar with Andrew Bonar's work, A *Commentary on Leviticus*,[4] or Matthew Henry's commentary will be aware of the wealth of gospel truth contained in Leviticus. The sacrifices are as follows:

- The burnt offering;
- The meal offering;
- The peace offering;
- The sin offering;
- The trespass offering.

Why were there five different sacrifices or offerings specified in Leviticus? Would not the burnt offering by itself have been sufficient? The simple answer is that sin touches every aspect of our being and nature and is so complex that no single sacrifice could possibly portray and cover every aspect. No matter what form sin takes, it separates men from God — even if it is unintentional or done in ignorance (Lev. 4:22,27). Regardless of how communion with God is broken, it must be restored; it can be restored, of course, only when God's wrath is appeased and the curse of sin is removed. That means atonement must be made for sin — and atonement is made only by offering an acceptable sacrifice.

Sin and its consequences

As the details concerning the burnt offering are contemplated, one surely must be thoroughly disgusted; the picture is one of unmitigated violence. Had there been animal-rights activists in those days, all kinds of vehement opposition and vigorous protests would have erupted over the way in which the sacrificial animals were slaughtered. In skinning the sacrificial victim, for example, the skin was actually beaten off. The animal was dead, of course, but the picture is graphic. In describing this action, some of the older translations use the word 'flay' — actually, that is a more accurate term. The apostle Peter says that by the 'stripes', or scourging, of the Lord Jesus Christ, we are healed (1 Peter 2:24, quoting Isa. 53:5). When turtle doves were brought for sacrifice, the priest literally wrung off their heads. The death of the sacrificial victim was awful; the action was one of wrath and destruction. If the passage is read with any under-standing at all, one is repulsed at the violence involved. How much worse it must have been to have witnessed and partici-pated in it!

Why did God record that? Indeed, why did he *require* it? Those sacrifices were designed to portray the magnitude, the seriousness, the heinousness and the consequences of sin. They show that sin deserves nothing less than the wrath and curse of God. Sin merits condemnation and infinite punishment because it is against the God who is 'infinite, eternal and unchangeable in his ... holiness'. For this reason, the burnt offering was sacrificed *totally*; nothing was spared. The peace offering, on the other hand, was divided between God, the priest and the one who offered it. It typifies Christ, who, through the blood of his cross, established peace between God and man. He broke down the barriers and removed the enmity which separate men and, thereby, established peace (Eph. 2:11-22). Through the sacrificial work of Christ, reconciliation to God is accomplished and communion is established.

Identification and substitution

When an Israelite brought his sacrificial lamb to the entrance of the tabernacle, he identified with it by placing his hands on its head and confessing his sin. Then he killed it. In this act of *identification* with the sacrificial victim, the person acknowledged that this was precisely what he deserved. This took place at the entrance to the tabernacle because he was unworthy to enter the presence of God. Sinners were not, and are not, admitted into the presence of God — even with an acceptable sacrifice! These Old Testament sacrifices were intended, not only to picture the nature of sin and its awful consequences, but also to establish the principle of *substitution*. The sacrificial lamb died in place of, and on behalf of, the sinner.

Those Levitical sacrifices portrayed and prefigured the Lamb of God who 'bore our sins in his own body on the tree' (1 Peter 2:24). As we behold the Saviour suffering on Calvary, are we not appalled at the cruelty and repulsed by the violence? Wicked hands took him and did their worst. Though 'he was led as a lamb to the slaughter' (Isa. 53:7), he voluntarily offered himself 'an offering and a sacrifice to God' (Eph. 5:2). What he bore on that cross, he bore in our place. He 'who knew no sin [was made] to be sin for us' (2 Cor. 5:21). Since he went to the cross as our substitute, we need to grieve over our sinful condition; as he told the women of Jerusalem, 'Do not weep for me, but weep for yourselves and for your children' (Luke 23:28).

Bearing shame and scoffing rude,
In my place condemned he stood,
Sealed my pardon with his blood:
Hallelujah! What a Saviour![5]

Of the art I have seen, my favourite painting is Rembrandt's *Raising of the Cross*. I love that painting, not so much because of its artistry (though it is a masterpiece) as because of the concept it portrays. Besides Christ, one of the most prominent and central figures in the picture is Rembrandt himself; he is there, not as an observer, but as an active participant in putting Jesus Christ to death. That great artist understood that *his* sin was responsible for the death of the Lord. He understood the principles of identification with and substitution by the sacrificial victim – the Lamb of God.

The blood

Because sin is offensive to God, the consequence is death; nothing less than the ultimate sacrifice is sufficient to satisfy the demands of divine justice. If the penalty of sin is to be paid and atonement made, a life must be forfeited. And it is not just any life; the sacrificial victim must be 'without spot or blemish'. The satisfaction of justice demands the shedding of blood because, as the key verse of Leviticus says, 'For the life of the flesh is in the blood, and I have given it to you upon the altar to make atonement for your souls; for it is the blood that makes atonement for the soul' (Lev. 17:11). For atonement to be made for sin, the blood of the sacrifice must be spilled and presented as evidence that the penalty has been paid in full.

Because the life is in the blood, the Old Testament expressly and emphatically forbade the partaking of blood. In the light of that strong prohibition, how radical the words of Jesus must have sounded to his audience when he declared, 'Unless you eat the flesh of the Son of Man and *drink his blood*, you have no life in you'! (John 6:53, emphasis mine). The shedding of his blood was not enough in itself for sinners to be reconciled to God; they must *partake* of it. In other words, identification had to be total and absolute. While '... it is not possible that the blood of bulls and goats could take away sins' (Heb. 10:4), '... the blood of Jesus Christ [God's] Son cleanses us from all sin' (1 John 1:7). The shedding of his blood was, and is, effectual in reconciling God and man and in bringing them together in communion. Through the sacrificial, substitutionary death of the Lord Jesus Christ, the wrath of God is appeased and the guilt and curse of sin are removed.

Now picture an Israelite, who, being burdened by sin, brings an appropriate sacrifice to the door of the tabernacle. In keeping with the Levitical requirements, he places his hands on the head of the sacrificial victim, confesses his sin and kills it. He has done everything precisely as the Levitical law required; at that point, is he forgiven? Does he have access into the presence of God? The answer is 'No!' He is still a sinner; he cannot enter into the presence of God. An acceptable sacrifice is absolutely necessary but, in addition, he must have a qualified priest who will offer the sacrifice on the altar and present it to God on his behalf. He needs a qualified mediator to represent him before God and bring him into communion with God. That brings us to the next section in Leviticus, which concerns the priesthood.

2. The office of the priest (Lev. 8-10)

The consecration of the priest (Lev. 8)

An acceptable priest was not some self-appointed egotist who liked being in public view; the priest was chosen and approved by God: 'Every high priest taken from among men is appointed for men in things pertaining to God [in order to] offer both gifts and sacrifices for sins' (Heb. 5:1). He had to meet certain qualifications and was set aside from other duties for the sacred task entrusted to him. Consecration of the priest was a very solemn and sacred occasion. Every detail of the consecration and investiture of the high priest is significant. For example, instructions pertaining to the application of the blood of the sacrifice and the anointing oil to his right ear, right thumb and right big toe are given in Exodus 29. This symbolized the necessity for the priest to be cleansed of sin and anointed by the Spirit as he listened to the confession of sin, as he performed his tasks and as he walked before the Lord. Matthew Henry comments: ' "The blood seems to have been a token of forgiveness, the oil of healing," for God first forgiveth our iniquities and then healeth our diseases (Ps. 103:3). Wherever the blood of Christ is applied for justification the oil of the Spirit is applied for sanctification; for these two are inseparable and both necessary for our acceptance with God.'[6]

This anointing is mentioned in Leviticus 8 as Aaron and his sons were consecrated for their sacred task. While Aaron was appointed high priest and his descendants inherited the office by virtue of being born into the family, the Lord Jesus, on the other hand, was confirmed to the office of priest by an oath (Heb. 5:6;

7:17,21). The Lord Jesus is not only the perfect sacrifice; he is also our great High Priest. He mediates between us and God. As our great heavenly lawyer, he represents us before God's bar of justice, he pleads our case and he intercedes on our behalf.

The ministration of the priest (Lev. 9)

On the occasion of the consecration of Aaron and his sons, appropriate sacrifices were offered, both for their own sins and for the sins of the people. Details of Aaron's officiation at the altar of sacrifice are given. Because Moses and Aaron were approved and accepted by the Lord, they were qualified to go into the presence of God on behalf of the people. Then, 'Moses and Aaron went into the tabernacle of meeting, and came out and blessed the people. Then the glory of the LORD appeared to all the people, and the fire came out from before the LORD and consumed the burnt offering' (Lev. 9:23-24). The sacrifice was accepted and the sin of the people forgiven — then the glory of God appeared. God's glory is evident when sinners are forgiven and reconciled to him.

The Old Testament sacrifices had to be repeated daily, because '... it is not possible that the blood of bulls and goats could take away sins' (Heb. 10:4) and the people needed to be reminded constantly of the magnitude and heinousness of sin — and the penalty it deserves. Commentators have pointed out that there was no chair in the tabernacle, for the work of the priest was never done; he could never sit down. Christ, on the other hand, as our great High Priest, having 'offered one sacrifice for sins for ever, sat down at the right hand of God' (Heb. 10:12). His work is ended; it is complete. In his presenting his substitutionary death on Calvary to satisfy the demands of divine justice, the wrath of God was appeased and the curse of sin removed for those whom he represents. Reconciliation to God is, therefore, on the basis of an *acceptable sacrifice* and the ministration, or mediation, of a *qualified priest*. The mediation of the Lord Jesus Christ, as our High Priest, has opened the way for us to enter the presence of God and have communion with him. In one of his great hymns, John Newton expressed both aspects:

He has washed us with his blood,
He presents our souls to God.[7]

Having identified the Redeemer of God's elect as the Lord Jesus Christ, the catechism proceeds to ask, 'How does Christ execute the office of a priest?' The answer summarizes his gracious work: 'Christ executes the office of a priest, in his once offering up of himself a sacrifice to satisfy divine justice, and reconcile us to God; and in making continual intercession for us.'[8]

As our Priest, Jesus Christ is *qualified*; as the sacrifice, he is *acceptable* to God. He has satisfied fully the demands of divine justice, he has reconciled us to God and he brings us into communion with God. Christ is, of course, not only our great High Priest; he is also our Prophet and King. Because he is truly God and truly man, he is the perfect mediator. As *God*, he reveals God to us; he executes the office of Prophet. As *man*, he represents us before God; he is our Priest.

A violation of the priesthood (Lev. 10)

Nadab and Abihu, the two sons of Aaron who had experienced the 'Old Testament transfiguration' on Mt Sinai with Moses, Aaron and seventy elders, entered the tabernacle and offered 'strange fire' on the altar. After all that they had seen and experienced of the power and majesty of God, one wonders how they could find the audacity to do such a thing. While we do not know what the 'strange fire' was, evidently they ignored God's explicit instructions concerning their function and duties as priests. Perhaps they thought that their privilege on the mountain gave them special liberties, or that God's instructions were merely suggestions. Possibly, they found an easier and more convenient method of kindling fire on the altar. At any rate, in this, they followed the way of Cain, who thought that he could approach God on his own terms. The violation was so serious and contemptuous that God struck them down immediately and instructed their father, Aaron, not even to mourn for them.

By way of contrast, when Moses and Aaron went into the tabernacle, 'fire came out from before the LORD and consumed the burnt offering' (Lev. 9:24). When Nadab and Abihu tried to 'do it their way', the 'fire went out from the LORD and devoured them' (Lev. 10:2) — not their offering! Similar incidents are recorded in Numbers chapters 11 and 16 (see also Rev. 20:9). The sacrifice must be acceptable, the priest must be approved and the work must be carried out according to God's instructions.

Apart from the consecration of the priests, this is one of two actual historical events recorded in Leviticus. The other concerns a half-Israelite who blasphemed the name of God (Lev. 24:10-16). God ordered that he be taken outside the camp and stoned. Significantly, both these events concern people who did not take God's instructions seriously. On both occasions, neither feared God or obeyed his Word. Both events are recorded for our benefit and admonition — to impress on us that sin can, and often does, dictate how we worship and work. Sin destroys communion with God.

Sadly, a lot of strange fire is being kindled within the church these days in an effort to attract and appeal to contemporary sinners. A church in our neighbourhood, for example, advertises 'Country Western Worship — Singing and Dancing'. (Incidentally, the pastor is a woman!) Another church recently had 'Baseball Sunday' for the beginning of the baseball season. The pastor and ushers were dressed in baseball uniforms and the church 'game plan' for the year was presented. After the 'service' a picnic lunch was followed by a baseball game. Some, it seems, have forgotten the lesson of Nadab and Abihu. That which is acceptable, pleasing and convenient to sinners might readily be an abomination to God. With so much 'do-it-yourself' religion around these days, we need to be sure that our approach to God is on his terms — otherwise, instead of invoking his favour, we

might discover that we have incurred his displeasure. We may
not be presumptuous when it comes to communion with God.
The psalmist prayed, 'Keep back your servant also from presumptuous sins' (Ps. 19:13).

3. The laws of purity (Lev. I I – I 5)

Surely, it is no coincidence that the presumption of Nadab and
Abihu is followed by laws of purity! These laws concern such
matters as food, childbirth and leprosy. Such passages are often
passed over casually and treated as irrelevant. While these
Levitical laws concern outward practical matters, they conveyed
important spiritual truth. Those who have been reconciled to
God and enjoy communion with him are called to live pure,
holy lives. Holiness goes much deeper than outward appearances
and external behaviour.

Food

The laws regulating food are appropriate. Health authorities
today are expressing more and more concern that people are
eating themselves to death with 'junk food'. My doctor advises
me to watch my diet and get more exercise. Since our bodies are
the temple of the Holy Spirit, we need to watch our diet. These
laws regulating diet also teach us valuable lessons concerning
good spiritual health. The apostle advised Timothy to 'be
nourished in the words of faith and of [sound] doctrine' and to
exercise himself in 'godliness' (1 Tim. 4:6,8). We must avoid
filling our minds with spiritual 'junk food'. Rather, we need to
meditate on the law of the Lord and think on those things which
are lovely, pure and of good report.

Childbirth

The laws relating to childbirth are brief. The penalty imposed on the woman because of the Fall was: 'I will greatly multiply your sorrow and your conception; in pain you shall bring forth children' (Gen. 3:16). Undoubtedly, the reason for this was to impress upon her that she brought another sinner into the world, who, if not brought to know God, would increase the sin problem. (Paul's comment in 1 Timothy 2:15 concerning a woman being 'saved in childbearing' needs to be considered in the light of this. In other words, if she continues 'in faith, love, and holiness, with self-control,' she will help solve the problem.)

The reason why a woman was regarded as unclean following childbirth was to 'signify the pollution of sin which we are all conceived and born in (Ps. 51:5)'.[9] 'Now that the nature of man is degenerated the propagation of that nature is laid under these marks of disgrace, because of the sin and corruption that are propagated with it, and in remembrance of the curse upon the woman that was first in the transgression... And the exclusion of the woman for so many days from the sanctuary, and all participation of the holy things, signified that our original corruption ... would have excluded us for ever from the enjoyment of God and his favours if he had not graciously provided for our purifying.'[10]

Leprosy

Numerous disorders are categorized as 'leprosy'. Israel had to be very strict to prevent contagious diseases from spreading. The people did well to heed God's instructions to avoid exposure or contamination. In Old Testament times, lepers were doomed to a life of separation, misery and death. Leprosy should not be seen merely as a physical disease, however. Throughout Scripture, it is used to illustrate sin; like lepers, sinners are unclean, without hope of a human remedy, and are utterly helpless. James says that we are to keep ourselves 'unspotted from the world' (James 1:27) — an expression relating to leprosy. We must avoid spiritual contamination and defilement. Obviously, that has direct application to us today, when the most depraved forms of wickedness can be imported directly into our homes through television, videos, magazines, and the like.

Significantly, the words 'holy' and 'holiness' appear 168 times in Leviticus. God is morally perfect. He is 'infinite, eternal, and unchangeable in his ... holiness'. He requires his people to be holy. As we have already noted, three times in Leviticus he declares, 'Be holy; for I am holy' (Lev. 11:44,45; 19:2). Holiness is not an option for us; if we, as sinful people, are to stand before God and enjoy communion with him, we must, as the author of Hebrews says, 'Pursue ... holiness, without which no one will see the Lord' (Heb. 12:14).

Who, then, can come into God's presence? As the psalmist asks, 'Who may ascend into the hill of the LORD? Or who may stand in his holy place?' (Ps. 24:3). The answer is: 'He who has clean hands and a pure heart' (which is a poetic way of saying 'those who have been cleansed from the defilement of sin'). Only those whose sins have been atoned for by the blood of Christ, who have been forgiven and cleansed of sinful defilement and who are clothed in the righteousness of Christ — they alone are able to stand in God's presence and enjoy communion with him. (The rest of the psalm shows that the effect, or result, is holy living.)

4. The Day of Atonement (Lev. 16)

The Day of Atonement was the most sacred day in the Jewish calendar; it fell on the tenth day of the seventh month. Significantly, the chapter begins with a reminder of the sin of Nadab and Abihu, the sons of Aaron who offered strange fire on the altar. Undoubtedly, the reason for that reminder was the fact that the Day of Atonement was a very solemn occasion; there was no room for carelessness or presumption. What was the Day of Atonement all about?

When Moses was instructed by God to build the tabernacle, he was told to build it exactly as God described. Later, when Solomon built the temple, the same pattern was used but it was much more elaborate and ornate. In offering the *daily* sacrifices, the priests went into the Holy Place with the blood of the sacrificial victim and sprinkled it *in front of the veil*. They never went into the Holy of Holies, where the ark of the covenant was kept. As we have seen, that room was, as it were, the throne room of God. On the Day of Atonement, however, the high priest made elaborate preparations and changed his ornate priestly clothing for a simple white linen robe. Because the Old Testament high priest was a sinner, he had to offer a sacrifice for his own sin. These elaborate preparations and rituals were designed to show that no man, not even Aaron, could enter the presence of God without atonement having been made for his sin. 'Without shedding of blood there is no remission' (Heb. 9:22). After the preparation, he took the blood of the sacrifice, entered behind the veil into the Holy of Holies, and sprinkled the blood on the mercy seat.

On the Day of Atonement a unique sacrifice involving two goats carried special significance. One goat was offered as a sin offering for all Israel. Aaron placed both hands on the head of the other goat and confessed the sins of Israel; it was then led away to a remote and uninhabited part of the wilderness and released. The two aspects of this important sacrifice illustrate two fundamental concepts. Theologians speak of propitiation and expiation. Both words have the same meaning – to be 'well-disposed' or 'favourable towards'. As we have seen, sin is an offence against God; it has incurred his wrath. The first goat signified the means by which God's wrath is appeased. Propitiation is that which satisfies divine justice and brings the favour of God. The second goat illustrated expiation – that is, the removal of sin. In other words, this sacrifice prefigured the work of Christ in appeasing the wrath of God and in removing 'as far as the east is from the west ... our transgressions from us' (Ps.

103:12) and '[casting] all our sins into the depths of the sea' (Micah 7:19).

Here the instructions focus on the preparation and ministration of the high priest; he did not act for himself, however, but on behalf of the whole nation — for the people of God! (Lev. 16:17). His reappearance indicated that the sacrifice had been acceptable and that the people were forgiven. When he reappeared, he did so in his ornate priestly robes. Every fiftieth year, the trumpet was blown on this sacred day to announce the year of jubilee. In that year, all debts were cancelled and slaves were set free. The year of jubilee was directly tied to the Day of Atonement.

All of this is a graphic picture of the return of the Lord Jesus Christ when salvation will be consummated. Unlike the Old Testament priest, our Lord did not need to make any sacrifice for his sin, because he had none. When he came to this earth, he laid aside his royal splendour and took 'the form of a bondservant, and coming in the likeness of men ... he humbled himself and became obedient to the point of death, even the death of the cross' (Phil 2:7-8). He came in the poorest of circumstances and lived amongst sinners. When he had offered himself as a sacrifice for sins, he arose from the grave and ascended into the Holy of Holies — the presence of God — where he lives to make intercession for us. There he pleads our case, not on the basis of who we are or what we have done, but on the fact that his blood was shed for our sins. As Charles Wesley expressed it:

Five bleeding wounds he bears,
Received on Calvary;
They pour effectual prayers,
They strongly plead for me.[11]

When our Lord returns from the presence of God, he will come robed in all his glorious splendour and majesty (Heb. 9:28). At that point, the trumpet will sound to announce that the year of jubilee has fully come; all debts have been cancelled, the slaves will be completely set free and his ransomed ones will be welcomed home.

At that point, our redemption will be complete and we shall be in communion with our Lord for ever. This will be accomplished because our Lord, as the only qualified High Priest; offered an appropriate sacrifice on our behalf. He is the perfect mediator between God and man. Because of his sacrificial work and his mediation at the right hand of God, the wrath of God is appeased, the curse of sin is removed, mercy is extended, forgiveness granted and communion with God is restored — and we are able to stand in the presence of the Lord with confidence.

11.
The blessing of communion with God

The theme of Leviticus is the holiness of God. He is 'infinite, eternal, and unchangeable in his ... holiness'.[1] That is, God is absolutely morally perfect. When God made man in his own image, he did so in order that man should have communion with him. Our 'chief end is to glorify and enjoy God for ever'.[2] To have communion with God, however, necessitates that man be holy as he is holy; we must be perfect as he is perfect. Communion with God is not merely desirable or optional; we cannot truly live without a conscious relationship to, and communion with, our Maker. Man has been deceived, of course, into thinking that he can live independently of God. The fact remains that we must have communion with God.

In these studies in Leviticus, we began with man in sin; sin is the barrier to communion with God. We considered also the person and work of Christ. As our great High Priest, he offered himself as a sacrifice to satisfy the demands of divine justice and to reconcile us to God. Being both God and man — one person with two natures — the Lord Jesus Christ is able to mediate between God and man and bring us into communion with God. He is the appropriate sacrifice for sin and the only qualified priest to represent us before God. He is the basis for communion with God.

When a sinner embraces the Saviour 'as he is offered to us in the gospel', he receives new life: '... if anyone is in Christ, he is a new creation; old things have passed away; behold, all things have become new' (2 Cor. 5:17). What does that mean? In Christ, he discovers the meaning of life and no longer needs to search for something to fill and satisfy the emptiness of his soul. It means that he is now 'under new management'! He lives under new rules; instead of obeying the dictates of the world, the devil and the flesh, he now lives under the authority of God's Word. From its principles and precepts, he begins to gain a new perspective, learn new values and establish new goals. He has a new allegiance, new desires and new ambitions. The thoughts of his mind, the desires of his heart and the intent of his will all begin to undergo a change. Life begins to take a new direction; instead of being consumed by the pursuit of pleasures and treasures in this life, he begins to live in the light of eternity. Whereas he once hated God and rebelled against his law, he now has the desire to know God and to please him. His new purpose and aim in life is to 'glorify and enjoy God'. He longs to know him, worship him and serve him — he desires communion with him. With the psalmist, he says, 'As the deer pants for the water brooks, so pants my soul for you, O God' (Ps. 42:1).

While that is the *direction* of every true believer, none of us has yet arrived. We are not yet perfect! We have a lot of growing, changing and maturing to do. Someone has said, 'Never make a goal out of God's starting point.' There is a race to be run and a crown to be won. While we have been *declared* righteous in Christ (justified), we still need to be *made* righteous (sanctified). The Christian life is one of growth and development towards the goal of being made like Christ. Spiritual growth does not happen automatically, however. Now that communion with God is established, we need to understand how to *maintain* communion with God. What must be done to ensure that there is growth in grace and in the knowledge of our Lord?

The principle of separation

In the previous chapter, I drew attention to the laws of purity given in Leviticus 11–15. The laws in those chapters concern things which defile a person and prevent communion with God. They concern *separation from* things which hinder communion. In the second half of Leviticus, chapters 17–27, there are additional laws. There is some repetition but, as a general observation, chapter 20 includes the requirement to distinguish between 'the clean and the unclean'. One of the marks of holiness is the ability to discern. These laws concern the kind of life which is to characterize those who are redeemed. They emphasize the necessity for holiness in daily life; they concern *separation to* God.

Within the church today two extremes exist concerning separation. On the one hand, some refuse to have fellowship with anyone or anything with which they disagree; they are exclusive. On the other hand, in some segments of the church, separation is conspicuous by its absence; it is not even a consideration for many people. Many dismiss separation as a concern of religious fundamentalists or extremists. Separation is a biblical mandate, however; it is not a matter which can be ignored or treated as irrelevant. God says, 'You shall be holy, for I the LORD your God am holy' (Lev. 19:2). He also says, 'Consecrate [or "Sanctify"] yourselves therefore, and be holy, for I am the LORD your God. And you shall keep my statutes, and perform them: I am the LORD who sanctifies you' (Lev. 20:7). If communion with God is to be experienced and enjoyed, all forms of spiritual defilement and contamination must be avoided and believers must separate themselves to the Lord.

We face a problem, however, concerning limits. What are the limits? What may we as Christians do or not do? The problem is compounded by the fact that the moment limits are defined, we are on the road to Pharisaism rather than holiness. When a list of 'dos and don'ts' is produced, attention is focused on outward performance rather than inward motivation.

Outward performance without inward motivation is hypocrisy;
those who follow this course become nothing more than
'whitewashed tombs ... full of dead men's bones' (Matt.
23:27). True holiness proceeds from the heart; it concerns
much more than outward compliance and external activity. I
tend to believe that the question of separation is not such a big
question as it is often made out to be; for the soul in communion with God, separation to God is a privilege and a delight.
This is not a matter of trying to justify one's ideas and excuse
questionable behaviour; for those walking with God, the desire
of the heart will be to avoid anything which hinders or mars
the relationship and to foster those things which will enhance
it. When the heart is right, the motivation will determine the
performance.

Having said all that, I do not mean to imply that the Scriptures are silent on the matter. As James says, we are to 'keep
[ourselves] unspotted from the world' (James 1:27). We are not
to walk as those who are in 'darkness', but 'as children of light'
(Eph. 4:18; 5:8).

> [We must not] be bound together with unbelievers; for
> what partnership have righteousness and lawlessness, or
> what fellowship has light with darkness? Or what har-
> mony has Christ with Belial, or what has a believer in
> common with an unbeliever? Or what agreement has the
> temple of God with idols? For we are the temple of the
> living God; just as God said,
>
> 'I will dwell in them and walk among them;
> And I will be their God, and they shall be my people.
> Therefore, come out from their midst and be separate,'
>   says the Lord.
> 'And do not touch what is unclean;
> And I will welcome you'
>   (2 Cor. 6:14-17, NASB).

The writer to the Hebrews says, 'Pursue ... holiness, without which no one will see the Lord' (Heb. 12:14). Holiness does not happen automatically; it does not come about by some sort of spiritual osmosis. How then is it pursued? While we are not sanctified (made holy) by human effort (Gal. 3:3), we have the responsibility to use the means of grace which God has provided for us. Godliness comes through personal discipline in the means of grace.

The seven convocations of Israel

In ancient Israel, God appointed and ordained seven holy convocations for the benefit of his people. They are listed for us in Leviticus 23. (Sometimes those special occasions are referred to as the 'Feasts of Israel' — though the Day of Atonement was a time of fasting!) The purpose of those convocations was fourfold:

> 1. They were occasions for thanksgiving to God for his blessings and provision.
> 2. They were occasions for commemorating special events in Israel's history.
> 3. They provided occasions for instruction concerning God's purpose for his people.
> 4. They carried a prophetic perspective concerning the future.

Those seven convocations were actually the means of grace for those living under the old dispensation; they are listed in chronological order in Leviticus 23. They are important to us because they prefigure successive steps in the redemption purchased by Jesus Christ our Lord. God has given to us certain means of grace; he has provided occasions, opportunities, resources and privileges by which our spiritual life and maturity are enhanced and by which we 'grow in the grace and knowledge of our Lord' (2 Peter 3:18). Those means of grace which God has ordained and provided for us include such things as the preaching of the Word of God, corporate worship, the sacraments, private and corporate prayer and the communion of the saints. In our use of the means of grace, the *substance* of those things which were foreshadowed in ancient Israel must always be our focus. In other words, to maintain communion with God, so far as we are concerned, depends upon the proper use of the means of grace which God has given to us. Conversely, the neglect of the means of grace will result in spiritual barrenness. In speaking of the 'proper' use, I am emphasizing the importance of the motivation and content, not merely on just keeping the form or ritual.

Well, what were the convocations of Israel and what did each of them foreshadow?

1. The Sabbath (Lev. 23:1-3)

The Sabbath heads the list to remind us of the importance and place of the Lord's Day. No command in Scripture is given greater emphasis, yet it was, and still is, the most commonly ignored and broken. Even the sacred work of constructing the tabernacle was to be suspended on the Sabbath. Proper observance of the Lord's Day was, and is, indicative of a person's commitment to, and love for, the Lord. The Sabbath was, and is, the occasion for regular, consistent and corporate worship of God. After six days of labour in which one deals with mundane physical and material matters, it is important to stop to look up in order to keep things in proper perspective, to assess one's values and to maintain right priorities. We cannot maintain communion with God if we do not take time to hear his Word, commune with him and fellowship with those of like mind. There is so much that needs to be said about the Lord's Day; at this point, let me say simply that it is one of the most basic means of grace. It is our opportunity to keep our focus on the one whom we love and serve. To pursue holiness, we should make proper and full use of the Lord's Day.

2. The Passover (Lev. 23:4-5)

The Passover marked the beginning of the national life of Israel: 'This month shall be your beginning of months' (Exod. 12:2). God's people were spared judgement when the angel of death passed through Egypt. The Passover was to be observed each year to remind the Israelites of their deliverance from the land of bondage by the mighty hand of God. Essentially, the annual observance was the same as that initial observance in Egypt. Each household was to take a lamb without spot or blemish, kill it at the appropriate time, apply the blood to the door and feast upon the lamb with bitter herbs inside their homes. Because they were coupled together in observance, the Feast of Un-leavened Bread needs to be considered alongside the Passover; as might be expected, they are tied together in their significance.

3. The Feast of Unleavened Bread (Lev. 23:6-14)

This feast began the day after the Passover and lasted for one week. On the second day, the first sheaf of the barley crop was offered to the Lord in recognition of the fact that he had pro-vided the harvest. (Barley was, of course, the first crop to ripen.) When taken with the Passover, this significant act took place on the third day.

The Passover is a graphic picture of our redemption from sin; it points to the 'Lamb of God who takes away the sin of the world' (John 1:29). By the application of his shed blood, judge-ment is averted and deliverance from the dominion, power and bondage of sin is assured. That much is obvious, but what is the significance of the presentation of the sheaf of barley at the Feast of Unleavened Bread? As I have said, it was an act of thanks-giving that God had provided the harvest. It was more than that, however. It, too, points to Christ. In 1 Corinthians 15, that great chapter concerning the resurrection, we read, 'Now Christ is risen from the dead, and has become the *first fruits* of those who have fallen asleep' (1 Cor. 15:20, emphasis mine). The apostle relates the presentation of the barley sheaf to the resurrection of Christ — that is why it was offered on the third day following the Passover. For this reason, the two feasts are coupled together; they cannot be separated. Obviously, the apostle had both convocations in mind when he wrote, 'Christ, our Passover, was sacrificed for us. Therefore, let us keep the feast, not with old leaven, nor with the leaven of malice and wickedness, but with the unleavened bread of sincerity and truth' (1 Cor. 5:7-8).

The Feast of Unleavened Bread not only pointed to the resurrection of Christ but it anticipated the ingathering of the entire harvest — the first fruit was the guarantee that the harvest was to come. Together the Passover and the Feast of Unleavened Bread speak of the death and resurrection of Christ. This is the ground upon which we have communion with God; it is the only basis upon which we may come before him. This is the reason why we should observe and celebrate the Lord's Supper regularly; it is one of the important means of grace that God has given for our spiritual development and growth in grace.

4. The Feast of Pentecost (Lev. 23:15-22)

In Exodus 23:16, this convocation is called 'the Feast of Harvest'. It was celebrated seven weeks — or fifty days — after the Passover. Pentecost was a time of great joy celebrating the completion of harvest; all the crops were gathered in. Several thank-offerings were prescribed. Instructions in this passage in Leviticus include the requirement to leave gleanings in the harvest fields for the poor and strangers. This was a reminder that God's people are to be considerate, compassionate and generous.

In discussing the giving of the law at Mt Sinai, I mentioned that Jewish tradition holds that the law was given fifty days after the Passover. That is not certain, but it is entirely possible. If it is

so, the relationship between the giving of the law on Mt Sinai
and the New Testament Day of Pentecost is quite remarkable. At
Sinai, God gave his Word; at Pentecost, people heard God's
Word in their respective languages. Further, did not our Lord
tell his disciples that the fields are white and ready to harvest?
(John 4:35). Pentecost concerns the gathering of the harvest. The
fact that gleanings were to be left in the fields for the poor and
for strangers reminds us that none is to be neglected or forgotten. The Bread of Life is to be made available for all. The Feast
of Pentecost points to the proclamation and hearing of the Word
of God as a means of grace for our spiritual growth. You will not
advance in holiness unless you give heed to the Word of God
and share it with others.

5. The Feast of Trumpets (Lev. 23:23-25)

The convocations were held in the autumn and the spring. The
convocations of which I have already spoken were in the autumn
— around the time of harvest. There was an interval, therefore, of
about five months between Pentecost and the Feast of Trumpets.
The seventh month was in the springtime and it was a particularly special month. Three important convocations were held
during this month. Incidentally, the demands which God places
on his people are not burdensome. The convocations were held
at times when the weather was neither too hot nor too cold for
the journey up to Jerusalem (actually, only three convocations
required going to Jerusalem). The time of year made the occasions and activities pleasant and reasonable. Further, the fact
that God required his people to observe the seventh day, the
seventh month, the seventh year and every seventh seven-year
period suggests something of the importance that God attaches
to regular and consistent spiritual observance.

The Feast of Trumpets marked the beginning of the *civil* year.
It was held on the first day of the seventh month — ten days
before the Day of Atonement. In Israel, there was a clear distinction between the sacred and the secular. The significance of this

convocation is not particularly clear. It could, for example, point to creation, when 'all the sons of God [angelic beings] shouted for joy' (Job 38:7). It might point back to the giving of the law on Mt Sinai when the trumpet was heard and grew louder and louder. Possibly it was to remind the people of the importance of obedience to the law, especially as the books for the fiscal year were closed. Jewish writers suggest that the significance was to remind the people at the beginning of the civil or fiscal year 'to shake off their drowsiness, to search and try their ways, and to amend them'.[3] This is possible in view of the fact that the Day of Atonement was at hand. The sound of the trumpet from morning till evening was 'to awaken them to prepare for that day by sincere and serious repentance, that it might be indeed a day of atonement'.[4] Matthew Henry also suggests that this feast 'was typical of the preaching of the gospel, by which joyful sound souls were to be called in to serve and keep a spiritual feast to him'.[5] Isaiah says that the conversion of the nations will be heralded by the blowing of the trumpet (Isa. 27:13). And does not the sound of the trumpet remind us of the return of our Lord, when the trumpet will sound and the dead in Christ will be raised? (1 Thess. 4:16).

Whatever the intended meaning, this feast was a special time of joy and rejoicing; it was a time of wonderful fellowship. One of the means of grace which God has given to us for our spiritual growth is the communion of the saints — when we delight in fellowship with other believers! As members of the Body of Christ, we are to encourage, comfort and love one another. We are commanded to build one another up in the faith, to bear one another's burdens, and to speak to one another in psalms, hymns and spiritual songs. We have much more in common than the weather, the football scores, or the latest Hollywood production! We need one another; our times together should be times of joy and rejoicing in what our Lord and Saviour has done for us, what he means to us and what we look forward to in faith. The writer to the Hebrews exhorts us: '... not forsaking the assembling of ourselves together, as is the manner of some, but exhorting one another, and so much the more as you see the Day approaching' (Heb. 10:25). Possibly, this convocation is intended to remind us of the importance of the communion of the saints — especially as the Day of Atonement draws near.

6. The Day of Atonement (Lev. 16; 23:26-32)

Many details concerning the Day of Atonement were given in chapter 16; this, the most solemn occasion in Israel's calendar, is included here in the proper sequence of convocations. Actually, like the Sabbath, it was a time of fasting. The people humbled themselves before the Lord. In the previous chapter, we noted that the Day of Atonement was the one occasion during the entire year when the high priest entered the Holy of Holies with the blood of the sacrifice. Also, both the sabbatical year and the year of jubilee were announced by the blowing of the trumpet on the Day of Atonement.

The Day of Atonement presents a graphic picture of the culmination of our redemption. Our great High Priest has entered the Holy of Holies with his own blood. His blood is evidence that the penalty for our sin has been paid in full — atonement has been made for sin. When the Lord Jesus re-appears, he will come robed in splendour and majesty. For those who are prepared and await his return, that will be the beginning of the eternal jubilee when the redeemed will finally possess their eternal inheritance in Christ.

7. The Feast of Tabernacles (Lev. 23:33-44)

In Exodus 23:16, this is called the 'Feast of Ingathering'. It too was held in the seventh month, from the fifteenth to the twenty-second. During the eight days of celebration, the Israelites lived in booths made from branches to remind them of the years their fathers had spent in the wilderness when they had no perma-nent dwelling place — they were 'pilgrims and strangers'. This was to remind them of the hardship that their fathers had endured — to remind them that 'This world is not our home; we're just a-passing through.'

The eighth and final day of the feast was marked by special celebration as the people anticipated returning to their homes. Sometimes it was referred to as 'the great day of the feast'. On that day, the priests took the sacred vessels of the temple down to the Pool of Siloam, filled them with water and, as they returned to the temple in procession, they chanted Isaiah 12:

> ... with joy you will draw water
> From the wells of salvation...
> Cry out and shout, O inhabitant of Zion,
> For great is the Holy One of Israel in your midst!
>   (Isa. 12:3,6).

The Gospel writer tells us that on the great day of the feast, one stepped out of the crowd and cried, 'If anyone thirsts, let him come to me and drink' (John 7:37). The Holy One of Israel was in their midst! As the final convocation of the year, the Feast of Tabernacles, reminded God's people, not only of the hardship of the journey, but also of the anticipated rest. It reminds us of the stream of living water that flows from the throne of God and satisfies our thirsty souls. It reminds us of the one who stands in the midst of his people.

The means of grace

The convocations of ancient Israel were ordained of God; they were the means of grace designed to teach them, and us, the whole scope of redemption. These convocations were the means by which believing Israelites maintained communion with God; they pointed forward to various aspects of redemption in sequence. They are recorded for our instruction and admonition; they remind us of our need to use the means of grace that God has given to us by which we maintain and enjoy communion with our God. 'Blessed are the people,' says the psalmist, 'who know the joyful sound!' (That is, the blast of the trumpet and the shout for joy on feast days.) 'They walk, O LORD, in the light of your countenance. In your name they rejoice all day long' (Ps. 89:15-16).

In passing, I should mention that the book of Esther speaks of the *Feast of Purim*. That feast was instituted at a later date to commemorate the deliverance of God's people from annihilation. The fact that God records it suggests that there may be special occasions or circumstances when God's goodness and mercy should be especially acknowledged. The celebrations of birthdays, anniversaries, or other significant or special events can, and should, be a time of special thanksgiving and praise to God.

Those who embrace Jesus Christ as Saviour are brought into communion with God. To maintain and continue in communion, the means of grace which God has ordained and placed at our disposal must be used. We need to use the Lord's Day for the purpose for which it is intended, take full advantage of the preaching of the Word of God, gather together with God's people for prayer and praise and practise the many injunctions relating to the communion of the saints. By the use of these respective means we are reminded of the many facets of our redemption and their eternal significance. To maintain communion with God, we must be obedient, keep the right perspective, and be consistent.

The closing section of Leviticus

Before leaving Leviticus, a couple more observations need to be made. The first section of Leviticus (chapters 1–16), which shows the basis of communion with God, ends with the Day of Atonement; it shows the complete spectrum of redemption. The second section (chapters 17–27), which shows how communion with God is maintained, essentially ends with the year of jubilee (chapter 25). Our debts are already cancelled in Christ and the joy which is experienced with God now will be fully realized on that day when our great High Priest returns and all the ransomed are gathered home.

Promises and warnings

The two final chapters of Leviticus (26–27) are often regarded as appendices. While chapter 26 gives a series of instructions and warnings, this is not an appendix or afterthought. After the reminders of the sin of Nadab and Abihu and of the half-Israelite who blasphemed the name of God, surely instructions and warnings concerning presumption, indifference and carelessness are appropriate. Significantly, emphasis is laid on the Second and Fourth Commandments in chapter 26 — that is, warnings against idolatry and Sabbath-breaking. Nothing is a greater insult or more offensive to God than images designed to assist in the worship of God. Breaking the Sabbath also destroys communion with God in that priority is given to things of less importance. As Matthew Henry says, 'As nothing tends more to corrupt religion than the use of images in devotion, so nothing contributes more to the support of it than *keeping the sabbaths* and *reverencing the sanctuary.* These make up very much of the instrumental part of religion, by which the essentials are kept up.'[6] 'The way to have God's ordinances fixed among us, as a nail in a sure place, is to cleave closely to the institution of them.'[7]

Obedience to these commands is accompanied by God's gracious promise: 'I will walk among you and be your God, and you shall be my people' (Lev. 26:12). Centuries later, when Israel became divided, King Jeroboam set up a new system of feasts for the people which 'he had devised in his own heart' (1 Kings 12:33). He did so because he did not want his people going to Jerusalem, of course. In setting up his system, he maintained the ritual of religion, but destroyed the meaning and significance of that which God had ordained. He had a form of godliness but

denied the power thereof (2 Tim. 3:5). Communion with God is
a serious matter; we dare not trifle with spiritual matters, act
carelessly or presumptuously, or neglect spiritual opportunities
and responsibilities. We do well to take heed to use God's
appointed means of grace — in keeping with his instructions.

Fulfilling vows

The making and keeping of vows is the subject of chapter 27.
Again, I believe that to regard this chapter as an appendix is a
mistake. Christianity is a religion of truth. God the Father is
true; the Lord Jesus Christ is the truth; the Holy Spirit is the
Spirit of truth, and God's Word is true. That means not only
that he speaks the truth, but also that he is true in his being and
character. He is 'infinite, eternal and unchangeable ... in his
truth'.[8] In one sense, the purpose of our redemption is to make
us, who are sinners, corrupt in nature and sinful in behaviour,
to be people who are true — that is, people who not only speak
the truth, but who are also inwardly true, people whose 'yes' is
'yes' and whose 'no' is 'no' (Matt. 5:37). As David said, 'You
desire truth in the inward parts' (Ps. 51:6). In other words, when
our redemption is real and our communion with God is genuine, we will become like our God — a people who are true
inwardly. As we maintain communion with God, we shall be
people of integrity who fulfil our vows to both God and man.
Truth in the innermost being is the result and fruit of communion with the God of truth.

Part IV.
Numbers — The goodness and severity of God

12.
The importance of leadership, order and discipline

Though God planned the redemption of his people from before the foundation of the world and initiated it at the gate of the Garden of Eden when he slew animals to make a covering for Adam and Eve, the actual implementation of his plan began when he covenanted with Abraham to make of him a great nation and promised that in him 'all the families of the earth [would] be blessed' (Gen. 12:3). Some were redeemed long before the call of Abraham, of course; the Messianic line began with Seth, the son of Adam, and included such great men as Enoch and Noah. In the fulness of time, that foundational promise was fulfilled in the person and through the work of Jesus Christ.

Already, we have seen that God's people are *chosen* by a sovereign God, *redeemed* by a powerful God and brought into *fellowship* with a holy God. The redemption of ancient Israel from the land of bondage typifies, or pictures, God's work in planning, initiating and accomplishing the redemption purchased by Jesus Christ. Eternal salvation is all of God; because of his greatness, goodness and grace, he accomplished for his people what they could not do for themselves.

Salvation from the bondage of sin is, however, only the beginning; there is a journey ahead – a life to be lived. Having been brought into fellowship and communion with God, one might expect that subsequently everything would be pleasant, easy and free of problems. Instead, an inhospitable wilderness, filled with dangers, trials, hardships and adversity, lies ahead. When God delivered his people from the bondage of Egypt, he did not thrust them into the wilderness and leave them to fend for themselves and to depend on their own wisdom and strength for their sustenance.

Why does God take his people into a wilderness? There are two reasons, at least. First, hardship and adversity are necessary to test and strengthen God's people and bring them to maturity; like trees, they need the winds of adversity and the heat of affliction to make them strong and to cause them to put down roots deeper into the source of life. They must also learn that God alone is sufficient and dependable; he can be trusted regardless of external conditions or circumstances. In other words, God's people must learn that their happiness does not depend on what happens. The patriarch Job, having been stripped of his wealth, his health and his friends, said, 'Though he slay me, yet will I trust him' (Job 13:15). Asaph learned the lesson; after contemplating the prosperity of the wicked, he became envious. He regained his perspective in the sanctuary and then declared, 'Whom have I in heaven but you? And there is none upon earth that I desire besides you' (Ps. 73:25). God's people must learn to prove his sufficiency when circumstances are adverse. Genuine religion is not always seen in fun-packed activities or problem-free experiences. Wilderness experiences are necessary and valuable. The book of Numbers concerns the wilderness experiences of those who have been redeemed. Important principles concerning Christian living are to be learned from this great book.

In due course, we shall see that the apostle Paul cited several historical events from the book of Numbers to instruct and warn the Christians in Corinth. There were close parallels between the behaviour of 'the congregation in the wilderness' (Acts 7:38) and that of believers in Corinth. He says that the things recorded in Numbers were written for our example and admonition (1 Cor. 10:6,11). As God's people journey through the wilderness of life and encounter all kinds of challenges, adverse circumstances and unexpected situations, they must learn to trust God – who always does what is right and good.

Background and overview of Numbers

To appreciate the message of Numbers, some background material is needed.

The period of time covered

Israel arrived at Mt Sinai at the beginning of the third month following the institution of the Passover in Egypt. The tabernacle was erected on the first day of the second year, after they had spent almost one year at Mt Sinai (Exod. 40:17). The events recorded in Numbers began on the first day of the second month of the second year (Num. 1:1). That means, of course, that the period of time covered in Leviticus is just one month; as we have seen, only a couple of historical events are recorded in Leviticus – the rest is instruction. At the end of Numbers, the Israelites are about to cross the Jordan River and occupy Jericho (Num. 36:13) – an event which took place forty years after the Exodus. The book of Numbers, then, covers a period of about thirty-nine years between Mt Sinai and the promised land – the years of the wilderness wanderings.

The place where the events happened

Twice in Deuteronomy, Moses refers to 'that great and terrible wilderness' (Deut. 1:19; 8:15); in the second of those passages

he speaks of 'the fiery serpents and scorpions and thirsty land
where there was no water'. It was not the sort of place one would
select for a picnic! If the people took their eyes off God and
forgot about his goodness, as they frequently did, they had
reason to murmur and complain. Had they recognized the
goodness of God in providing their daily food, in protecting
them from dangers and enemies and manifesting his glorious
presence 'to cheer and to guide', the circumstances would have
been immaterial. When God was with them, they did not need
to fear or fret. Because God is infinite in his goodness, they
could commit their lives into his hands with complete confidence, knowing that 'As for God, his way is perfect' (Ps. 18:30).

Traditional route of the Exodus

Outline of Numbers

The book may be outlined according to specific geographical locations at which certain events took place and which punctuated the progress of the Israelites towards the promised land:

1. Israel at Mt Sinai (1:1 – 10:10).
2. From Mt Sinai to Kadesh (10:11 – 14:45).
3. The years of wilderness wandering (15:1 – 19:22).
4. The events of the fortieth year (20:1 – 36:13).

The goodness and severity of God

When the Westminster divines defined God in the *Shorter Catechism*, they stated that 'God is infinite, eternal, and unchangeable in his ... goodness.'[1] Surprisingly, they said nothing about his mercy, love, or grace. They knew that mercy, love and grace are encompassed in God's goodness. That is, because God is good, he is merciful, loving and gracious. Goodness is generally not understood in contemporary society; when used as a moral attribute, it has lost its essential meaning. This is not surprising, of course; whenever God, who is the standard by which goodness is determined, is ignored or dismissed as irrelevant, goodness becomes whatever sinful men want to make it. Goodness is understood and appreciated only as it relates to God and is observed as he leads and instructs his people.

There are two sides or aspects to God's goodness. On the one hand, God is good in dwelling among his people, in providing for their needs, and in protecting them from their enemies. His goodness must never be construed as weakness, however; throughout Numbers, he chastised and punished his people for their unbelief, rebellion and disobedience. That is not because of any flaw or lapse in his goodness but, because '... whom the LORD loves he chastens' (Heb. 12:6). While the

Israelites could rejoice in God's presence, provision and protection, one of the greatest evidences of his goodness was his patience with them. In spite of their unbelief and disobedience, he was patient and long-suffering. Even when God acted in severity and chastised them, he was still 'infinite, eternal and unchangeable in his goodness'. The theme of Numbers, then, may be expressed in the words of the apostle Paul when he speaks of the 'goodness and severity of God' (Rom. 11:22).

The goodness of God in providing leadership for his people

Another expression of God's goodness was his provision of capable leadership for his people. God has not redeemed a mass of individuals and sent them forth to 'do their own thing'. While he leads his people individually, he does not lead them independently. Though 'The LORD is my Shepherd' (Ps. 23:1, emphasis mine), 'He [feeds and leads] his flock like a Shepherd' (Isa. 40:11). There is, in other words, a corporate aspect to redemption. As Ephesians 2 shows, believers are reconciled, not only to God through the work of Christ, but also to one another. The church is the object of the redemption purchased by Christ (Eph. 5:25); it is precious to him. God leads his people as an army and he is glorified when they dwell together in unity. To ensure order and unity within the body, God gave righteous, gifted leaders.

There was no place or provision in Israel for 'do-it-yourself' religion in which individuals acted independently, or claimed that God had spoken to them personally or led them subjectively. What confusion and chaos there would have been had the people simply followed the pillar of cloud! One can imagine the jostling for position, the neglect of the elderly and the weak, and the friction and animosity which would have arisen as various members of the community fought over places to pitch their tents. The logistics of moving such a multitude must have been extremely complicated — especially without modern means of communication!

God chose, prepared and commissioned Moses for the monumental task of leading the Israelites out of Egypt. He was one of the greatest men of history, not merely because of innate ability and wisdom, but because he knew God, he loved God and he communed with God; the phrase, 'The LORD spoke to Moses', appears eighty-five times in Numbers alone. Moses was constantly in communion with God. He did not lead Israel single-handed, however. Prepared, qualified men were chosen and appointed to lead each of the tribes; responsible leadership was committed to them to organize, to maintain order and to exercise righteous judgement. For people to dwell together in unity, they needed to know how they related to each other and where they fitted into the structure. Working together as a body was not a matter of blind obedience or conformity; it was for the good of every individual. The body provided security, instruction, encouragement, help and love. As Bunyan says, 'This house was built by the Lord of the hill, and he built it for the relief and security of pilgrims.'[2]

Godly leadership is one of God's gifts to his church (Eph. 4:11-16). God calls his people to submission to the leadership which he has chosen and ordained. Such leaders are responsible, of course, to determine God's will and to 'judge righteous judgement'. Because the choice of godly leaders is so important, no local church should 'lay hands on anyone hastily' (1 Tim. 5:22). Before choosing a pastor or elders in the church, members should make sure that nominees have been called by God and that they are properly qualified. God is not the author of confusion; he requires that all things be done properly and in an orderly manner (1 Cor. 14:40). As we shall see, some tried to take the leadership of Israel into their own hands and God judged them severely.

While Moses was the commander-in-chief, he had a well-regimented organization. At the outset, the names of the leaders of each of the tribes are listed (Num. 1:5-15). Why does God record names of people about whom we know virtually nothing? Why did he include their names in his Word for all eternity? Is it not to impress upon us the fact that God knows his people by name and that he places honour and importance on positions of leadership among his people? In Scripture, names are important because they describe character. Significantly, here, as in many other places in Scripture, the names of the fathers are given. Some of the names reveal very little; others suggest a great deal. Even a casual reading of these names suggests something of the greatness of many of the leaders of Israel and of their family heritage. Of particular note is the leader of Judah, Nahshon, who is named in the genealogy of Jesus (Matt. 1:4); his name means 'oracle' — a reminder that Jesus, who also came from the tribe of Judah, is 'the Word'.

Tribe	Leader	Meaning	The son of	Meaning
Reuben	Elizur	God is a rock	Shedeur	Shedder of light
Simeon	Shelumiel	God is peace	Zurishaddai	Almighty is a rock
Judah	Nahshon	Oracle	Amminadad	My people is willing
Issachar	Nethanel	God gives	Zuar	Little
Zebulun	Eliab	God is Father	Helon	Strong
Ephraim	Elishama	God is hearer	Ammihud	My people is honourable
Manasseh	Gamaliel	God is recompenser	Pedahzur	The rock delivers
Benjamin	Abidan	Father of judgement	Gideoni	(unknown)
Dan	Ahiezer	Helping brother	Ammishaddai	My people is mighty
Asher	Pagiel	God meets	Ochran	Troubler
Gad	Eliasaph	God is gatherer	Deuel	God is knowing
Naphtali	Ahira	Brother of evil	Enan	Fountain

How good our God is in calling his people by name! Jesus said that the Good Shepherd 'calls his own sheep by name and leads them out. And when he brings out his own sheep, he goes before them and the sheep follow him, for they know his voice' (John 10:3-4). How does the Good Shepherd lead his sheep? He gives them qualified, capable leaders who get their instructions from him. How good and gracious God was, and is, to give his people leaders to organize and direct them in an orderly manner!

One is reminded of Bunyan's magnificent description of a godly pastor in his immortal work, *Pilgrim's Progress*. When Christian arrived at the House of Interpreter, he was shown a portrait 'of a very grave person... It had eyes lifted up to heaven, the best of books in his hand, the law of truth was written upon its lips, the world was behind his back, it stood as if it pleaded with men, and a crown of gold did hang over his head.' After explaining the meaning of this portrait, Interpreter said, 'I have showed thee this picture first, because the man whose picture this is, is the only man whom the Lord of the place whither thou art going hath authorized to be thy guide in all difficult places thou mayest meet with in the way; wherefore take good heed to what I have showed thee, and bear well in thy mind what thou hast seen; lest, in thy journey, thou meet with some that pretend to lead thee right, but their way goes down to death.'[3] Bunyan understood the importance of godly, qualified and authorized leadership.

A major turning point for Israel took place when the people decided at Kadesh not to proceed to conquer and possess the promised land (Num. 14). Evidently, the leaders of Israel failed at that point to exercise responsible spiritual leadership; their failure, as we shall see, led to chaos and rebellion. That does not negate the importance of God-ordained leadership or relieve God's people of their duty to be submissive to those under whom God has placed them; on the contrary, it magnifies the importance of wise, godly leadership. Undoubtedly, Joshua and Caleb could have taken matters into their own hands at that point and found adequate justification for doing so; instead, they waited patiently for God to work — and they had to wait another thirty-eight years. Genuine faith is patient. A lot can be learned from the book of Numbers!

The numbering of the tribes

Following this list of leaders, the number of men in each of the tribes over twenty years of age is given. As with the list of names, most people today, I suppose, pay very little attention to this data. It is important, nevertheless. At the end of the forty years of wandering in the wilderness a second census, or numbering, was taken. A comparison of those numbers is important and reveals, or suggests, some interesting possibilities. The comparison is as follows:

Tribe	Chapter 1	Chapter 26	Decrease	Increase
Reuben	46,500	43,730	2,770	
Simeon	59,300	22,200	37,100	
Gad	45,650	40,500	5,150	
Judah	74,600	76,500		1,900
Issachar	54,400	64,300		9,900
Zebulun	57,400	60,500		3,100
Ephraim	40,500	32,500	8,000	
Manasseh	32,200	57,700		20,500
Benjamin	35,400	45,600		10,200
Dan	62,700	64,400		1,700
Asher	41,500	53,400		11,900
Naphtali	53,400	45,400	8,000	
Totals	603,550	601,730	61,020	59,200
Net decrease			1,820	

These numbers are in round figures because they concern military regiments and battalions — these were the men eligible for military service. Since there were 603,550 military men at Mt Sinai, with women, children and the elderly, the total number must have been about 2,500,000. Significantly, while these people multiplied greatly while in Egyptian slavery, they actually decreased in number during the forty-year period in the wilderness. I will comment on the dramatic decline in the tribe of Simeon in a later chapter.

The Levites

The tribe of Levi is not included; it was set aside for the service of God. The Levites were chosen in place of the firstborn who had been spared when the angel of death passed through Egypt (Num. 3:12). The reason for that substitution is given in Exodus. While Moses was on the mountain, the people made and erected the golden calf and were engaged in revelry and idolatry. In righteous anger, Moses broke the tablets of the law. His own tribe, the tribe of Levi, stood with him and began to execute judgement. Although Aaron (a Levite) was responsible, the Levites defended the honour of the Lord (Exod. 32:25-29). Here, the reason for God's choice of Levi is given in a simple, direct comment; God says, 'I am the LORD.' He is sovereign and chooses whomsoever he pleases. There were, however, 273 more firstborn Israelites than Levites. God did not say, 'Well, that is near enough!' He is precise and specific; there had to be an exact correspondence. The additional 273 Israelites had to be redeemed by the payment of five shekels each to Aaron, the high priest. Undoubtedly, the numbers involved carried greater significance than is generally recognized; later, Moses declared:

> When the Most High gave the nations their inheritance,
> When he separated the sons of man,
> He set the boundaries of the peoples
> *According to the number* of the sons of Israel
> (Deut. 32:8, NASB, emphasis mine).

Matthew Henry says somewhere, 'Known unto God are all his works beforehand, and there is an exact proportion between them, and so it will appear when they come to be compared.'

The tribe of Levi was made up of four family groups; each family had designated responsibilities concerning the tabernacle and its function:

1. The *sons of Aaron* were the priestly family responsible for ministry within the tabernacle.
2. The *Kohathites* were responsible for transporting the sacred vessels and furnishings of the tabernacle, including the ark of the covenant.
3. The *Gershonites* were responsible for transporting the curtains and coverings of the tabernacle. (That, incidentally, was no small thing; some of the curtains were made from the skins of animals and were very heavy.)
4. The *Merarites* were responsible for transporting the heavy structural beams and posts of the tabernacle.

Clearly, some families had greater responsibilities and privileges than others but each aspect of the work was important and needed to be done. Apparently, they worked well together until one of the Kohathites (of all people!) began to envy and challenge the leadership roles of Moses and Aaron (Num. 16). More of that in a later chapter.

Order and discipline in submission to leadership

The third stanza of the hymn, 'Onward Christian Soldiers', begins with the words: 'Like a mighty army moves the church of God.' How does an army move? It moves in a systematic and orderly manner, under the command of officers. Sad to say, much of the church today is anything but orderly or systematic. Often, the authority of leadership is challenged and undermined; there is a clamouring for recognition and position and submission to leadership is lacking. To be sure, the leadership is not always what it should be. In some sectors of the Christian church individualism, independence and informality have been almost canonized. Many professing Christians, it seems, consider themselves to be free to believe what they like, behave as they want and to reject the authority of their leaders. God's people, however, are to be submissive to leaders, orderly in worship and disciplined in personal conduct. Numbers has many important lessons for God's people in modern times!

The goodness of God in establishing order for his people

Israel was still encamped at Mt Sinai when the instructions in Numbers 1:1 – 10:10 were given. These chapters concern the organization of God's people. There are two important aspects:

> 1. The *outward formation* of the camp (Num. 1:1 – 4:49).
> 2. The *inward condition* of the people (Num. 5:1 – 10:10).

Admittedly, some parts of Numbers are difficult to read; to wade through the names, numbers of people and the details concerning the arrangement of the camp can make laborious reading. It is all important, nevertheless. This was not a nomadic family wandering around the wilderness looking for a good campsite. The logistics involved in the movement and encampment of such a host of people must have been phenomenal. Even with the advantage of a public address system or other modern means of communication it would still have been a monumental task. Without such means, there had to be a very high level of order and organization.

The organization of the camp

The tabernacle was always pitched at the centre of the encampment of all the tribes. The pillar of cloud and fire (the Shekinah glory — the visible presence of God) rested on the tabernacle. God was in the midst of his people — he was at the centre of their camp.

Immediately surrounding the tabernacle were the families of *Levites*, the custodians and ministers of the tabernacle. The sons of Aaron camped immediately before the front entrance. On the perimeter, three tribes camped on each side. Of the three tribes on each side, the central one, in each case, bore the standard and held the leadership position. Of particular importance is the position of the tribe of Judah — the tribe through which God's promised Messiah was to come.

			(North)			
	Asher		Dan		Naphtali	
Benjamin						Issachar
			Merarites			
Ephraim (West)	*Gershonites*		**Tabernacle**	*Aaron*		Judah (East)
			Kohathites			
Manasseh						Zebulun
	Gad		**Reuben** (South)		Simeon	

The encampment of the tribes of Israel

Whenever the pillar of cloud moved from over the tabernacle, the camp packed up and moved in an orderly fashion; nothing was done haphazardly or carelessly. When the encampment moved:

- *Judah* led the way with Issachar and Zebulun.
- The *two families of Levites* (Merarites and Gershonites) followed with the structure and curtains of the tabernacle. (When they arrived at the new site, the tabernacle could be

erected by the time the Kohathites arrived with the ark of the covenant.)

- Another three tribes followed.
- Central to the whole procession were the *Kohathites* bearing the ark of the covenant. The ark of the covenant was central to the people even when they moved.
- Finally, six tribes followed the ark.

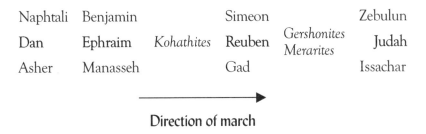

Direction of march

All of this might appear to be remote and quite unrelated to us. What possible relevance does it have? If nothing else, it should teach us that God intends — indeed, requires — his people to be orderly, obedient and disciplined.

I was only a child when World War II broke out; having grown up in the country, I had never seen a large crowd of people. The pictures in the newspapers of soldiers marching off to battle, and the enormous crowds lining the streets to send them on their way, left an indelible impression on my young mind. I was not impressed by the crowds who broke through barriers, however, but by the order and discipline of the soldiers. The contrast between the jostling crowds, which needed to be controlled by force, and the disciplined battalions of men in line, in step, with their eyes straight ahead, could not have been greater. There was tremendous dignity in their order and discipline. For weeks I marched around with a stick over my shoulder pretending that I was the best soldier in the world. While the organization of God's people these days is of a different order to that of Israel (a bit more military precision might not come amiss in some churches!), what a blessing it is to have brethren work together in unity — each fulfilling his role!

The inward condition of the people

This first section of Numbers not only concerns the outward formation of the camp of Israel; it also addresses the inward condition of the people (5:1 - 10:10). Good organization is important, but it is not sufficient in itself, nor is it the desired end. The attitude of the mind and the condition of the heart are of primary importance. Someone has said, 'Happy is the man who is outwardly acceptable to man and inwardly acceptable to God.' Like much of Leviticus, these chapters give miscellaneous regulations concerning such things as uncleanness, restitution of stolen property, jealousy and the purification of the Levites. According to Numbers, cleanliness is not next to godliness; it is part of godliness! In the lives of God's people there is no room for carelessness, disorder, impurity, or individualism. God's people were, and are, to be 'a holy nation' — a people who are orderly, disciplined and pure.

God's goodness in protecting his people and providing for their needs

God's power and protection

Before reaching Mt Sinai, at the beginning of their wilderness experience, the Israelites were ruthlessly attacked by Amalekites (Exod. 17). On that occasion, Israel achieved a decisive victory; their victory was not due to their superior power or wisdom, however; it was due to the intercession of Moses, the skill of Joshua and, above all, the power of their God. After their victory, Moses built an altar and named it 'Jehovah-Nissi' — 'the LORD our Banner'.

We are not told whether other enemies were encountered during the wilderness years. (Actually, we are told very little about what happened during those wilderness years; almost half of Numbers is devoted to events of the final year.) As they advanced towards the promised land in the fortieth year, however, they came into conflict with the King of Arad, with Sihon the King of the Amorites, and with Og, King of Bashan. These kings terrorized the rest of the Canaanites; God, in his goodness, assured Moses, 'Do not fear [Og], for I have delivered him into your hand, with all his people and his land; and you shall do to him as you did to Sihon king of the Amorites' (Num. 21:34).

The dangers encountered in the wilderness consisted, not only of hostile nations, but also of harsh natural conditions. Later Moses makes special mention of the serpents and scorpions in 'the great and terrible wilderness'. As we shall see, God unleashed the serpents on one occasion as a judgement on the people for their murmuring and complaining. At other times, he restrained these venomous pests and protected the people he loved.

God's provision

God's goodness is seen also in his continual provision for the needs of his people. He provided their daily bread. The Israelites were instructed to gather manna each morning (Exod. 16). If any of them attempted to store the manna, it went bad. They were, however, to gather enough manna on the sixth day for the Sabbath as well. Each week, God, in his providential goodness, preserved their food for the day of rest. The daily sustenance of that great multitude of people depended entirely on the goodness of God. Gordon Keddie says, 'In Sinai, Israelites woke every morning knowing for sure that if they could not trust God, they would go to bed hungry. The manna was indeed as dependable as the Lord who sent it, but every scrap that the Israelites ate reminded them that they had to trust the Lord, wholly, exclusively, for absolutely everything, every single day.'[4]

God proved that he can be trusted. Even when the people complained and murmured against his provision of manna, he gave them their desire for meat by sending them an abundance of quails (Num. 11). To be sure, it was a judicial measure; God 'gave them their request, but sent leanness into their soul' (Ps. 106:15). Nevertheless, he sustained them those forty years in the wilderness.

God's presence

Throughout Numbers, God went before his people in a pillar of cloud and fire; he was visibly present in their midst as he guided them every step of the way through the wilderness. God's goodness was evident in his abiding presence. On a couple of occasions, God threatened to withdraw his presence. At the crisis concerning the golden calf, he threatened to withdraw and leave. Moses knew that he could not proceed unless God was with him. He prayed, therefore, 'I pray, if I have found grace in your sight, show me now your way, that I may know you and that I may find grace in your sight. And consider that this nation is your people.' And God said, 'My presence will go with you, and I will give you rest.' Moses responded by saying, 'How then will it be known that your people and I have found grace in your sight, except you go with us? So we shall be separate [NASB, distinguished], your people and I, from all the people who are upon the face of the earth' (Exod. 33:13-14,16). If God were not with them, they would be no different from any other group or nation. That which distinguishes God's people and makes them unique is the presence of God in their midst.

Later, when Israel turned back from occupying the promised land at Kadesh-Barnea, God threatened to destroy them for their unbelief. Again, Moses went before the Lord to intercede for them. He expressed his concern for God's reputation and glory; he was afraid that the Canaanites would hear about their retreat and conclude that God was unable to accomplish what he had begun. Moses prayed, 'They have heard that you, LORD, are

among these people; that you, LORD, are seen face to face and
your cloud stands above them; and you go before them in a
pillar of cloud by day and in a pillar of fire by night' (Num.
14:14).

In spite of their disobedience, God did not withdraw his
presence from his people; he continued to go before them and to
show them the way. Today, God is present among his people by
his Holy Spirit; he guides them into the truth of his Word and
'leads [them] in the paths of righteousness for his name's sake'
(Ps. 23:3). His presence is evident, however, not in physical signs
and wonders, nor in noise and confusion, but where there is
truth, unity and genuine love. While God has promised 'never
to leave nor forsake' his people, he does remove his hand of
blessing where there is unfaithfulness and disobedience — as he
threatened to do with the church at Ephesus (Rev. 2:5).

The message of Numbers for today

Those ancient people had God's *power* to protect them, his
provision to sustain them and his *presence* to guide them. More
than that, in his goodness, he gave them godly human leadership and practical instructions for their good. Because God is
good, he is a God of order.

In spite of all these expressions of God's goodness, the
people always seemed to be complaining and murmuring about
something. They objected to the difficulties they encountered, to
the continual manna, and they complained about the leadership
of Moses and Aaron. Many times, it seems, they tried the
patience of God to the limit. As we shall see, on occasions, God
had to deal with them severely; but, even then, his disciplinary
measures were expressions of his goodness. It is the 'goodness of
God' that 'leads ... to repentance' (Rom. 2:4).

God is 'infinite, eternal, and unchangeable ... in his goodness'. His people can trust him completely at all times and under
all circumstances. In the light of his goodness, how are God's

people to live as they journey through the wilderness? In teaching us about the goodness of God, the book of Numbers establishes the foundational principle that 'The just shall live by faith.'

Faith always has an object; one does not simply 'have faith'. Faith means to take someone at his word. Whether or not a person's word is believable depends on his knowledge and his character. If he does not know the facts, his word, though spoken with the best of motives with all sincerity, must be treated with caution. If, on the other hand, he is a notorious liar, his word must be treated with suspicion and questioned. With God, there is no limitation to his knowledge and there is no defect in his character. His Word can be trusted even when he takes us into a wilderness. The life of faith implies obedience and demands personal discipline and orderliness. The message of Numbers may be summed up in the words of the familiar hymn:

> When we walk with the Lord
> In the light of his Word,
> What a glory he sheds on our way!
> While we do his good will
> He abides with us still,
> And with all who will trust and obey.
>
> But we never can prove
> The delights of his love
> Until all on the altar we lay.
> For the favour he shows
> And the joy he bestows
> Are for them who will trust and obey.

13.
The importance of faith and obedience

Recently, the board of Biblical Foundations International, the Christian organization with which I minister, believed that God wanted us to undertake a certain project and, accordingly, took a significant step involving a large sum of money. Since BFI does not appeal for funds, if the Lord did not send sufficient money, we would have been in a dire predicament – we would have found ourselves in a practical wilderness with no visible means of support. (It was crucial, of course, for us to determine that the matter was according to the will of God. I am thankful to say that subsequent events proved it to be God's will and not merely human desire or presumption.) One dear Christian brother, whom we respect greatly, heard of the decision and declared, 'In this country we live by legal tender.' While we do not criticize or condemn brethren who disagree with our policies, we find it difficult to comprehend how those who appeal to the Christian public for funds and live 'by legal tender' ever prove the goodness and sufficiency of God in practical ways.

As we saw in the previous chapters, faith always has an object; it is to act upon someone's word. Whether a person's word is credible and believable depends, of course, on his character and knowledge. If he lacks integrity, his word must be questioned or doubted. If his knowledge is deficient, his word, though uttered sincerely, must be treated with caution. God's Word, of course, can be trusted completely because there is no flaw in his character and his knowledge is comprehensive. What God has promised, he will perform. Since his Word is trustworthy, God's people can commit their lives into his hands with complete confidence, knowing that whatever he does, it is good and right. To have faith in God is to act in confidence on his Word. The basic principle of the Christian life is stated four times throughout the Scriptures: 'The just shall live by faith' (Hab. 2:4; Rom. 1:17; Gal. 3:11; Heb. 10:38). In other words, the call to live by faith is a call to obedience to the Word of God. The twin principles of faith and obedience are inseparable.

Because all God's people are called to live by faith, the principle is stated and applied from the outset. In the books of the Pentateuch, the principle and practice of faith are developed systematically:

- In Genesis, the principle of faith is established.
- In Exodus, faith is applied to worship and obedience.
- In Leviticus, the principle of faith is applied to worship.
- In Numbers, the principle of faith is applied to obedience.
- In Deuteronomy, the practice of faith in daily life is stressed.

Abraham was called to live by faith and although his faith faltered at times, he believed God's promise and acted accordingly. Though he died without seeing God's covenantal promise fulfilled, he believed that the word of the Lord was sure and that, in his time, God would make from him a great nation. Numerous times throughout the New Testament Abraham is cited as the father of faith.

Although most of what occurred during the five centuries between the promise and the Exodus is passed over without comment, no doubt faithful Israelites throughout those centuries expected God to fulfil his Word and lived in expectation of it. When God declared the month in which he instituted the Passover to be the beginning of Israel's existence as a nation, no doubt people like Amram and Jochebed, Moses' parents, rejoiced greatly. They actually saw God's plan begin to be fulfilled. As the Israelites witnessed God's great power in judgement on Egypt, at the division of the Red Sea and at Mt Sinai, one would have thought that their faith would have been unshakeable. For those who had experienced those spectacular events, and more, surely any doubts or fears would have been dispelled thereafter! Spectacular signs and wonders, however, though impressive and awesome, do not produce faith or generate obedience.

Faith tested in the wilderness

Now that Israel was in the wilderness, how were they to find their way through such rough and inhospitable territory? How could so many people and animals survive in such desolate, inhospitable and unproductive land? Humanly speaking, their situation was hopeless; it was utterly impossible. God had not thrust his people into the wilderness to fend for themselves and to eke out an existence as best they could, however. In his goodness, his *presence* went before them to guide them, his *power* was present to protect them and his *provision* was adequate to sustain them. God would not forsake them or fail them, but they had to believe him; they had to live by faith. They were cast entirely upon God's goodness; they had to depend entirely on his Word. Ironically, sometimes trusting God in situations like that which they faced at the Red Sea is easier than dependence on him to supply personal daily needs.

For faith to be strengthened, it must be proved and tested. When we are put to the test, two responses are possible: either we must stake everything on the Word of God, or we must take matters into our own hands. We can always try to provide for our daily needs apart from God; we can depend upon our own wisdom and ability. That alternative, however, is clearly akin to the course taken by Adam and Eve. In essence, it is to question and doubt God's integrity and goodness. It is to affirm that man is wiser, more capable, and more dependable than God. Lack of faith in God, or unbelief in his Word, is a far greater sin than most people, it seems, realize or recognize. (Incidentally, many banks in the US have a sticker on the door assuring customers that 'This bank is guaranteed by the FDIC' — a government insurance system. They want customers to know that their savings are secure. When I see that sign, I think to myself, 'And who guarantees the government?')

The second section of Numbers (10:11 - 14:45) covers the journey of the Israelites from Mt Sinai to Kadesh-Barnea (the exact location of which is unknown; most likely it was somewhere near the southern end of the Dead Sea). Probably, that journey took a short period of time; only three encampments en route are recorded. At Kadesh, the Israelites sent spies into the promised land to investigate. Because they did not trust God to enable them to overcome the obstacles, they spent the next thirty-eight years wandering in the wilderness. Those wilderness years are covered briefly in the third section of Numbers (chapters 15-19). During those years, the sins of unbelief and disobedience reigned.

Though the only certain factor in the wilderness was God, the primary problem of the people was lack of confidence and trust in God. Could he be trusted for daily bread? Even after their spectacular deliverance and awesome experiences of God's power, many of them, no doubt, engaged in 'What if ...?' speculation. 'What if God forgets us and leaves us here?' 'What shall we do if there is no manna tomorrow morning?' 'What if the Amalekites launch a retaliatory attack for their defeat at Rephidim?' 'Where are we going to get new clothing when we need it?' Christians today can look from afar and easily criticize those Israelites (after all, we know the outcome); it is not uncommon, however, to hear similar questions and comments:

'With announced cutbacks in the company, I am afraid I might lose my job!' 'With the stock market so unstable, what shall we do if it crashes? We could easily lose our home!' 'What if the insurance company will not pay our hospital bills?' 'What shall we do?' 'Where can we turn?' The future is filled with uncertainties; we do not know the way ahead. We do not know what a day may bring forth.

If we allow our minds to dwell on the uncertainties of life, inevitably we shall begin to question God's goodness and doubt his word. When such questions are entertained, the precarious nature of circumstances becomes increasingly magnified and exaggerated until it becomes cause for alarm. Confidence in God gives way to uncertainty, insecurity and fear. Fear, in turn, is expressed in discontent, murmuring and complaint. Fear for the future demands alternative plans. When the Israelites turned back from the promised land, some accused God of malevolence; they proposed a change of leadership and desired to return to Egypt. Calvin says, 'Men will never be obedient to God's precepts, unless their distrust of him is corrected, and will be always ingenious in laying hold of pretexts for disobedience.'[1]

In all, Moses records ten occasions when the Israelites complained and rebelled in the wilderness (Num. 14:22). Of the four occasions recorded in *Exodus*, no mention is made of God's acting in judgement against them (see Exod. 14:11; 15:24; 16:2; 17:2). God threatened to destroy them, of course, when Aaron erected the golden calf at Mt Sinai; on that occasion, they were spared because of the intercession of Moses (Exod. 32). Of the six incidents of murmuring, complaining and disobedience recorded in *Numbers*, however, all but one called forth a severe response from God. Why the difference? The occasions recorded in Exodus happened before God gave the moral law. After they had experienced the awesome power of God's holy presence at Mt Sinai, and now that they were in possession of his holy law, to distrust him and complain about his provision was a serious offence against his wisdom, power and holiness. Those incidents of complaint and rebellion recorded in Numbers reveal a serious lack of faith — the people did not take God at his word.

1. The departure from Sinai (Num. 11:1)

After they had spent a year at Mt Sinai, the time had come for the people to move towards the promised land. No doubt, having become familiar with the environment, they enjoyed a degree of security in being settled there. Now, '... the cloud was taken up from above the tabernacle of the Testimony. And the children of Israel set out from the Wilderness of Sinai on their journeys... So they started out for the first time according to the command of the LORD by the hand of Moses' (Num. 10:11-13).

For a year, they had not faced unknown territory or uncertain circumstances. The command to move was unsettling and they began to murmur against God. One can almost hear their questions and comments: 'Why should we have to move when we have just become reasonably settled and comfortable in this locality?' 'Why do we have to go through all the hard work of packing up camp when we don't know where we are going or what lies ahead?' Matthew Henry says, 'They had received from God excellent laws and ordinances, and yet no sooner had they departed from the mount of the Lord than they began to quarrel with God himself.'[2]

Another aspect of their complaint concerned their *food*; they despised the manna and longed for the food of Egypt. Again, Matthew Henry's comment is appropriate: 'They magnified the plenty and dainties they had had in Egypt (v. 5), as if God had done them a great deal of wrong in taking them thence. While they were in Egypt they sighed by reason of their burdens, for their lives were made bitter to them with hard bondage; and yet now they talk of Egypt as if they had lived like princes.'[3]

Had they forgotten the bondage of Egypt so soon? Was the lash of their taskmasters in Egypt preferable to their liberty in the Lord? The specific complaint was the lack of meat; one wonders why they didn't butcher some of the livestock that they had with them. Were the provisions of Egypt actually superior to those given by the Lord? 'His yoke is easy, his burden is light,' and his provision is sufficient. Surely, whenever God's people complain about his leading and provision, it reveals an evil heart of unbelief.

'Now when the people complained, it displeased the LORD; for the LORD heard it, and his anger was aroused. So the fire of the Lord burned among them, and consumed some in the outskirts of the camp' (Num. 11:1). No doubt those who complained were procrastinating and dawdling along disregarding order and organization – they were 'on the outskirts of the camp'. Not only was their attitude wrong, but their behaviour affected the whole body of people. God acted in severity against the rebels and consumed them. The fire died out, however, when Moses prayed. Those who were spared needed to realize the seriousness of unbelief and disobedience; they needed to know that God is not only a God of judgement but also a God of mercy.

2. The report of the spies and the people's unbelief (Num. 14:2)

When Israel arrived at Kadesh-Barnea, the Lord told Moses to send twelve leaders to spy out the promised land (Num. 13:1). When Moses recounts the incident in Deuteronomy, however, he attributes the decision to send spies to the will of the people (Deut. 1:22). There are several possible explanations for the difference; we can say confidently that this is not a contradiction. Most probably, Moses took the matter to the Lord and he approved the plan because he knew the secret discontent which prompted the request and the open rebellion which would result if the proposal were rejected and denied.

God had promised the land to the descendants of Abraham; it had already been deeded to them by God. No doubt, the testimony of Jacob concerning the productivity of the land had been transmitted to each generation.

The spies acknowledged that the land was good and productive. They even brought back a bunch of grapes as evidence! Particular mention is made of their visit to Hebron, where the patriarchs were buried. Abraham had received a favourable reception there when he bought a burial plot for Sarah (Gen. 23). The spies, however, encountered the sons of Anak there. Evidently, the sons of Anak were formidable foes; they are mentioned three times in chapter 13, several times in Deuteronomy and also in Joshua. In Numbers 13:22 and Joshua 15:14, the sons of Anak are named; they were:

Ahiman — meaning, 'brother of man'.
Sheshai — meaning, 'noble' or 'free'.
Talmai — meaning, 'bold' or 'spirited'.

While the majority of the spies were impressed with the land, they reported that it could not be conquered and occupied because of the giants who lived in well-fortified cities. They reckoned that the enemies were far too powerful for them to overcome and conquer. Caleb and Joshua, the two spies who brought the minority report, believed God and spoke confidently of success (Num. 13:30; 14:6-10). Caleb spoke as though it were already accomplished. Forty years later, as an old man, he still expressed that same confidence (Josh. 14:8-12) and specifically requested that he be allowed to conquer the hill country of Hebron so that he could drive out the Anakim. So we read, 'Caleb drove out the three sons of Anak from there: Sheshai, Ahiman, and Talmai, the children of Anak' (Josh. 15:14).

The people waited forty days for the spies to bring back their report; ironically, they could not wait forty days for Moses to bring them the law of the Lord! The ten spies were unbelieving and pessimistic; they dissuaded the people from attempting the conquest. What a predicament that decision caused! What an indictment their unbelief was against the Lord! 'In effect,' says Matthew Henry, 'they charge that God who is love itself with the worst of malice, and eternal Truth with the basest hypocrisy, suggesting that all the kind things he had said to them, and done for them, hitherto, were intended only to decoy them into a snare, and to cover a secret design carried all along to ruin them. Daring impudence! ... Sinners are enemies to themselves; and those that walk not in God's counsels consult their own mischief and ruin.'[4]

After their foolish decision not to proceed, God threatened to disinherit Israel and raise up a new nation from Moses (Num. 14:12). This was one of the two occasions when God threatened to destroy his people before they reached the promised land. Moses pleaded for them, however, on the basis of God's character and the covenant that he had made with Abraham. In his prayer, he says, ' "The LORD is longsuffering and abundant in mercy, forgiving iniquity and transgression; but he by no means clears the guilty, visiting the iniquity of the fathers on the children to the third and fourth generation." Pardon the iniquity of this people, I pray, according to the greatness of your mercy, just as you have forgiven this people, from Egypt even until now' (Num. 14:18-19).

Had it not been for the intercession of Moses, God would have left them to find out how foolish their wisdom and how weak their strength really were. Moses did not ask that they should be spared chastisement and correction, but that God would not disinherit them. He was fearful that reproach would fall upon God's name. Nevertheless, the people murmured against the leadership of Moses and Aaron and some made plans to return to Egypt. If the hazards of the conquest of Canaan and the perils of the wilderness were great, how much greater the hazards and peril of returning to Egypt! Surely, such a foolish course of action would have been disastrous. How readily the welfare of a people is jeopardized by unbelief! The Israelites did not realize that 'They would succeed against their enemies if they did not make God their enemy.'[5]

When they recognized their sin, some of them determined to undertake the conquest of the land; the problem was that God did not approve of their plans and did not go with them. 'They

now desire the land which they had despised, and put a
confidence in the promise which they had distrusted.'[6] They
were defeated by the Amalekites at a place called Hormah — 'a
place of destruction' (Num. 14:45). Significantly, at the end of
the wilderness wanderings, thirty-eight years later, when the new
generation was preparing to possess the land, their first victory
was at Hormah (Num. 21:3). God often takes his people back to
the place of defeat and there gives them the victory. At this first
encounter, however, the Israelites suffered defeat; it was the
beginning of their punishment for unbelief. Even though Moses
and Aaron prayed, the punishment of the people was not
averted, just deferred. Those above twenty years of age, except
Caleb and Joshua, were sentenced to spend the rest of their years
in the wilderness.

Though the punishment was severe, it must not be forgotten
that God continued with his people and provided for their needs
throughout those wilderness years. He might have cast them off
and abandoned them to fend for themselves after their unbelief
and disobedience — and would have been perfectly just in doing
so. But God did not forsake them utterly; he did not lure them
into the desert to destroy them. In fact, he told them to return to
the Red Sea. Why would he take them back there?

3. Korah's rebellion (Num. 16:2)

The next two incidents of murmuring and complaining are
recorded in Numbers 16. These two occasions are related;
because of the nature of them and their importance, I plan to
devote a significant portion of the next chapter to them. I will,
therefore, simply mention them here.

In Numbers 16:2 Korah led an insurrection against the
leadership of Moses and Aaron. God dealt with the rebels
severely.

4. Complaints about the judgement of Korah and his followers (Num. 16:41)

As a result of God's judgement upon Korah and his companions, the people murmured; they considered that the punishment had been too harsh and was, therefore, unfair and unjust.

5. Rebellion at Kadesh provokes Moses to strike the rock (Num. 20:2)

At this point, the forty years in the wilderness were past and the new generation was preparing to possess the land. Their faith needed to be tested and it was tested in the same way as that of their fathers; there was no water. Not surprisingly, their response was the same as that of their fathers. They not only grumbled and complained about their need, but also they expressed a wish that they had died in the wilderness. 'They wished they had died as malefactors by the hands of divine justice, rather than thus seem for a while to be neglected by the divine mercy.'[7]

This incident immediately followed the death of Miriam, but rather than offering condolences to Moses and Aaron, the people only expressed concern for their own present need. Again, they murmured against Moses and Aaron and blamed them for their predicament. On this occasion, God instructed Moses to speak to the rock; instead, in disgust, Moses struck it twice. One wonders whether or not Moses had concluded that the second generation, like their fathers, would be forbidden from entering the land because of their unbelief. Moses was held accountable for his rash behaviour; he had, of course, acted in full view of the entire congregation. As the leader, he was responsible to set an example. In spite of the murmuring of the people and the action of Moses, God, in his goodness, provided the needed water. The judgement this time was pronounced against Moses: because of his unbelief, he would not enter the promised land.

6. Complaints about the manna lead to the plague of fiery serpents (Num. 21:4)

The people returned to Hormah, where the King of Arad attacked them and took some of them captive. On this occasion, however, they cried out to the Lord; he answered their prayer and gave them a resounding victory. Instead of pressing on with renewed vigour and determination, however, they became discouraged, or impatient, and complained against God and Moses. They wanted the 'milk and honey' of the land immediately because they detested the manna which God, in his goodness, continued to send. A plague of snakes was sent among them as judgement for their sin. In his mercy, God provided a remedy which, significantly, pointed to the one who would come in the fulness of time to restore those bitten by that old serpent, the devil. As Moses lifted up the brass serpent in the wilderness, Jesus Christ was lifted up to draw men unto him (John 3:14).

The Lord's chastisement of his people

God did not ignore or excuse the unbelief and disobedience of his ancient people — just as he does not excuse these things in his people today. In perfect justice and faithfulness, God chastises and disciplines disobedient children by appropriate means. Though he judges severely, he does so for the good of his people. Because many people do not understand the importance of God's chastising hand, they react negatively to it. God's severity is never in opposition to his goodness. Many objections arise because people do not understand God's moral perfection and they fail to realize the enormity of the sin of unbelief. God never acts impulsively or indiscriminately; he always acts righteously and justly. Because God is 'infinite in his wisdom, goodness and justice', he acts in the best interests of his people — even when he deals with them in severity. 'Whom the LORD loves he chastens' (Heb. 12:6). And, as we have seen, along with the execution of God's justice, there is mercy.

In addressing the problems in the church at Corinth, the apostle Paul cites five historical incidents from the Old Testament and says that 'These things became our examples' (1 Cor. 10:6). For added emphasis, he repeats: 'All these things happened to them as examples, and they were written for our admonition' (1 Cor. 10:11). Four of these events are taken from the book of Numbers. Significantly, the apostle does not list the events in chronological order; it would be wrong to assume, however, that he chose them arbitrarily or carelessly. The Corinthian Christians were not practising what they professed; Paul selects these events, therefore, to illustrate progressive steps in spiritual decline. Obviously, Paul believed that Old Testament events have important lessons for Christians.

1. Evil cravings (1 Cor. 10:6)

'We should not lust after evil things as they also lusted.' Paul is referring to Numbers 11:4, where the 'mixed multitude who were among them yielded to intense craving' and longed for 'the fish ... the cucumbers, the melons, the leeks, the onions, and the garlic' of Egypt. Their dissatisfaction with God's provision for their daily needs led to an inordinate desire and appetite for those things which were not in the will of God for them at that time. There is no indication that, in the first instance, the people expressed their craving verbally; it says, that they 'became like those who complain' (Num. 11:1, NASB) . If this rendering is correct and they simply murmured in their hearts, 'The LORD heard it.'

Initially, spiritual decline begins with an inordinate craving in the heart; there is no outward expression. James says that 'Each one is tempted when he is drawn away by his own desires and enticed. Then, when desire has conceived, it gives birth to sin; and sin, when it is full-grown, brings forth death' (James 1:14-15).

2. The golden calf (1 Cor. 10:7)

'Do not become idolaters as were some of them.' Paul quotes Exodus 32:6 and, in doing so, reveals that the occasion in view is the making of the golden calf at Mt Sinai (Exod. 32:1-6). Lust grows like a cancerous tumour in the heart until the object of desire becomes the consuming passion, resulting in idolatry.

3. Sexual immorality (1 Cor. 10:8)

'Nor let us commit sexual immorality, as some of them did, and in one day twenty-three thousand fell.' The number of people involved identifies the occasion as the one recorded in Numbers 25:1-3. It concerns that enigmatic prophet, Balaam, who was hired by the King of Moab to curse Israel. When he failed to achieve his mission, apparently he devised a system of doctrine by which his malicious purpose would be served. His pernicious doctrine is described by our Lord in his letter to the church at Pergamum. He said, 'You have there those who hold the doctrine of Balaam, who taught Balak to put a stumbling block before the children of Israel, to eat things sacrificed to idols, and to commit sexual immorality' (Rev. 2:14). Idolatry has tremendous appeal and attraction to a lustful heart; idols can easily be manipulated to permit anything. When a person produces a god in his imagination, he can practise immorality with an easy conscience — that is, his god allows it! The Old Testament prophets frequently described Israel's departure from the Lord as spiritual adultery or fornication. When it comes to one's spiritual commitment and allegiance, the fundamental question is: 'Whom do you love?'

4. Testing God and the plague of fiery serpents (1 Cor. 10:9)

'Nor let us tempt Christ, as some of them also tempted, and were destroyed by serpents.' Obviously, Paul is referring to the incident recorded in Numbers 21:4-5. The craving of the heart leads to idolatry, and idolatry leads to immorality. The next step in spiritual decline is to blame the Lord. 'To test God is to insist that he prove that he is trustworthy.'[8] Such audacity is to test, or try, the patience of God. God is patient and long-suffering; his Spirit will not always strive with presumptuous, rebellious men, however (Gen. 6:3).

Significantly, Paul uses this event at this point to remind his readers that, by implication, a remedy exists for those who 'look'. As the hymn-writer says, 'There is life for a look at the Crucified One.' Jesus Christ is the only remedy for those who have the poison of sin coursing through their veins.

5. Murmuring (1 Cor. 10:10)

'Nor murmur, as some of them also murmured, and were destroyed by the destroyer.' Apparently, the apostle is referring to Numbers 14:1-3, where the Israelites were turned away from the promised land and sentenced to die in the wilderness. Many people, no doubt, would consider this to be the least serious sin. Probably most people murmur and complain at times; can it be such a great sin? Surely a little grumbling or murmuring isn't too bad! Murmuring is a very serious expression of unbelief; it offends God because it is the practical denial of his sovereign wisdom, his mighty power and his righteous character. Murmurings about conditions or circumstances are ultimately complaints against God's goodness. Those who grumbled against Moses actually grumbled against God. 'Men murmur against God's providences,' says Thomas Watson, 'because they distrust his promises.' After the grumbling at Kadesh, the Israelites passed the point of no return; God left them in the wilderness to die. Their situation was like that of Esau, of whom we read, 'When he wanted to inherit the blessing, he was rejected, for he found no place for repentance, though he sought it diligently with tears' (Heb. 12:17).

A call to repentance and faith

While the goodness of God is seen in his provision for daily needs, his protection from enemies, his presence 'to cheer and to guide' and his patience with us in our rebellion and disobedience, we must never presume on God's goodness. While God disciplines his children by bringing temporal punishments on them for their unbelief, disobedience, rebellion and sin, even then, his chastisement is not vindictive nor vengeful; in his goodness, it is designed to bring us to repentance. 'The goodness of God leads ... to repentance' (Rom. 2:4).

'The just shall live by faith.' While the inclination of the human heart is unbelief and disobedience, God, in his mercy and grace, generates faith and enables his people to respond to his Word in obedience. Christians have no excuse to be disobedient, rebellious, or complaining. Having warned the Corinthians of the steps and dangers of spiritual decline, the apostle proceeds to say, 'No temptation has overtaken you except such as is common to man; but God is faithful, who will not allow you to be tempted beyond what you are able, but with the temptation will also make the way of escape, that you may be able to bear it' (1 Cor. 10:13).

'Therefore we must give the more earnest heed to the things we have heard, lest we drift away' (Heb. 2:1).

'Therefore, since a promise remains of entering his rest, let us fear lest any of you seem to have come short of it' (Heb. 4:1).

14.
Serious challenges to faith

Those Israelites who left Egypt under Moses had known nothing other than the hardship and oppression of slavery. When people are slaves, they have what might be called a 'pernicious', or evil, freedom. That is, they are free from the necessity to think. They do not need to organize their lives, discipline themselves, or plan for the future. So long as they do what they are told, they do not have to think about anything; their lives are planned for them.

That which keeps slaves going is hope — hope that some day they will be free. Faithful Israelites had a hope which was based on the promises of God; they looked for the day when they would occupy the land which God had promised to their fathers. Evidently, Amram and Jochebed, Moses' parents, had their hope set on God's promise as they took action to preserve the son whom God had given to them.

When slaves are emancipated they have to begin to think for themselves and to take responsibility for their own lives; they have to plan, organize and discipline themselves. Another problem that arises with liberation relates to the nature of freedom. Apparently, some of the Israelites failed to understand that they had been redeemed from Egyptian slavery, not to do as they pleased, but to fulfil a God-given purpose. In Egypt, they had no option but to obey; they were forced to submit. In the wilderness, they were still under authority; they needed to obey God. Unlike the slave conditions in Egypt, obedience to God was not from compulsion or of necessity; it was to be voluntary and done willingly. During the year at Mt Sinai, God gave his people the righteous requirements for holy and orderly living. Even though God was good to them, submission, obedience and trust did not come readily or naturally.

Perhaps some of the Israelites thought that, having been delivered from Egypt, they would face no more problems and have no more difficulties. Once a person has been redeemed, he is not exempt from hardship or problems; as we have seen, faith must be tested. Many of the children of Israel had not learned to trust God and they frequently expressed discontent with their conditions, God's provision for their needs and their leadership. All of that was bad and exceedingly serious; their attitude implied that God did not know what he was doing, that he was unrighteous in doing it and that he could not be trusted any more than the Egyptians — or indeed that he could be trusted less! At the least hardship, the immediate reaction of an un-believing heart is to look for the cause everywhere except in the right place and to blame everyone except the right person. The problem does not lie with God, the leadership, the organization, or the circumstances; the problem is within the heart. 'The want of original righteousness, and the corruption of [the] whole nature'[1] cause people to doubt God's wisdom, power and goodness and to distrust his men, his methods and his motives.

As we have seen, one of the greatest crises in the history of Israel took place at Kadesh-Barnea when the majority of the twelve spies returned with a negative report concerning posses-sion of the land. Even after their deliverance at the Red Sea and their encounter with God at Mt Sinai, and with the Shekinah glory in their midst, they faltered in faith; they still did not believe that God could, or would, do the impossible. The majority lost sight of their mighty God — and when people lose sight of God, they are already defeated. The results were disas-trous. Because of disobedience, those above twenty years of age were sentenced to wander in the wilderness until they died. Their unbelief did not suddenly happen, of course; the seeds of discontent were sown long before their arrival at Kadesh. Much earlier, they had expressed their discontent with the conditions, the food and the leadership which God, in his goodness, had provided. They reaped what they had sown; through their unbelief, they missed the blessing of the inheritance that God had promised. God has not told us much about those years in the wilderness; probably there was not much worth telling! Only one event is recorded from the thirty-seven years following Kadesh.

Korah's rebellion

Soon after the verdict at Kadesh, Korah is named as the ring-leader in an insurrection. He is the first of two individuals that I want to consider in this chapter; the other is the prophet Balaam. These two individuals are classical examples of apostates. Korah, on the one hand, challenged the *leadership* of Moses and the priesthood of Aaron; Balaam, on the other hand, perverted the *teaching* of Moses. Their influence was substantial; sinful hearts and minds are readily influenced and enticed away from true faith and obedience by ambitious and covetous people. In writing to Timothy, the apostle said, 'Pay close attention to *yourself* and to your *teaching*' (1 Tim. 4:16, NASB, emphasis mine).

The persons involved

Korah was a Kohathite; that is, he was from one of the families of Levites (Exod. 6:16). While the Merarites and the Gershonites, the other two families of Levites, were responsible for dismantling, transporting and re-erecting the supports and coverings of the tabernacle, the Kohathites had the unique privilege of transporting the ark of the covenant and other sacred items of furniture whenever the tabernacle was moved (Num. 4). When they approached those sacred items, however, they were

to do so at the appointment and direction of Aaron (Num. 4:17-
20). The family of Aaron was, of course, responsible for the
ministry of the tabernacle; they officiated in the sacrifices and
mediated on behalf of the people before God.

What were the people to do now that they had been turned
back from the promised land? Having been sentenced to die in
the wilderness, some began to make plans to return to Egypt
(Num. 14:1-4). They advocated that a new leader should be
chosen. One can readily imagine the comments: 'Moses actually
has brought us into the wilderness to die' (cf. Exod. 17:3). 'That
is poor leadership! And, by the way, who made Moses the leader
and Aaron, his brother, the high priest? Obviously, this is a
collaboration between brothers! We need someone who will do
what the majority wants.'

Korah seized the opportunity to agitate for change; his feeling
seems to have been that the priesthood should have belonged to
his family and that he himself should have been high priest.[2]
While Korah sought to depose and replace Aaron, Dathan and
Abiram, of the tribe of Reuben, the eldest son of Jacob, collabor-
ated with him in an apparent attempt to overthrow Moses and
seize the power of leadership. Traditionally, because the eldest
son in a family was the one through whom the family name and
inheritance were kept and passed on, Reuben should have
received a double portion of the inheritance and had the right of
leadership. Because of the sin of Reuben, however, 'No judge,
prophet, nor prince, is found of that tribe, nor any person of
renown except Dathan and Abiram, who were noted for their
impious rebellion against Moses.'[3] Undoubtedly, Korah encouraged them to assert their rights and usurp the leadership. In
speaking specifically of this event, the psalmist says that 'They
envied Moses in the camp, and Aaron the saint of the LORD'
(Ps. 106:16).

In the arrangement of the camp, the Kohathites and the
Reubenites were camped next to each other on the south side of
the tabernacle. God lays the primary responsibility and blame for
the insurrection on Korah. As the instigator, his relationship to,

and contact with, his neighbours, gave him ample opportunity to sow seeds of discord among brethren. One can almost hear him say, 'Obviously, Moses and Aaron have taken these positions on themselves [Num. 16:3]. What right do they have to these positions? Who do they think they are? We are as good as them! We deserve better leadership!'

The nature of the rebellion

The ways in which Korah and his company rationalized, projected blame and manipulated the truth to make their case would merit my devoting an entire chapter to this theme. The sacred record states that 'They rose up before Moses with some of the children of Israel, two hundred and fifty leaders of the congregation, representatives of the congregation, men of renown. They gathered together against Moses and Aaron, and said to them, "You take too much upon yourselves, for all the congregation is holy, every one of them, and the LORD is among them. Why then do you exalt yourselves above the assembly of the LORD?"' (Num. 16:2-3).

The charges brought against Moses were as follows:

1. They charge [Moses] with having done them a great deal of wrong in bringing them out of Egypt, invidiously calling that *a land flowing with milk and honey* (v. 13). Ungrateful wretches, to represent that as an injury to them that was really the greatest favour that was ever bestowed upon any people!

2. They charge him with the design upon their lives, that he intended to *kill them in the wilderness*, though they were so well provided for.

3. They charge him with a design upon their liberties, that he meant to enslave them, by *making himself a prince over them*.

4. They charge him with cheating them, raising their expectations of a good land, and then defeating them

(v. 14): *Thou hast not brought us*, as thou promisedst us, *into a land that floweth with milk and honey.* It was purely their own fault that they were not now in Canaan, and yet Moses must bear the blame.[4]

Evidently, this rebellious trio even set up their own tabernacle (headquarters) where 'they hung out their flag of defiance against Moses'.[5] (Reference is made twice to the 'tabernacle of Korah, Dathan, and Abiram' — Num. 16:24, 27, AV — though some versions use the word 'tents' and understand it as referring to their dwellings. The appearance of Korah with 250 of his followers equipped with censers to burn incense suggests some organized preparation.)

When this insurrection surfaced, Moses summoned Dathan and Abiram to appear before him but, with an air of insolence, they defied his order (Num. 16:12). Matthew Henry comments: 'Had not their heads been wretchedly heated and their hearts hardened, they might have considered that, if they regarded not [the messengers of Moses], Moses could soon in God's name send messengers of death for them. But thus the God of this world *blinds the minds of those that believe not.*'[6]

Strange, is it not, how those with selfish, ambitious and impure motives can build a case by character assassination? Like Korah and his company, evildoers impute guilt to others, attribute ulterior motives to them and accuse them of the very things of which they themselves are guilty. They described Egypt as a 'land flowing with milk and honey' (Num. 16:13). 'How outrageous the insult to divine majesty thus to describe Egypt in the very terms in which God himself had often spoken of the land of promise.'[7]

By implying and attributing unworthy motives to those whom God had called and ordained to sacred responsibilities, Korah and his companions tried to undermine the integrity of Moses. While they denigrated God's chosen leaders, on the one hand, they also exaggerated the spiritual condition of the people. The Scripture implies that almost the entire nation turned back

in unbelief at Kadesh. If one may say such a thing, the under-
statement of the Bible is 1 Corinthians 10:5, where Paul says
that God was not pleased with 'most' of the people in the
wilderness. In fact it was *all* except Caleb and Joshua! Obviously,
the pursuit of holiness by the majority left much to be desired!
Yet Korah and his followers had the audacity to ignore their sin
and declare that everyone in the entire congregation was holy.
Truly, the Lord was in their midst, as they claimed, but his
presence was due to his goodness, not their holiness. How
skilfully sinners manipulate and pervert the truth to accomplish
their own ambitious desires!

Judgement on the rebels

The destruction of these rebels seems to have taken place in two
phases. Dathan and Abiram and their possessions were evidently consumed in an earthquake. The earth opened; they fell
into the pit, and the earth closed on them (Num. 16:31-34).
'The cleaving of the earth was as wonderful, and as much above
the power of nature, as the cleaving of the sea, and the closing of
the earth again more so than the closing of the waters.'[8]
    Korah and those who coveted the priestly office, on the other
hand, were commanded to appear before the Lord with their
censers to burn incense. 'The command for them ... was in effect
the same as saying, "Perform the office of priests, as you see fit to
deny my claim to it as a right." '[9]
    Had they forgotten the swift punishment brought upon
Nadab and Abihu for offering 'strange fire on the altar'? Surely,
that comparatively recent event should have convinced them that
God is serious about the ministry in his sanctuary. They should
have known that God does not tolerate intrusion into his ways
or self-appointed priests. As with Nadab and Abihu, Korah and
250 of his men were consumed by fire (Num. 16:35). God
vindicated the leaders whom he had chosen. Unbelief and
disobedience, if not confessed immediately and dealt with
properly will, inevitably, lead to apostasy.

God's vindication of the leaders he had appointed

Korah attempted to introduce a democratic system of government which, if implemented, would have produced anarchy and
chaos. He wanted a system in which 'everyone [could do that
which is] right in his own eyes' (Judg. 21:25). Several years ago, a
prominent member of a church of which I was pastor declared at
a congregational meeting that 'The church should operate on the
principles of the constitution of the United States.' I do not
doubt that his comment was made in ignorance but, like Korah,
he wanted a form of government where everyone supposedly
had an equal voice and where every opinion was equally valid.
God does not govern his people by popular opinion or preference. Not every person in the church is holy or spiritually mature
and, therefore, not everyone is capable of determining the Lord's
will. God gives leaders to his people to guide them and instruct
them. Christians are, therefore, to 'obey [their] leaders, and
submit to them; for they keep watch over [their] souls, as those
who will give an account. Let them do this with joy and not with
grief, for this would be unprofitable for [those whom they are
appointed to lead]' (Heb. 13:17, NASB).

This event had a sequel. Apparently, Korah and his companions had many sympathizers; the next day the people began to
murmur against Moses and Aaron, accusing them of killing the
Lord's people (Num. 16:41). As a result, the Lord dealt severely
with them by sending a plague in which another 14,700 died
(Num. 16:49). This number suggests something of the extent
and impact of Korah's influence. To vindicate God's righteousness and the holy office of the priesthood, Aaron was instructed
to take his rod, along with twelve others (one rod for each of the
tribes), and place them in front of the ark of the covenant. To
remove any question or suspicion of deception, or sleight of
hand, God caused Aaron's rod to bud, blossom and bear ripe
almonds all at the same time. Subsequently, the rod was placed
in the ark of the covenant as a perpetual reminder that the Lord

had vindicated the leadership of Moses and the priesthood of Aaron (Heb. 9:4).

By way of contrast, before becoming King of Israel, David was pursued relentlessly by King Saul; David would have had good reason to retaliate and kill Saul. On a couple of occasions, the situation was reversed; David had the opportunity to take Saul's life. Had he done so, David would have been acclaimed as a greater national hero than he was. He recognized, however, that such matters must be left in the Lord's hands; he refused to 'stretch out [his] hand against him, seeing he is the anointed of the LORD' (1 Sam. 24:6).

What lessons may be derived from this complex of events! In our day, individualism and independence have been emphasized within society and in the church to such an extent that people imagine that they have better understanding and greater insight, are far more qualified and capable, and are as righteous or holy as anyone else; they believe, therefore, that they can give better leadership and direction than the leaders whom God has chosen and ordained. Generally, such people reveal that they have no comprehension of the meaning or significance of the call of God. Leaders called by God do not lord it over the flock (1 Peter 5:3). Moses is a wonderful example of humble, godly leadership. He always seems to have been on his face before the Lord interceding for the people. In this context, one cannot help but think again of Bunyan's magnificent portrait of the man of God shown to Christian at the House of Interpreter: 'This is the only man whom the Lord of the place whither thou art going hath authorized to be thy Guide in all difficult places thou may'st meet within the Way.'[10]

The error of Balaam

The background

The events of the fortieth year in the wilderness are recorded in chapters 20-36. The generation that had grown up in the wilderness began to move towards the promised land. To reach Canaan, they needed to pass through several small nations east of the Dead Sea.

From Kadesh, Moses sent messengers to *Edom* to request permission to pass through their territory. We learn later that God had instructed Moses not to detest an Edomite because the Edomites were brothers to the Israelites (Deut. 23:7). That is, they were descendants of Esau, the twin brother of Jacob. Moses appealed to Edom on the basis of that relationship. Although it was to Edom's advantage to favour them, now that Israel was about to inherit the blessing of Esau's stolen birthright, hatred revived and permission was denied. Israel 'might have justified their passing through any man's ground ... yet God would have [them] respect the Edomites'.[11] Israel had, therefore, to circum-navigate Edom. This inconvenience brought discouragement and complaint; as a result, God chastened his people by sending the plague of snakes. Moses says that the wilderness was filled with serpents and scorpions (Deut. 8:15); how good God was in protecting his people from their venomous bites up to that point! And, when he used the serpents to chastise his people, he graciously provided a remedy.

The Israelites also sought permission to pass through the territory occupied by the *Amorites*. Sihon, King of the Amorites and Og, King of Bashan, responded by launching successive attacks against them. The Lord gave the Israelites tremendous victories over both kingdoms. Those were significant conquests; they are referred to repeatedly in the Old Testament and re-garded as the standard by which other battles were compared or measured. If Sihon and Og could be overthrown, nothing could

stop Israel; those victories were such that the rest of the Canaanites were terrified. Perhaps Sihon and Og were considered such
formidable foes because Og, at least, was a giant; his bed was
about six feet (or 1.8 metres) wide and thirteen and a half feet (or
4.11 metres) long (Deut. 3:11).

Having wrought a great victory over Sihon and Og, Israel
needed to pass through Moab. God had specifically told Israel
not to harm the Moabites or take anything from them. Permission to pass through their territory was respectfully requested.
Balak, King of the Moabites, however, was terrified. He knew
that his gods were helpless to protect him from such a formidable foe. He called on a notorious prophet named Balaam to
come to his aid and place the people of Israel under a curse.

Balaam's defiance of God's revealed will

Apparently, Balaam lived in the same region from which God
had called Abraham (Num. 22:5). From his pronouncements
upon Israel, it would appear that he was familiar with the
covenantal promise which had been given to Abraham — though
God could have put the words in his mouth at the time! At any
rate, God explicitly told Balaam not to go. Being enticed by great
reward, however, he determined in his heart to go to curse those
whom God had promised to bless.

As with Korah, much could be said about this covetous
prophet as he struggled between his convictions and his corruption. The apostle Peter says of Korah that he 'loved the wages of
unrighteousness' (2 Peter 2:15). As Balaam journeyed towards
Moab, his donkey kept trying to deviate from the path. He beat
his mount and would, in his anger, have killed it. Eventually, the
Lord opened his eyes to see an angel standing with his sword
drawn blocking the pathway; at that point, his donkey rebuked
him for his madness. 'How vainly did Balaam boast that he was
a man whose *eyes were open*, and that he saw *the visions of the
Almighty* (ch. 24:3,4), when the ass he rode on saw more than he

did, his eyes being blinded with covetousness and ambition and dazzled with the rewards of divination.'[12]

But Balaam was committed to doing what he surely knew would end in disaster. Did he really believe that he could curse those whom God had promised to bless? Did his covetous heart cause him to ignore what God had declared to Abraham? God declared, 'I will curse him who curses you' (Gen. 12:3). Obviously, he did not believe what God had declared. How could anyone defy what God had spoken without considering the terrible consequences? When Balaam arrived in Moab, ironically, he organized a series of seven sacrifices as if he expected to change God's opinion and win his favour. As Samuel told Saul, however, 'To obey is better than sacrifice... For rebellion is as the sin of witchcraft' (1 Sam. 15:22-23).

Every time Balaam opened his mouth to curse the people of God, he pronounced a blessing. Those blessings are reminiscent of the covenantal and Messianic promises given to Abraham and Jacob. He said, for example:

Who can count the dust of Jacob,
Or number one-fourth of Israel?

God had promised Abraham that his seed would be as numerous as the dust of the earth
                                              (Num. 23:10; cf. Gen. 13:16).

Again, Balaam said:

Blessed is he who blesses you,
And cursed is he who curses you
                                              (Num. 24:9; cf. Gen. 12:3).

A Star shall come out of Jacob;
A Sceptre shall rise out of Israel
                                              (Num. 24:17; cf. Gen. 49:10).

Balaam leads the Israelites into sin

How such a disobedient prophet could utter such things is difficult to understand. At any rate, he failed to fulfil his contract with Balak and hence was deprived of the rich reward he had been promised. Balak was angry. Balaam, however, was not prepared to let the prospect of riches slip through his fingers so easily. He devised a scheme to achieve the same objective and so obtain the reward. A little compromise and a slightly different emphasis or interpretation would enable him to 'have his cake and eat it too'. The corruption of the human heart is such that it is ingenious in devising ways and means to achieve its ambitions and desires. As the apostle Paul says, the unrighteous are given over to a depraved mind and they become 'inventors of evil things' (Rom. 1:28,30). From Numbers 31 and other passages of Scripture, we learn that, having failed to accomplish his objective, Balaam developed a perverted doctrine. He manipulated the truth to accomplish his pernicious goal. In his letter to the church at Pergamum (Rev. 2:12-17), our Lord declares that some within that body held the doctrine of Balaam. He says that Balaam 'taught Balak to put a stumbling block before the children of Israel, to eat things sacrificed to idols, and to commit sexual immorality' (Rev. 2:14).

Being acquainted with the covenantal promise God had given to Abraham, Balaam knew that the Israelites were God's chosen people. Evidently, he succeeding in persuading the Israelites that since they were chosen by God and enjoyed his special favour, they could do whatever they pleased. As God's elect, they could, according to him, sin with impunity. At the same time, he encouraged the women of Moab to entice the men of Israel into idolatry and adultery knowing that God would judge them for their sin. 'The people began to commit harlotry with the women of Moab. They invited the people to the sacrifices of their gods, and the people ate and bowed down to their gods' (Num. 25:1-2).

Balaam knew that what could not be achieved through
military might or superstitious incantations is readily accomplished through the enticements of the heart: 'If Balak had
drawn his armed men against them to fight them, Israel had
bravely resisted, and no doubt had been more than conquerors;
but now that he sends his beautiful women among them, and
invites them to his idolatrous feasts, the Israelites basely yield,
and are shamefully overcome; those are smitten with his harlots
that could not be smitten with his sword. We are more endan-
gered by the charms of a smiling world than by the terrors of a
frowning world... Those that have broken the fences of modesty
will never be held by the bonds of piety... Israel's whoredoms
did that which Balaam's enchantments could not do, they set
God against them.'[13]

Judgement on those who sinned

As a result of their wicked exploits, God chastised his people
severely: 24,000 of them died by a plague. The Moabites and
Midianites did not escape God's judgement in this matter, of
course. While God's people experienced a plague for their sin,
the Moabites fell under the sword. Israel attacked the Midianites,
killed their five kings, and 'Balaam the son of Beor they also
killed with the sword' (Num. 31:8). Gaining the whole world
and losing his soul was an exceedingly poor bargain! The
difference between these two forms of punishment is significant.
Punishment by the sword is final whereas, with a plague, a
remedy is possible. Did King David understand this when he
sinned in numbering the people? He chose three days of pesti-
lence because, in doing so, he cast himself entirely upon the
mercy of the Lord rather than place himself into the hands of
men (2 Sam. 24:10-25).

Previously, I drew attention to the significant decrease in the
tribe of Simeon; the tribe declined from 59,300 to 22,200 — a
decrease of 37,100. Some suggest that the tribe of Simeon was
primarily involved in the sin at Baal-peor in Moab; as a result,

they suffered the greatest loss when God sent judgement upon
their sin. Possibly, it is significant also that the tribes of Reuben
and Gad, which were camped on the same side of the tabernacle
as Simeon, suffered losses also.

The warnings for God's people today

The teaching of Balaam shows the power and serious consequences of false doctrine. Error and falsehood have tremendous
attraction because 'Men [love] darkness rather than light because
their deeds [are] evil' (John 3:19). False teaching can be made to
conform to sinful desires and enable people to live as they please
without any pangs of conscience. False doctrine undermines the
necessity for obedience to God's revealed will and for the
discipline of godly living. Sadly, much that is taught in the
church today is compromised to make people comfortable in
their sin.

The rebellion of Korah led to disorder and discontent among
God's people; the error of Balaam led to idolatry and immorality. Both were terribly destructive. In his goodness, God has
recorded these matters for our instruction and warning. Constantly, the enemy of men's souls attacks both the leadership and
the doctrine of the church. If either or both can be destroyed,
God's redemptive purpose can be hindered. In his short epistle,
Jude instructs us to 'contend earnestly for the faith which was
once for all delivered to the saints' (Jude 3). We are to do so in
view of apostates who creep in and 'turn the grace of our God
into lewdness [NASB, "licentiousness"] and deny the only Lord
God and our Lord Jesus Christ' (Jude 4). An apostate is, of
course, one who knows the truth but subverts it and deliberately
misuses it. Significantly, Jude proceeds to cite Cain, Balaam and
Korah as the three classical examples of apostates. Apostates, he
says, 'have gone in the way of Cain, have run greedily in the
error of Balaam for profit, and perished in the rebellion of
Korah' (Jude 11). In my book, Let Us Make Man, I have shown

that these three individuals are negative examples of the offices of our Lord as Prophet, Priest and King. The '*way* of Cain' stands in complete contrast to Jesus, who is 'the *way*'. 'The *error* of Balaam is antithetical to our Lord, who is 'the *truth*'. And the *rebellion* of Korah is opposite to 'the *life*' given by our Lord Jesus (John 14:6).

The theme of Numbers is the goodness and severity of God as he guides and instructs his people through the wilderness. There are many dangers in the wilderness, not the least of which are the Korahs and Balaams who pervert the methods and message of God to accomplish their own sinful ambitions. God's people are to live by faith; they can trust the living God in every circumstance and under every condition because he is 'infinite, eternal, and unchangeable in his ... goodness'.[14]

Part V.
Deuteronomy — The faithfulness of God

15.
God's faithfulness in keeping his covenant

Moses, the servant of God

The life history of the vast majority of people could be summarized, no doubt, in two brief statements: 'He (or she) was born' and 'He (or she) died.' What transpires between those two points for most, it seems, is of no particular importance or significance — they are born and they die! When Moses died, God said to Joshua, 'Moses my servant is dead' (Josh. 1:2). In using the epithet, 'my servant', God gave him the greatest tribute and compliment that can be paid to any man. Moses had *served* God; he had fulfilled the purpose for which God made him and, in doing so, he had glorified God and enjoyed him. What a dramatic, purposeful life Moses had! He was one of the greatest men ever to have lived.

His preparation for leadership

Though born into Egyptian slavery, Moses' parents, Amram and Jochebed (Exod. 6:20), were godly people of the tribe of Levi. When God gave them their third child, the Israelites were under orders to destroy all their baby boys. The divine commentary says that 'By faith Moses, when he was born, was hidden three months by his parents, because they saw he was a beautiful child; and they were not afraid of the king's command' (Heb. 11:23). When his parents could keep him no longer, they placed him in a little waterproofed bassinet, launched him onto the river and entrusted him to the sovereign care, mercy and power of God. In the providence of God, Moses was rescued from the Nile by Pharaoh's daughter and given back to his mother to rear. One can only imagine how lovingly that godly woman cared for her child and prayed earnestly day by day that God would use him in his redemptive plan. No doubt, because she was a godly woman, she had an attitude similar to that of Hannah who, with her eye of faith fixed on the coming Messiah, prayed, 'O LORD of hosts, if you will ... give your maidservant a male child, then I will give him to the LORD all the days of his life' (1 Sam. 1:11). (Hannah's prayer contains the first use of the word 'anointed' — 'Messiah' — in the Old Testament.)

While being educated in the schools of Egypt, Moses had opportunity to observe the affliction of the Israelites; he was well acquainted with their sorrow and grief. When he killed an Egyptian in his defence of an Israelite, he no doubt expected that his own people would rally behind him; after all, it was evident that they had an ally in the king's court. When he attempted to mediate between two Israelites the following day, however, one responded by saying, 'Who made you a prince and a judge over us? Do you intend to kill me as you killed the Egyptian?' (Exod. 2:14). 'In the malice of that Israelite he saw not only the rejection of his leadership but the certainty of his betrayal. No Egyptian was witness to his stroke of liberation, but his own people were ready to use his deed against him.'[1]

Consequently, he became an exile in a remote corner of the desert for another forty years. He learned things in the wilderness school of God which he could never have learned in the schools of Egypt. He was being prepared for one of the most important roles ever given to any man. At eighty years of age, God called to him from out of a burning bush and sent him back to Egypt to liberate the people.

The responsibilities and burdens of leadership

His reappearance in Egypt, however, brought greater affliction and increased burdens for the Israelites. Not surprisingly, they murmured and complained against him. In due course, under the mighty hand of God, divine judgements were called down on the Egyptians and Pharaoh was forced to let Israel go. Even though the people had experienced the powerful hand of God at the Red Sea, they were no sooner out of Egypt than they were complaining about the bitter water at Marah and the lack of water at Rephidim — where Moses was instructed to strike the rock. At Sinai, while he was on the mountain receiving the law, his brother, Aaron, was making a golden calf which he declared to be the god that had brought them out of bondage. In exasperation and righteous indignation, Moses dashed the tablets of law to the ground but soon afterwards pleaded with God to spare the people whom he had redeemed.

After a year at Mt Sinai, the encampment moved to Kadesh-Barnea, where twelve spies were sent to investigate the promised land. The spies returned with the report that the land 'flowed with milk and honey', but that it was also filled with giants who lived in well-fortified cities. In unbelief, the people murmured against Moses and refused to proceed to conquer and possess the land. That brought a serious challenge to Moses' leadership by Korah. Again, Moses pleaded with God to spare the people. God answered his prayer but, because of their unbelief and disobedience, the Israelites spent the next forty years wandering in the desert. 'Though the Mosaic history records little more than the first and last year of the forty, yet it seems by this general account that the rest of the years were not much better, but one continued provocation.'[2] Later, as the new generation proceeded towards the promised land, they encountered the error promulgated by Balaam and the heinous sin which he instigated.

For forty years, Moses had borne the burden of those people, and what a task it proved to be! No wonder he needed eighty years' preparation! At the outset of Deuteronomy, he speaks of that burden and says, 'I spoke to you at that time, saying: "I alone am not able to bear you... How can I alone bear your problems and your burdens and your complaints?"' (Deut. 1:9-12).

Leadership is often a thankless and lonely task. People who aspire to positions of leadership frequently do not realize the cost involved; it necessitates thorough preparation, total commitment and extraordinary perseverance. Most of us, no doubt, would have despaired and abandoned the task at Mt Sinai — if not before! We would have judged it to be a lost cause. Even though those people were unbelieving, disobedient and rebellious, Moses carried them on his heart. On numerous occasions, he was broken-hearted, he wept over them and he pleaded with God to spare them. At Sinai and Kadesh, God says that he would have cast off the Israelites had it not been for the inter-cession of Moses. 'Moses had come to such full knowledge of God, that the man who wrote the last page of the book of Deuteronomy had to say of him that he was a prophet who knew God "face to face".'[3]

Moses' final message to the people

Moses endured the trials and opposition those forty years because he was the servant of God. Now the time had come for Moses to leave them. Visualize that dear old prophet with the rod of God in his hand as he stands before the multitude to deliver his farewell address. If you had been in Moses' shoes what would you have said? 'No man ever addressed an audience under more impressive circumstances than did Moses; and no audience ever had greater reason to give heed to the words of wisdom spoken in their hearing. Again and again we feel in them that passionate yearning and intense earnestness which are so fully in keeping with the circumstances in which they were uttered.'[4]

Moses reminisces about the past, not in a rambling, purpose-less, or pointless manner — as one might expect of a man 120 years of age. These are not the memoirs of an old man who has lived an eventful life; it is as much the Word of the living God as that uttered from the lofty heights of Sinai. His message is filled with pathos and concern. While many laws, including the Ten Commandments, are repeated in Deuteronomy ('Deuteronomy' means 'Second Law'), the book is not merely repetition. It was appropriate, of course, that the law should be repeated. As Matthew Henry says, 'What God has said once we have need to hear twice.'[5] Philosopher George Santayana is reported to have said, 'Those who cannot remember the past are condemned to repeat it.'[6] Moses was addressing the new generation which needed to have the law repeated, explained and applied. 'Moses began to explain [or expound the] law' (Deut. 1:5).

Concerning the authorship of Deuteronomy, O. T. Allis says, 'No book of the Pentateuch — we might perhaps say, no book of the Bible — gives clearer indication of authorship and occasion than does Deuteronomy.'[7] Ironically, no book of the Bible has been attacked more vigorously by critics. This is not surprising, of course; the more evident God's Word is, the more concerted the efforts are to discredit it. Further, because Deuteronomy emphasizes the practical application of the Word of God to daily life, Satan has been, and continues to be, rigorous in his opposition to it. He does all within his power to prevent people from hearing and doing God's law. The entrance of God's Word brings light (Ps. 119:130). It is noteworthy that Jesus quoted from Deuteronomy in response to the temptations of Satan in the wilderness.

An outline of Deuteronomy

Though it is beyond my purpose to expound the book, the message of Deuteronomy is quite systematic in its development. In *Explore the Book*,[8] Sidlow Baxter outlines Deuteronomy as follows:

I. Looking backward (Deut. 1-9)

Review of the way since Sinai (Deut. 1-3).
Review of the law from Sinai (Deut. 4-11).

II. Looking forward (Deut. 12-34)

Final rules and warnings to Israel, before entering the
   earthly inheritance (Deut. 12-30).
Final words and actions of Moses, before entering the
   heavenly inheritance (Deut. 31-34).

God's faithfulness to his covenant

The theme of Deuteronomy is the faithfulness of God. Faithfulness concerns a person's word. Does he mean what he says? Is
his word reliable? Is he dependable and trustworthy? Will he
perform what he promises? When Satan asked Eve, 'Has God
said ...?', he was not seeking information but setting the context
to insinuate that God does not mean what he says. He was
attempting to persuade Eve that God is not true to his word —
that he is not faithful. In the book of Deuteronomy, Moses not
only wants us to know *what* God said (the content), but also that
he keeps his word. As Moses rehearsed the past and reviewed
what God had done, he shows that God is faithful: 'Therefore
know that the LORD your God, he is God, *the faithful God* who
keeps [his] covenant and mercy for a thousand generations with
those who love him and keep his commandments' (Deut. 7:9,
emphasis mine).
       God has not simply spoken and declared his righteous will,
(that would, of course, in itself be sufficient reason for obedience
from his creatures), but he made a covenant with the fathers,
Abraham, Isaac and Jacob. That is, he placed himself under legal
obligation to do what he promised. As Hebrews makes clear, he

swore by himself because there was none greater by whom he could swear (Heb. 6:13): 'God, determining to show more abundantly to the heirs of promise the immutability of his counsel, confirmed it by an oath, that by two immutable things, in which it is impossible for God to lie, we might have strong consolation, who have fled for refuge to lay hold of the hope set before us' (Heb. 6:17-18).

If God were to default on his word, his being would be at stake. He himself is the guarantor of the covenant; his word is absolutely reliable and trustworthy because it depends on his eternal being and perfect character. His word is sure! Moses believed that God would never violate his covenant; he would fulfil his word and accomplish what he had promised. It is not surprising, therefore, to find that the theme of the covenant is prominent throughout Deuteronomy. At the outset of his message to the new generation, Moses repeated what God had said as their fathers had departed from Sinai: 'I have set the land before you; go in and possess the land which the LORD *swore to your fathers* — to *Abraham, Isaac,* and *Jacob* — to give to them and their descendants after them' (Deut. 1:8, emphasis mine). Also, he says, '(... for the LORD your God is a merciful God), he will not forsake you nor destroy you, nor forget *the covenant of your fathers which he swore to them'* (Deut. 4:31, emphasis mine).

About thirty such statements appear throughout the book. 'The LORD did not make this covenant with our fathers, but with us, those who are here today' (Deut. 5:3). Being confident of God's faithfulness, Moses reminded the people of the wonders which he performed in judging the Egyptians (Deut. 1:30) — that was, of course, to accomplish what he had promised.

Occasionally, when people enter into a contract or legal agreement, they have regrets about what they have done. Because a contract is legally binding, they recognize that they are obliged to keep the terms. And, while they might remain faithful legally, they fulfil their obligation reluctantly and grudgingly. In such circumstances, a wrong spirit or attitude prevails. With all the unbelief, disobedience, murmuring and rebellion of the children of Israel, one is tempted to think that God surely must have regretted placing himself under legal obligation to redeem them. (I speak as a foolish man.) Since he made the covenant, he was bound to fulfil it, of course, but he had no regrets; he fulfilled it willingly and gladly. The fact that God chose to redeem rebellious, disobedient, complaining sinners serves to magnify the wonder and greatness of his goodness and grace. God was, and is, faithful in keeping his promise, and he does so lovingly and graciously.

The covenant love of God

God says that the reason he made his covenant with Abraham and his descendants was because of his great compassion and love towards them. As we have just seen from Deut. 4:31, '(... the LORD your God is a *merciful* God), he will not forsake you nor destroy you, nor forget the covenant of your fathers which he swore to them' (emphasis mine). 'Because *he loved* your fathers, therefore he chose their descendants after them; and he brought you out of Egypt with his Presence, with his mighty power' (Deut. 4:37, emphasis mine). 'The LORD did not set his love on you nor choose you because you were more in number than any other people, for you were the least of all peoples; but *because the LORD loves you, and because he would keep the oath* which he swore to your fathers... Therefore know that the LORD your God, he is God, *the faithful God* who keeps covenant and mercy for a thousand generations with those who love him and keep his commandments' (Deut. 7:7-9, emphasis mine). 'On your fathers did the LORD *set his affection to love them*, and he chose their descendants after them, even you above all peoples' (Deut. 10:15, NASB, emphasis mine).

Deuteronomy is filled with the love and compassion of God. As we noted in chapter 1, God's covenantal promise concerns the gospel. God 'preached the gospel to [Abraham]' (Gal. 3:8). At Pentecost, the apostle Peter declared, 'The promise is to you and to your children, and to all who are afar off, as many as the Lord our God will call' (Acts 2:39). That covenant which God made with Abraham, concerns, not just ancient Israel, but all whom the Lord God will call — and he has called them because of his love.

According to Campbell Morgan, the *permanent values* of Deuteronomy are:

1. God's *love* of man the motive of his government.
2. Man's *love* of God the motive of his obedience.[9]

How did God manifest his love towards his people? Evidences of his love towards Israel as a nation are plentiful in Exodus and Numbers, of course. Were it not for his love, he might have ignored their plight and left them in Egypt to cope as best they could under the lash of their masters. He manifested his love in protecting them from the plagues, in delivering them from slavery, in guiding them through the wilderness, in providing for their needs and in protecting them from danger.

An additional aspect is noted in Deuteronomy, however; God's love was evidenced in that he imparted his wisdom to them. Moses says, 'What great nation is there that has God so near to it, as the LORD our God is to us, for whatever reason we may call upon him? And what great nation is there that has such statutes and righteous judgements as are in all this law which I set before you this day?' (Deut. 4:7-8). 'Did any people ever hear the voice of God speaking out of the midst of the fire, as you have heard, and live?' (Deut. 4:33).

Matthew Henry adds, 'When God made himself known to them at Horeb he did it by a voice of words which sounded in their ears, to teach them that *faith comes by hearing*, and God in the word is nigh us.'[10]

The giving of the law as an expression of God's love

In what way is the giving of God's Word an expression of his love? Contrary to the practice of many parents these days, love is not expressed by allowing a child to do whatever he wants. The corruption of the human heart is such that, when a person is left to himself, he will deny truth, be morally perverse and act violently and wickedly. No worse fate can overtake any individual or nation than for God to give them up (Rom. 1:24,26,28) and let them do as they please. Sinful human beings need principles to direct their lives and restrain their passions. As we shall see, we also need a change of heart; we need inner motivation. God, in love, gave the moral law to govern his people and, thereby, lead them 'in the paths of righteousness for his name's sake' (Ps. 23:3).

Some, these days, find the relationship of law and love a contradiction. Several decades ago, the Professor of Social Ethics at the Episcopal Theology School in Massachusetts, Joseph Fletcher, made a name for himself by advocating what became known as 'situation ethics'. His approach was to apply pragmatism to ethics — that is, to say that how a person acts on a given occasion is determined, not by moral laws, but by the situation in which he finds himself. Fletcher based his ethics, so he claimed, on love. And, as might be expected, he opposed and denigrated any thought of absolute law. In his system, law and love are antithetical and irreconcilable. That is, however, a totally false antithesis. To be sure, law without love can be inconsiderate, harsh and unrelenting. Love without law, on the other hand, is nothing but subjective, selfish sentimentality — it becomes whatever one wants to make it! An important relationship exists between law and love; they need each other. Love tempers the law and allows for extenuating circumstances. Law, on the other hand, gives content, meaning and direction to love. 'Love is,' says the apostle, 'the fulfilment of the law' (Rom. 13:10). According to our Lord, the primary expression of love is obedience. 'If you love me,' he said, '[you will] keep my commandments' (John

14:15). This relationship between law and love is evident in Deuteronomy.

Why did God not reveal himself in his majestic glory so that the people could see him? Surely, such an experience would never be forgotten! On the contrary, Moses was instructed to warn the people against crossing the boundary established at the foot of Sinai in any attempt to gaze on God (Exod. 19:21). Any visual revelation was always limited to the *effects* of God's presence — as when he revealed himself to Moses when he hid him in the rock (Exod. 33:12-23), in the fire on Mt Sinai, or the Shekinah glory. He has never revealed himself visibly because we, as sinful beings, cannot look upon the majesty and purity of God and live.

An unbelieving heart desires and demands visual objects and sensational experiences to excite the senses. Although the Pharisees had many prophecies concerning Messiah, they still wanted signs (see for example, Luke 11:29). Rather than live by faith, the recipients of the book of Hebrews were tempted to return to the Old Testament system which had been fulfilled in Christ — that is, to things which could be seen, heard and touched. Visual experiences leave impressions and produce certain effects, but they cannot convey principles or transform a life; they do not provide the necessary content for righteous living. We need to know what duty God requires of us. In love, God has given his law as 'a lamp to [our] feet and a light to [our] path' (Ps. 119:105).

Love for God the motive for obedience

In Deuteronomy love for God is commanded. He does not demand obedience as an Egyptian tyrant or despot; he commands his people to love him, not for his benefit or satisfaction, but for their good: 'You shall love the LORD your God with all your heart, with all your soul, and with all your strength' (Deut. 6:5). 'What does the LORD your God require of you, but to fear the LORD your God, to walk in all his ways and to love him, to serve the LORD your God with all your heart and with all your soul, and to keep the commandments of the LORD and his statutes which I command you today for your good?' (Deut. 10:12-13, emphasis mine). 'Therefore you shall love the LORD your God, and keep his charge, his statutes, his judgements, and his commandments always' (Deut. 11:1).

While God will never forget his covenant, or fail to keep his word, his people are apt to become careless, forget and act presumptuously. Moses exhorted the people, therefore, not to forget God's covenantal promise: 'Take heed to yourselves, lest you forget the covenant of the LORD your God which he made with you' (Deut. 4:23). God's purpose and plan was not, and is not, to make his people prosperous, comfortable and contented with this life, but to accomplish the redemption of sinners throughout the world. Hence, he blesses them that they, in turn, might be a blessing to others (Ps. 67:1-2). With every promise and privilege comes responsibility, however. Like ancient Israel, we are apt to forget why God has called and blessed us. To be a blessing to others, we must love the Lord our God with all our hearts, minds and strength.

Love for the Lord is shown by obedience to his revealed will – his holy law. The repetition of the law is significant as it relates to Christian experience. As at Mt Sinai, the terror of the law must first be realized – that is, the moral perfection required by the law must be seen and all 'want of conformity unto and transgression of'[11] it must be acknowledged. Sinners must realize that they stand under the condemnation and penalty of the law. At that point, the law is the schoolmaster to bring them to Christ (Gal. 3:24). In him, the terror of the law has been removed and there is 'now no condemnation to those who are in Christ Jesus' (Rom. 8:1). That does not mean, however, that the purpose of the law is accomplished. The repetition of the law in Deuteronomy serves to remind God's people that instruction and guidance in 'the paths of righteousness' are needed. Here, God does not speak with the terrors of Sinai but in the quiet and tender tones of a loving Father. The response of the true believer is: 'Oh, how I love your law! It is my meditation all the day' (Ps. 119:97).

At Mt Sinai, the Israelites gave a tremendous expression of commitment and resolved to be obedient. They said, 'All that the LORD has spoken we will do' (Exod. 19:8). Before long, however, they were murmuring and complaining about their conditions and circumstances. Either they had spoken impulsively without understanding the implications, or they were genuinely sincere but lacked the power to keep their word. Probably both! Though Israel had been chosen by God's grace, redeemed by his powerful hand, protected by his holy presence and sustained by his infinite goodness, their response was one of doubt, unbelief and disobedience.

In sending the twelve spies to investigate the promised land, Israel seems to have acted in unbelief; Matthew Henry says, 'Moses had given them God's word ... but they could not find in their hearts to rely upon that; human policy goes further with them than divine wisdom... As if it were not enough that they were sure of a God before them, they must send men before them.'[12]

The consequence of that initial act of unbelief was expressed when they adopted the majority opinion and turned away from conquest and occupation of the land. Not only was that generation banished to the wilderness for the rest of their days, but their unbelief produced dissension and unrest. Worst of all, they projected the blame on God and interpreted his love and goodness as hatred. In rehearsing that event, Moses says, 'You would not go up, but rebelled against the command of the LORD your God; and you complained in your tents, and said, "Because the LORD hates us, he has brought us out of the land of Egypt to deliver us into the hand of the Amorites, to destroy us"' (Deut. 1:26-27, emphasis mine).

No matter how much God might be blamed and accused by sinful men, he is faithful; he will not break his covenantal promise.

The law must be written on the heart

The law is good and sufficient in and of itself, but sinners lack
the necessary motivation and power to do what it requires. We
need the content of the law and a radical change of heart. When
God made his covenant with Abraham, he ordained the rite of
circumcision as a sign and seal. Circumcision was not merely an
external rite; it carried spiritual significance. The significance is
declared to be the necessity for a circumcised heart. Moses
understood that a change of heart was needed. (Significantly, the
prophet Jeremiah, who used Deuteronomy extensively, also
speaks about the importance of a circumcised heart — Jer. 4:4;
9:26.)

Moses says, 'Circumcise the foreskin of your heart, and be stiff-
necked no longer' (Deut. 10:16, emphasis mine). 'And the
LORD your God will circumcise your heart and the heart of your
descendants, to love the LORD your God with all your heart and
with all your soul, that you may live' (Deut. 30:6, emphasis
mine).

While the ancient Israelites promised obedience, they lacked
the power to perform. They knew what was required but they
could not do it. God's law must be written on the heart. Having
repeated the Ten Commandments, God said through his
servant Moses, 'Oh, that they had such a heart in them that they
would fear me and always keep all my commandments, that it
might be well with them and with their children for ever!' (Deut.
5:29, emphasis mine).

As we shall see, successful training of children (Deut. 6)
requires that the law must first be written on the heart of the
parent. Before one can teach God's law effectively, it must be
internalized. While God graciously enabled many Old Testament saints to live righteous lives, for the most part, his law
remained written on tablets of stone. Some of the prophets
looked forward to the time when the law would be written on
the hearts of God's people. For example, Jeremiah declared,
'Behold, the days are coming, says the LORD, when I will make a

new covenant with the house of Israel and with the house of Judah — not according to the covenant that I made with their fathers in the day that I took them by the hand to lead them out of the land of Egypt, my covenant which they broke, though I was a husband to them, says the LORD. But this is the covenant that I will make with the house of Israel after those days, says the LORD: I will put my law in their minds, and *write it on their hearts*; and I will be their God, and they shall be my people' (Jer. 31:31-33, emphasis mine). The book of Hebrews shows that the problem did not lie with the covenant but with the people (Heb. 8:8).

Thank God, 'When the fulness of the time had come, God sent forth his Son ... and [he] sent forth the Spirit of his Son into [our] hearts' (Gal. 4:4,6). The Lord Jesus came 'in the likeness of sinful flesh ... that the righteous requirement of the law might be fulfilled in us [so that we no longer] walk according to the flesh but according to the Spirit' (Rom. 8:3-4). The Holy Spirit came to dwell within his people so that the law might be written, not just on tablets of stone, but also on the 'tablets of flesh, that is, of the heart' (2 Cor. 3:3). With the psalmist, we can say, 'I delight to do your will, O my God, and your law is within my heart' (Ps. 40:8). He writes his law on our hearts so that we might be living epistles to be 'known and read by all men' (2 Cor. 3:2). When a believer is faced with temptation, opposition, or persecution, he will, when governed by the law of God and motivated by the Spirit of God, stand on truth, maintain his integrity and do what is right. In other words, the righteousness of the law will be evident to a watching world.

God will always be faithful to his covenant

As Moses rehearsed the events of the past, he recognized God's faithfulness in keeping his covenant. About five hundred years later, God reiterated his covenantal promise to King David. He said:

I will not break off my lovingkindness from [David],
Nor deal falsely in my faithfulness.
My covenant I will not violate.
Nor will I alter the utterance of my lips.
Once I have sworn by my holiness;
I will not lie to David

(Ps. 89:33-35, NASB).

16.
God's faithfulness in instructing his people

In the mid-seventies, I was privileged to pastor a church in one of the south-eastern suburbs of Melbourne which had a reputation as an evangelical, Bible-believing, mission-minded church. Soon after my arrival, however, I learned that only four people in the congregation had read the entire Bible. Consequently, we implemented a plan to encourage all the members to read God's Word through as a congregation in one year. Everyone became quite enthusiastic and many of them not only read the Bible themselves but encouraged their relatives, friends, neighbours and missionaries to join in the exercise. By the end of the year, about double the number of the membership had read the Bible through. As a result, personal conversations changed dramatically; instead of incidental talk about the weather, the football or cricket scores and other mundane matters, the people began sharing what they had learned from the Scriptures. God was pleased to bless that simple plan; a few people came to faith in Christ and some members were so blessed that they continued to read the Bible through each year after that.

The leaders of that church, like many elders, I suppose, assumed that the members studied the Scriptures and were well acquainted with the contents and teachings of the Bible. Such an assumption was ill-founded; pastoral issues and problems revealed that many were not nearly as well versed in the Word of God or committed to Christ as the leaders supposed. Jesus spoke of the necessity of having his Word abide in us (John 15:7). His Word cannot abide in us, of course, if we do not abide in it. In other words, regular, consistent and systematic reading and study of the Scriptures are essential for spiritual growth and development. Without the knowledge of the principles and precepts of the Word of God, an individual or a church will be spiritually malnourished. Where spiritual malnutrition exists, the spiritual immune system breaks down — resulting in loss of discernment, commitment, love and conviction. This, in turn, results in the decline or reversal of biblical values, priorities and standards, and makes one susceptible to temptation. Continual neglect of God's Word is, in essence, a declaration of confidence in self; one might as well say, 'I don't need my Maker's instructions, I am wise enough to set my own standards, competent enough to determine my direction in life and powerful enough to accomplish my own purpose.' This was, of course, the argument that was used by Satan in the Garden of Eden.

Having been born of slaves and reared in a wilderness, the generation of Israelites addressed by Moses on the plain of Moab had known nothing of a home which they could call their own. Their occupation and settlement of the promised land carried challenges, opportunities, demands and dangers which hitherto they had not known or encountered. Instruction in the law and its application was, therefore, especially necessary and appropriate. As we have seen, Moses had reminded them of God's faithfulness in keeping his covenant; he knew that God would *never* fail them. Having endured the rebellion and disobedience of their fathers in the wilderness, Moses' primary concern was now for them. If their future as a nation were to be guaranteed, they must build on the right foundation, focus on the right object and be obedient to God's law. It was imperative, therefore, that they clearly understood the principles and precepts of God's Word.

The God whose Word it is

Moses not only repeated the Ten Commandments on this occasion; he exhorted the people to give heed: 'Hear, O Israel, and be careful to observe it, that it may be well with you' (Deut. 6:3). Immediately afterwards, he makes that remarkable statement concerning God, commonly known as the *Shema* (meaning, 'Hear!'): 'Hear, O Israel: the LORD our God, the LORD is one!' (Deut. 6:4). The Jews interpreted this to mean that God is one numerically. It includes that idea, of course, but, having come out of Egypt, where almost everything was identified with a different god, and with the prospect of Canaan ahead, where some of the most abominable gods and idols were worshipped, the Israelites needed to know that there is 'one God only; the living and true God'. This God is *our* God' — an affirmation which appears many times in Deuteronomy (e.g., Deut. 6:4; 11:1,13,22; 13:3; 19:9; 30:6,16,20).

The Jews failed to understand that the God of Abraham, Isaac and Jacob is one but exists in three persons. The three persons of the Godhead are one in their relationship; they are one in mind, will, desire and purpose. Jesus declared, for example, 'He who has seen me has seen the Father... Believe me that I am in the Father and the Father in me' (John 14:9-11). Matthew Henry says, 'Happy they that have this one Lord for their God; for they have but one master to please, but one benefactor to seek to. It is better to have one fountain than a thousand cisterns, one all-sufficient God than a thousand insufficient ones.'[1]

Because there is only one God, the living and true God, his commandments are not merely suggestions or options. There is no alternative or substitute; his Word is law and it must be obeyed.

The law is for life

This God, in giving his law, declared, 'I am the LORD your God who brought you out of the land of Egypt' (Deut. 5:6). Having redeemed his people, God gave them his law. He did not make his laws arbitrarily or capriciously to repress or frustrate his people; he always has good reason for what he requires. He was never inconsiderate of his creatures or unmindful of their circumstances; what he required was, and is, not only for his glory, but also for their good. His law is good because, as the psalmist declares, it restores the soul, makes wise the simple, rejoices the heart, enlightens the eyes and warns of spiritual dangers (Ps. 19:7-11). God's Word instructs, teaches and counsels his people in righteousness, justice, goodness and truth so that they might enjoy the blessing of God and live life to the full. Not that life is obtained by keeping the law; no one, other than the Lord Jesus Christ, has perfectly kept all the righteous requirements of the law. Nevertheless, it provides the standard for righteous and successful living: 'Every commandment which I command you today you must be careful to observe, *that you may live* and multiply, and go in and possess the land of which the LORD swore to your fathers' (Deut. 8:1, emphasis mine).

Again Moses tells the people, '*The word* is very near you, in your mouth and in your heart, that you may do it. See, I have set before you today life and good, death and evil, in that I command you today to love the LORD your God, to walk in his ways, and to keep his commandments, his statutes, and his judgements, *that you may live* and multiply; and the LORD your God will bless you in the land... *I have set before you life and death,* blessing and cursing; therefore choose life, *that both you and your descendants may live;* that you may love the LORD your God, that you may obey his voice, and that you may cling to him, for he is your life and the length of your days; and *that you may [live]* in the land which the LORD swore to your fathers, to Abraham, Isaac, and Jacob, to give them' (Deut. 30:14-16,19-20, emphasis mine).

In Deuteronomy, the law is shown to be reasonable and beneficial; it is practical and not burdensome. Moses not only repeated the law and stressed its importance; he expounded it to show how application was to be made in daily situations and various circumstances. Since knowledge of the law was essential for the spiritual well-being of God's people, provision was made for consistent reading of, and adequate instruction in, it.

The responsibilities of the king

The King of Israel needed to understand that, unlike pagan kings, who were a law unto themselves, he was not above the law and that he would, like everyone else, be judged by it. Because of his unique responsibility for law and order, the king not only needed to know the law, but also to set a personal example of righteousness and justice. Indeed, additional specific laws are given to restrain kings from temptations and excesses to which they, by virtue of their office, were exposed. The king was not to multiply horses, have a plurality of wives, or accumulate silver and gold (Deut. 17:14-20). The king 'must carefully avoid everything that would divert him from God and religion'.[2] 'Riches, honours, and pleasures are the three great hindrances of godliness (the lusts of the flesh, the lusts of the eye, and the pride of life).'[3] No provision was made for the dichotomy claimed by contemporary politicians between their so-called private life and public performance.

The king was required, not only to read the law, but also to make a copy of it from the one held by the priests (Deut. 17:18). The priests were the custodians of the law; the copy entrusted to, and held by, them was the standard from which all copies were to be made and with which other copies were to be compared. If the king were to copy from another source, the possibility of error would be greater — and the law was too important to take that risk. Besides, in receiving it from the priests, there was a sense in which he was getting it directly from God. While the priests were the custodians of the law, the king was responsible to uphold and enforce it. He, above all people, needed to know and heed the law.

While Joshua, Moses' successor, was not a king, he was the leader of Israel. God's instructions to him are worthy of note. Having been assured that God would not fail or leave him, he was instructed by God to meditate in the law day and night, to give himself wholly to it and not to let it depart from his mouth (Josh. 1:8). As Matthew Henry says, 'All his orders to the people, and his judgement upon appeals made to him, must be consonant to the law of God.'[4] 'Those that make the word of God their rule, and conscientiously walk by that rule, shall both do well and speed well; it will furnish them with best maxims by which to order their conversation (Ps. 111:10); and it will entitle them to the best blessings.'[5]

The role of judges in administering the law

Judges were responsible to enforce the law; obviously they needed to know what was required in order to apply it righteously and justly. Knowledge of the law is implicit in the requirements and restrictions imposed on judges: 'You shall appoint judges ... and they shall judge the people with just judgement. You shall not pervert justice; you shall not show partiality, nor take a bribe, for a bribe blinds the eyes of the wise and twists the words of the righteous. You shall follow what is altogether just, that you may live and inherit the land which the LORD your God is giving you' (Deut. 16:18-20).

The Levites as teachers of the law

When Jacob blessed his sons (Gen. 49:1-28), he was not particularly favourable to Simeon and Levi. In fact, his remarks were anything but a blessing; he declared:

Instruments of cruelty [violence] are in their dwelling place.

Let not my soul enter their council;
Let not my honour be united to their assembly...
Cursed be their anger, for it is fierce;
And their wrath, for it is cruel!
I will divide them in Jacob
And *scatter them in Israel*

(Gen. 49:5-7, emphasis mine).

The curse pronounced by Jacob, however, was turned into a blessing by God. The Levites were not given an inheritance as were the other tribes; rather, they were dispersed to forty-eight cities throughout the land — six cities of refuge plus forty-two others (Num. 35:6-7).

'Of Levi', Moses said, 'They shall teach Jacob your judgements, and Israel your law' (Deut. 33:8,10). Matthew Henry comments: 'That each tribe might have the benefit of the Levites' dwelling among them, *to teach them the good knowledge of the Lord*; thus that light was diffused throughout all parts of the country, and none were left to sit in darkness.'[6]

The public reading of the law

At the beginning of each sabbatical year, the people were to rejoice before the Lord and to give attention to the reading of the law (Deut 31:10-13). No doubt, those servants who were released at that time and the people whose debts were cancelled had good reason to be thankful — not just for their release but for the benefit of righteous and just law which required their liberty. One of the great benefits of the sabbatical year was the opportunity it afforded the people to reconsider their purpose, to reassess their values and to review their priorities in the light of God's law. The sabbatical year was a regular occasion in which the people proved the trustworthiness and faithfulness of God. They had to know the Word of God and depend on it.

The instruction of children

Provision was made also for the instruction of children. One stated purpose for the reading of the law at the Feast of Tabernacles was to acquaint children and strangers with the requirements of the law. The instructions were clear: 'And Moses commanded them, saying: "At the end of every seven years, at the appointed time in the year of release, at the Feast of Tabernacles, when all Israel comes to appear before the LORD your God in the place which he chooses, you shall read this law before all Israel in their hearing. Gather the people together, men and women and little ones, and the stranger who is within your gates, that they may hear and that they may learn to fear the LORD your God and carefully observe all the words of this law, and that their children, who have not known it, may hear and learn to fear the LORD your God as long as you live in the land"' (Deut. 31:10-13).

Parents had, and still have, the unique responsibility to teach their children. God's law was to be 'written on the heart' of the parent so that the children were taught diligently. Parents were instructed to talk of God's law when they sat in the house, walked by the way, lay down and rose up (Deut. 6:7; see also 11:19). Those four activities represent between them just about everything a person does in the course of his daily life. The conversation was not intended to be a constant lecture in systematic theology – though at times systematic instruction in doctrine was appropriate. The emphasis was on practical theology. In any and every situation in which parents found themselves, they were to show how the law of God had to be applied towards God and man. Allis remarks, 'Let a single generation grow up in ignorance, and all the precious heritage which the fathers have received will be lost to their sons. The Bible is the best practical handbook of psychology and pedagogy in the world!'[7]

A young mother who started to teach her children at home told me that although at first she was most apprehensive about such a daunting task, she began to enjoy it as she found that she could turn every activity into a learning experience. A trip to the grocery store became an opportunity to teach mathematics, for example. That is the method of teaching implicit in this passage — as a teaching method, it cannot be improved upon. What a privilege parents have in leading their children in the knowledge of the Creator and the discovery of his creation! What a delight it is to watch their personalities develop and their understanding grow! Many parents miss the best years of their child's development and growth by committing them to an artificial environment in which they are often subjected to false ideas and ungodly practices long before they are mature enough to evaluate and discern them. In Israel, the children were to be thoroughly instructed in God's law and to be taught how to apply it by their parents. It is effective, of course, only to the extent to which the law of God is first written on the heart of the parent.

The general principle

In general, the Israelites were instructed to 'lay up these words in [their] heart and in [their] soul, and bind them as a sign on [their] hand, and they shall be as frontlets between [their] eyes' (Deut. 11:18). The Jews took this command very literally and made phylacteries to wear on the forehead and bind on the forearm. Obviously, this was not what was intended by this instruction; Jesus, in his denunciation of the Pharisees, used this as an illustration of their hypocrisy (Matt. 23:5). Rather, to apply God's Word to the soul, it needs to be bound to the mind and the hand. In other words, both thoughts and actions were, and are, to be regulated by the law of the Lord. Also, the law was to be written on the doorposts of their houses and on their gates (Deut. 6:9,11-20). The intention was not a pharisaical application, but to inform the stranger who entered the gate that the property and the household were regulated by, and functioned under, the law of God.

The importance and value of God's Word

'Moses began to explain this law' (Deut. 1:5). He wanted all Israel to know 'the whole counsel of God' and to apply it rigorously to every aspect of life. After 'Moses had completed writing the words of this law in a book, when they were finished, [he] commanded the Levites ... saying: "Take this Book of the law, and put it beside the ark of the covenant of the LORD your God"' (Deut. 31:24-26). It was to be kept securely and permanently; further, it was to be kept pure: 'You shall not add to the word which I command you, nor take [anything] from it' (Deut. 4:2). Genuine religion is based on truth — and truth never changes! In his Word, God has given us a body of truth; he has set before us the way of life and the way of death — we do well, therefore, to take heed!

Significantly, in response to Satan's temptation, Jesus quoted a foundational principle from Deuteronomy. He said, 'Man shall not live by bread alone; but by every word that proceeds from the mouth of God' (Matt. 4:4; Luke 4:4, quoting Deut. 8:3). Job understood the principle; he declared, 'I have not departed from the commandment of his lips; I have treasured the words of his mouth more than my necessary food' (Job 23:12). The Word of God is essential for right living.

> How firm a foundation, ye saints of the Lord,
> Is laid for your faith in his excellent Word!
> What more can he say than to you he has said,
> To you who for refuge to Jesus have fled?[8]

Someone has summarized the importance of God's Word in the following words:

> This book contains — the mind of God, the state of man, the way of salvation, the doom of sinners, and the happiness of believers. Its doctrines are holy, its precepts

are binding, its histories are true, and its decisions are immutable.

Read it to be wise, believe it to be safe, and practise it to be holy. It contains light to direct you, food to support you, and comfort to cheer you. It is the traveller's map, the pilgrim's staff, the pilot's compass, the soldier's sword, and the Christian's charter. Here, too, Heaven is opened, and the gates of Hell disclosed.

Christ is its Grand Subject, our good its design, and the glory of God its end. It should fill the memory, rule the heart, and guide the feet. Read it slowly, frequently, prayerfully. It is a mine of wealth, a paradise of glory, and a river of pleasure. It is given you in life, will be opened at the Judgement, and be remembered for ever. It involves the highest responsibility, will reward the greatest labour, and condemn all who trifle with its sacred contents. It is 'the Word of our God which shall stand for ever'.[9]

As Matthew Henry says, 'None must expect to receive favours from God's hand but those that are willing to receive the law from his mouth.'[10]

The purpose of God's Word

The purpose of the Word of God is not merely to *inform* us, but also to *transform* us. The facts or content of Scripture might be known, of course, without the person being motivated to do what is required. In other words, while the Scriptures teach us the path of life, they do not, in themselves, impart life. Jesus said to the Pharisees, 'You search the Scriptures, for in them you think you have eternal life; and these are they which testify of me' (John 5:39). In addition to the Scriptures, God's Spirit must transform the heart and bring about new desires and different motivation. The Spirit of God does not do his work in a vacuum; along with the information of the Word of God, he

changes the desires of the heart and renews the will unto obedience. The purpose of the transformation is to enable sinners to
please God, to worship him acceptably and to do his will from
the heart. The law by itself was, and is, as the apostle says, 'weak
through the flesh' (Rom. 8:3). That is, while people might be
well instructed in the law, in themselves, they lack the ability to
carry out its requirements.

God's Word teaches us how to worship God

Significantly, Moses was concerned, not only for thorough
instruction in the law, but also that the law be written on the
hearts of the people and, consequently, that they *worship* God
acceptably. The recognition of the worth of God should never be
a cold intellectual acknowledgement of his greatness but a
heartfelt expression of gratitude and adoration for his goodness
and grace. True worship occurs when the soul is 'lost in wonder,
love and praise'. Genuine worship proceeds from both the heart
and the mind. 'God is Spirit, and those who worship him must
worship in spirit and truth' (John 4:24). The law is fulfilled
when God's people love the Lord their God with all their heart,
mind, soul and strength.

The place of worship

Israel's worship was centred on the tabernacle; it was the place
were God met men and men met God. Since its construction,
the tabernacle had been located and remained at the centre of
Israel at all times. (Significantly, when Israel began to occupy the
land, the priests, rather than the Kohathites, carried the ark one
thousand cubits — more than one third of a mile — ahead of the
people.) Now that the conquest and settlement of the land was
imminent, what should be done with the tabernacle? Should it
remain in one place, or be moved periodically to the major cities

throughout the land? God, in his wisdom, knew that if the tabernacle were moved to various locations, sinful creatures, being what they are, would soon make every place where it was erected a sacred site. Coupled with that would come the temptation for each community to formulate its own peculiar concept of God. Obviously, that would defeat the purpose for which God had ordained the tabernacle.

When the Israelites occupied the land, they were ordered to destroy utterly all the sacred sites of the Canaanites (Deut. 12:2); they were not to replace them with sacred sites of their own. Matthew Henry comments: 'Let these pest-houses be demolished, as things they were afraid of. [Moses] begins the statutes that relate to divine worship with [the destruction of the sacred sites of the Canaanites], because there must be an abhorrence of that which is evil before there can be a steady adherence to that which is good (Rom. 12:9). The kingdom of God must be set up, both in persons and places, upon the ruins of the devil's kingdom; for they cannot stand together, nor can there be any communion between Christ and Belial.'[11]

Although Moses did not specify the permanent location for the tabernacle, nineteen times in Deuteronomy he speaks of the Lord *choosing* a place for his name. It is 'the place where the LORD your God chooses' (Deut. 12:5). 'Its location is left undetermined, and is not to be determined until "the Lord your God [gives] you rest from all your enemies round about, so that [you] dwell in safety" (verse 10). Apparently these conditions were not met until the time of David (2 Samuel 7:1)... God will choose it, not the Israelites themselves.'[12]

While the activities of daily life for every family were to be regulated by the law of the Lord, their focus was to be on the place where the Lord dwelt. God himself was to be the central unifying factor for the nation. (As we have seen previously, every male was required to go up to Jerusalem for three feasts each year.) As God's chosen people, Israel was to be united in their worship. 'The Lord our God is one'; his people are called to be one. At this point in God's great plan of redemption, the place was important; they needed to understand that there is only one place where God meets man and where man meets God — the place of the altar.

Matthew Henry writes:

> There is not any one particular precept (as I remember) in all the law of Moses so largely pressed and inculcated as this, by which they are all tied to bring their sacrifices to that one altar which was set up in the court of the tabernacle.
>
> All this stress is laid upon [the place]:
>
> 1. Because of the strange proneness there was in the hearts of the people to idolatry and superstition, and the danger of their being seduced by the many temptations which they would be surrounded with.
>
> 2. To prevent the introducing of corrupt customs into their worship and to preserve among them unity and brotherly love, that, meeting all in one place, they might continue both of one way and of one heart.
>
> 3. Because of the significancy of this appointment. They must keep to one place, in token of their belief of those two great truths, which we find together (1 Tim. 2:5), that *there is one God,* and *one Mediator between God and man.*[13]

At the conclusion of Solomon's reign, the nation divided. Jeroboam became king over Israel — that is, the northern kingdom composed of ten tribes. For Jeroboam, the place which the Lord had chosen was no longer acceptable because it was located in the southern kingdom, Judah. He proposed, therefore, that his people should worship God on their own turf. He did not want his people going up to Jerusalem; he modified the God-given system to suit the circumstances. Ostensibly, what he proposed was merely a modification of the religion of the fathers but, in reality, it was a new religion.

- He provided *new objects of worship* by making two golden calves.
- He designated Bethel and Dan as *new centres for worship*.
- He established a *new order of priests*. Instead of choosing Levites, he 'made priests from among the people'.
- He ordained a *new feast* similar to the feasts in Jerusalem, but they were held in the eighth month.
- He offered sacrifices on a *new* and different *altar* (1 Kings 12:28-33).

Jeroboam's modified religion might have been more convenient, but it was not regulated by the law of the Lord. Significantly, Israel never again had a righteous king after that.

A couple of centuries later, the Assyrians sought to integrate the various races. 'The king of Assyria brought people from Babylon, Cuthah, Ava, Hamath, and from Sepharvaim, and placed them in the cities of Samaria instead of the children of Israel' (2 Kings 17:24). As a result, the Samaritans were racially mixed. Because of this, the Jews avoided all contact with Samaritans. The Samaritans, being forbidden to enter Jerusalem, worshipped on Mt Gerizim — the mount of blessing. Several centuries later, the Lord Jesus sat beside a well and talked to a woman of Samaria. In response to her comment about the place of worship, Jesus said, 'The hour is coming when you will neither on this mountain, nor in Jerusalem, worship the Father' (John 4:21). God's people do not need to go up to Jerusalem to worship now, but their focus is on that place called Calvary — the place where 'one sacrifice for sins for ever' was made (Heb. 10:12). There, burdens are lifted and the dividing barriers are broken down; sinners are reconciled to God and to one another — they are made one in Christ (see Eph. 2:11-22).

The manner of worship

The place where God chose to put his name is important to those who worship the living God. *How* they worship is also important. The Second Commandment, as mentioned previously, concerns the *method* of worship; not surprisingly, this commandment is prominent in Deuteronomy. Obviously, Moses was burdened that the corrupt practices of the wicked Canaanites would contaminate and corrupt the worship of God's people. Undoubtedly, the Israelites understood that they were God's instrument of judgement upon the nations which they were to dispossess and that, therefore, Canaanite worship was unacceptable and displeasing to God. Nevertheless, the attraction of falsehood for the sinful heart and mind is great. In facing the idolatry of the Canaanites, the initial temptation would, no doubt, begin with curiosity. Investigation would produce fascination and empathy and, in the course of time, this would lead to identification with their idolatry.

As liberal scholars began to doubt the authority of God's Word early in this century, they took an interest in, and began to study, comparative religions. Soon after, we were told that all religions have some truth and that it is arrogant for Christians to claim that Christ is the only way to God. This led to dialogue with false religions, 'interfaith' exchanges and, in due course, to acceptance. While a person must understand the beliefs and customs of those whom God calls him to reach with the gospel, the danger of studying falsehood is real. The Israelites were explicitly forbidden from looking into the means and methods of Canaanite worship. 'Do not enquire after their gods, saying, "How did these nations serve their gods?"' (Deut. 12:30).

Matthew Henry says, 'Those that dare violate the second commandment will not long keep to the first. Strange worships open the door to strange deities.'[14] His further comment is also appropriate: 'Next to God's being, unity, and universal influence, it is necessary that we know and believe that he is an infinite Spirit; and therefore to represent him by an image in the making of it, to confine him to an image in the consecrating of it, and to worship him by an image in bowing down to it, *changes his truth into a lie* and *his glory into shame*.'[15]

Occasionally, when questions arise in ecclesiastical circles concerning worship, appeal is made to what is called the 'regulative principle'. On the one hand, Roman Catholics, Episcopalians and Lutherans have held that anything may be done in worship except that which is explicitly forbidden in Scripture. Reformed and Presbyterian churches, however, have taken a much stronger position; they insist that anything which is not commanded in Scripture is forbidden. (With the captivating entertainment offered in many churches these days, one wonders if the regulative principle means anything any more!) Purity of worship is not optional or incidental; true worship is not open for modification! 'Those enterprises which we undertake by a divine warrant, and prosecute by divine direction, we may expect to succeed in. If we take God's method, we shall have his blessing.'[16]

The Second and Fourth Commandments

As the observance of the First Commandment depends to a large degree on careful and faithful observance of the Second, the observance of the Third Commandment (reverence for God's name) depends on the faithful observance of the Fourth Commandment (observance of the Sabbath). Those who disregard the Sabbath day will, inevitably, dishonour God's name. The Second and Fourth Commandments are particularly crucial to sustained worship which is acceptable to God.

One notable change occurs in the repetition of the Ten Commandments in Deuteronomy concerning the reason for the observance of the Sabbath day. In Exodus 20, God's people were to observe the Sabbath day because of the pattern established by God at *creation* — he created the world in six days and rested on the seventh. In Deuteronomy 5, however, the Sabbath is to be kept because God redeemed his people from the land of bondage. Exodus looks back to *creation*; Deuteronomy looks forward to *redemption*. The first looks back to our *origin* and the latter looks forward to our *destiny*. As we have seen previously, these are the two points which give life meaning and purpose. To maintain the right direction in life, the Lord's Day provides regular intervals for us to examine and assess our direction and progress.

Some argue that every day is to be a holy day and that there is, therefore, no distinction; the law, they say, was fulfilled in Christ and we have no obligation to observe a special day. The arguments and counter-arguments have many facets and can become quite complex at times but, in my humble opinion, because the Sabbath is interwoven into every aspect of life in the Old Testament, one day of the week set aside for the worship of God is a necessity. Actually, one's attitude towards the Lord's Day reflects the attitude towards the Lord himself. Those who acknowledge that they owe their existence to the Creator and who have been redeemed from the bondage of sin will observe the Lord's Day because they love him.

Though Matthew Henry's comment concerns Leviticus 26, it is appropriate:

> The inculcating of those precepts of the law which were of the greatest consequence, and by which their obedience would be tried. They are the abstract of the second and fourth commandments, which, as they are by much the largest in the decalogue, so they are most frequently insisted on in other parts of the law. Moses, after many precepts, closes [Leviticus] with a special charge to observe these two great commandments.
>
> 1. 'Be sure you never worship images.'
> 2. 'Be sure you keep up a great veneration for the sabbaths and religious assemblies.'

As nothing tends more to corrupt religion than the use of images in devotion, so nothing contributes more to the support of it than keeping the sabbaths and reverencing the sanctuary. These make up very much the instrumental part of religion, by which the essentials of it are kept up. Therefore we find in the prophets that, next to the sin of idolatry, there is no sin for which the Jews are more frequently reproved and threatened than the profanation of the sabbath day.[17]

The book of Judges shows that not long after the death of Joshua, Israel, as a nation, became wicked and corrupt; the people ignored the instruction, profaned the Sabbath and embraced idolatry. As a result, God delivered them into the hands of their wicked neighbours for times of oppression and affliction to remind them that obedience brings blessing and rebellion brings a curse. When God called the judges, the issue in every case was *idolatry*; in summary, the Scripture says, 'The people served the LORD all the days of Joshua ... another generation arose after them who did not know the LORD nor the work which he had done for Israel. Then the children of Israel did evil in the sight of the LORD, and served the Baals; and they forsook the LORD God of their fathers, who had brought them out of the land of Egypt; and they followed other gods from among the gods of the people who were all around them, and they bowed down to them; and they provoked the LORD to anger' (Judg. 2:7-12).

The two outstanding themes of the book of Judges are the incorrigible wickedness of the people and the persistent mercifulness of the Lord. In spite of their continual rebellion, God was faithful; when they repented and turned to the Lord, he sent them a deliverer and, for a time, they enjoyed his blessing of peace. But then the cycle of rebellion, retribution, repentance and rest began all over again. If there is one thing which the message of Judges teaches us, it is that 'The law ... was weak through the flesh' (Rom. 8:3). Those ancient people failed, not for want of information or historical evidence, but for want of motivation. No one can be saved without the information of God's Word, but one cannot be saved merely by information. If that were possible, the answer to the sin problem would be education.

God's law written on the heart

After Israel had occupied the land for almost a millennium, the nation began to crumble; the people had forgotten the law of their God; they did not love him with all their heart. As a result of their disobedience, they were being taken into captivity by Babylon. God sent his prophets to remind the people of what Moses had written, but, recognizing human inability to please God, they anticipated a new covenant in which God's law would be written on the hearts of his people. They looked forward to the redemptive work of Messiah by which an inward transformation would be accomplished. Jeremiah said, 'Behold, the days are coming, says the LORD, when I will make a new covenant ... this is the covenant ... I will put my law in their *minds*, and write it *on their hearts*; and I will be their God, and they shall be my people' (Jer. 31:31-33, emphasis mine). Similarly, Ezekiel declared, 'I will sprinkle clean water on you, and you shall be clean; I will cleanse you from all your filthiness and from all your idols. I will give you a *new heart* and put *a new spirit within* you; I will take the heart of stone out of your flesh and give you a heart of flesh. I will put my Spirit *within* you and cause you to walk in my statutes, and you will keep my judgements and do *them*' (Ezek. 36:25-27, emphasis mine).

In the fulness of time, 'God [sent] his own Son in the likeness of sinful flesh [and] ... he condemned sin in the flesh, that the righteous requirement of the law might be *fulfilled in us* [so that we] do not walk according to the flesh, but according to the Spirit' (Rom. 8:3-4, emphasis mine).

In writing to the Corinthians, the apostle Paul says that we are 'a [letter] of Christ ... written not with ink but by the Spirit of the living God, not on tablets of stone but on tablets of flesh, that is, of the *heart*' (2 Cor. 3:3, emphasis mine). God writes his law '*in our hearts*' that we might be living letters to be 'known and read by all men' (2 Cor. 3:2, emphasis mine). Moses anticipated the coming of Christ and he wrote of him; he knew that Christ alone can transform a sinful heart and enable it to obey God's law — indeed, to love that law.

God is faithful: he has provided the information we need in order to live; he has provided the means of instruction; and, by his Spirit, he enables us to do his will from the heart. As responsible beings, however, he does not coerce us. In order to do his will and enjoy his blessing, we must 'keep [ourselves] from idols' (1 John 5:21) and make full use of the means of grace which he has ordained — particularly in the observance of his day, when we receive instruction in his Word. 'Man shall not live by bread alone; but man lives by every word that proceeds from the mouth of the LORD' (Deut. 8:3).

17.
God's faithfulness in warning of dangers

While the physical dangers of the wilderness were, no doubt, a constant threat and cause for fear, they were not to be compared to the dangers which the Israelites were about to encounter in the land to which the Lord was leading them. The well-fortified cities filled with giants which had proved too great an obstacle for their fathers were still there, of course, but they were of no concern to Moses; he knew that God was with his people. God would give the victory as readily as he had provided deliverance from the Egyptian taskmasters. Hence, when Moses spoke of their possession of the land, he spoke of it as an accomplished fact. It was the unseen spiritual dangers that concerned him. The people needed to be made aware of the temptations with which they would be confronted and which, should they succumb, would result in the loss of their calling and purpose and would take them back into bondage comparable to that which they had experienced in Egypt. They must, therefore, be diligent to remember God's covenant with them and observe the precepts of his law.

Throughout Deuteronomy, Moses frequently urged his audience to 'take heed', 'hearken' and 'keep' the law: '*Take heed to yourself*, and diligently keep yourself, lest you forget the things your eyes have seen, and lest they depart from your *heart* all the days of your life. And teach them to your children and your grandchildren' (Deut. 4:9, emphasis mine). '*Take heed to your-selves, lest you forget* the covenant of the LORD your God' (Deut. 4:23, emphasis mine).

The greatest danger of all lay within themselves. Sinners are their own worst enemies; they see themselves as wise enough to plan their lives, strong enough to accomplish their objectives and moral enough to do what they think is right. Self-interest, however, always conflicts with the calling and purpose of God. Pride and presumption were, and are, ever-present dangers. Beside the enticement of idolatry, as we saw in the previous chapter, the Israelites needed to watch diligently against pride in accomplished victories, satisfaction in accumulated possessions and fascination with falsehood.

The prophet Jeremiah declared:

Thus says the LORD:
Let not the *wise man* glory in his wisdom,
Let not the *mighty man* glory in his might,
Nor let the *rich man* glory in his riches;
But let him who glories glory in this,
That he understands and knows me,
That I am the LORD, exercising lovingkindness, judge-
    ment, and righteousness in the earth
                              (Jer. 9:23-24, emphasis mine).

The warnings given by Moses concern these three classifications of Jeremiah: 'wise men', 'mighty men' and 'rich men'. I want, however, to consider them in a different order.

The danger of pride and presumption

'Mighty men' attribute their successes to their strength. Having fought difficult battles and having gained victory after victory in the conquest of the land, the people could readily presume that they were invincible and that the victories were due to *their* military strategy and strength. After success at Jericho, for example, the little village of Ai appeared to be a 'pushover'; they presumed that victory was a foregone conclusion. Dr Noel Weeks says, 'Before the battle the danger is fear; after the battle it is pride.'[1] From the outset, God's people had to acknowledge that their victories were due to the sovereign power of God. Success in the future depended on their continued recognition of God's sovereignty and obedience to his law. Pride, on the other hand, would lead to presumption, which in turn would shift the focus to the wrong object and attribute the effect to the wrong cause.

Undoubtedly, the greatest example of presumption in the history of ancient Israel was the time when the ark of the covenant was taken from Shiloh into battle and was captured by the Philistines (1 Sam. 4). Significantly, the ark was never returned to Shiloh — that city of Ephraim 'did not know the day of her visitation' and foolishly forfeited her privilege as the place where God dwelt among his people. When Jeremiah reminded his generation of what happened at Shiloh, the leaders were furious and sought to kill him. It was in the context of, and in conjunction with, his reference to Shiloh, that the prophet spoke of the 'wise man', the 'mighty man' and the 'rich man'.

Back in the days when I had aspirations of playing football in high school, the coach constantly encouraged the team never to fear the opposition; he used to tell us, 'The bigger they are, the heavier they fall!' When a big player was brought down, there was a sense of power, superiority and pride: 'Look at me! I brought *him* down!' The greater the accomplishment or victory, the greater the temptation to pride. The formidable obstacle which caused the Israelites to fear and turn back from the conquest of Canaan was the 'sons of Anak'. Moses, in reminding the new generation of those fearsome foes, warned against self-righteous pride; he said, '... you heard it said, "Who can stand before the descendants of Anak?" Therefore understand today that the LORD your God is he who goes over before you as a consuming fire. He will destroy them and bring them down before you; so you shall drive them out and destroy them quickly, as the LORD has said to you. Do not think in your heart, after the LORD your God has cast them out before you, saying, *"Because of my righteousness* the LORD has brought me in to possess this land"' (Deut. 9:2-4, emphasis mine).

This matter of self-righteous pride is emphasized three times in as many verses (Deut. 9:4,5,6). Sinners are always ready to project blame, or to attribute success to their personal condition. If trouble or affliction comes, as with Job, an immediate reaction is to question the reason: 'What did he do wrong?' Conversely, when things go well, the cause is often attributed to personal goodness: 'He must have done something right!' At times, we are all tempted to think more highly of ourselves than we ought (Rom. 12:3), but, as the apostle Paul says, 'If anyone thinks himself to be something, when he is nothing, he deceives himself' (Gal. 6:3). The apostle himself acknowledged that 'when [he was] weak, then [he was] strong' (2 Cor. 12:10). That is to say, when he recognized his own inability and attributed his accomplishments to God, he had things in the right perspective. God's grace does not depend on human goodness or personal righteousness; his blessing is not due to favouritism. 'Let not the mighty man glory in his might.'

The danger of materialism

Material possessions are not inherently wrong; we live in a world where we not only come constantly into contact with material objects, but where they are necessary for our existence. (Incidentally, the addition of the suffix '-ism' to any noun makes it into a philosophical system or way of life. There is nothing wrong with being human, for example, but 'humanism' is a way of life in which man regards himself as independent, autonomous and self-sufficient.) Materialism has been a major problem ever since the Fall; it is actually the inversion of values in which the creation is placed above, or substituted for, the Creator. The materialist believes in, and lives only for, those things that can be placed in a test tube, held in the hand, or deposited in the bank. In other words, he ignores God, the ultimate reality, and believes that matter is all that matters; he treats *things* as ultimate reality and values them accordingly. A popular slogan appeared on bumper-stickers, coffee mugs, brass plaques, and the like, a few years ago declaring that 'The one with the most toys wins.' That is, of course, a materialistic value-statement based on the contemporary concept of reality.

Material things are attractive and have tremendous appeal because they are tangible — that is, they are perceived and experienced by the senses. Because things are encountered constantly and are used perpetually, we know them to be real; we depend on them — in fact, we cannot do without them. When a person depends *entirely* on things for his existence and sustenance, however, and thinks that life is possible apart from, and without reference to, God, he is a materialist. The person who believes that 'life consists in the abundance of things which he possesses' will make the acquisition and accumulation of things his goal and priority in life.

Materialism tends to great pride, of course; in the eyes of a world which has forgotten God, human importance is determined and measured by what a person possesses. As Matthew Henry says, 'When the estate rises, the mind is apt to rise with it, in self-conceit, self-complacency, and self-confidence... When men grow rich they are tempted to think religion a needless thing... We are basely ungrateful if the better God is to us the worse we are to him.'[2]

To keep things in proper perspective, six days of mundane labour must be balanced and regulated by one day of worship in which the true principles of righteousness, justice, goodness and truth are considered and applied. God must be acknowledged regularly as the ultimate reality to whom all things owe their origin and their existence, and from whom they derive their value. To work for the right reasons and objectives, the biblical perspective is imperative and must be maintained.

Sinners are strange creatures! When in need of food or water, like the ancient Israelites, we tend to murmur and complain; when there is abundant provision, we tend to take it for granted, ignore the source from which it comes, and become greedy for more. In other words, in both poverty and prosperity, we, as sinners, do not naturally acknowledge the Lord God — the source of all material blessings. Often when adversity or hardship arises, God is blamed; when prosperity comes, he is ignored. It is much easier to live by sight than by faith! While those who were about to occupy 'the land flowing with milk and honey' proved to be faithful to the Lord until the death of Joshua, the dangers of prosperity and affluence were acute. The abundance of the land which the Israelites were about to experience and enjoy carried unique responsibilities and dangers. Future generations would take their material possessions for granted and presume on the goodness of God. Moses' warning was appropriate for them — and us! 'Rich men' are tempted to forget God, trust in their resources and take pride in their possessions.

Immediately following his instruction concerning the teaching of God's law to children, Moses issued a warning concerning materialism. He was, as it were, impressing on his hearers that part of parental responsibility is to impart a right perspective and true values. Someone might be thoroughly taught the requirements and prohibitions of the law and, with the apostle Paul, be blameless in the observance of them (Phil. 3:6), but still have a covetous heart (Rom. 7:7). As we have seen, to be effectual, the law must be written on the heart. Moses warned, therefore, against the powerful attraction of materialism and the pride which accompanies it: '... when the LORD your God brings you into the land of which he swore to your fathers, to Abraham, Isaac, and Jacob, to give you large and beautiful cities which you did not build, houses full of all good things, which you did not fill, hewn-out wells which you did not dig, vineyards and olive

trees which you did not plant — when you have eaten and are full
— *then beware, lest you forget the* LORD who brought you out of the
land of Egypt, from the house of bondage' (Deut. 6:10-12,
emphasis mine). '[Beware lest] then you say in your heart, "My
power and *the might of my hand* have gained me this wealth"'
(Deut. 8:17).

When God blesses his people with material wealth, he does
so not merely for their sakes: he makes provision 'to confirm his
covenant'. He blesses them in order to make them a blessing.
The psalmist made this clear in Psalm 67 when he said:

God be merciful to us and bless us,
And cause his face to shine upon us,
That your way may be known on earth,
Your salvation among all nations

(Ps. 67:1-2).

Again, God exhorts his people: 'You *shall remember* the LORD
your God, for it is he who gives you power to get wealth, that he
may establish his covenant which he swore to your fathers...
Then it shall be, if you by any means *forget* the LORD your God,
and follow other gods, and serve them and worship them, I
testify against you this day that you shall surely perish' (Deut.
8:18-19, emphasis mine).

In Deuteronomy, God impresses upon his people the
importance of the covenant which he has made to redeem them.
If all the nations are to be blessed under that covenant, Israel
had the responsibility, not merely to enjoy and hoard the
blessings bestowed upon them by God, but, as God's people,
they were to use their resources so that the 'ends of the earth'
might hear also. They must keep that purpose in view and
depend entirely upon him to provide for their daily needs.

In his wilderness temptations, our Lord rebutted Satan by
saying, 'It is written [in Deuteronomy], "Man shall not live by
bread alone, but by every word that proceeds from the mouth of
God"' (Matt. 4:4). Soon afterwards, he delivered his Sermon on

the Mount, in which he categorically dismissed materialism by saying, 'You cannot serve God and mammon' (Matt. 6:24). He proceeded to say, 'Therefore I say to you, do not worry about your life, what you will eat or what you will drink; nor about your body, what you will put on. Is not life more than food and the body more than clothing? ... After all these things the Gentiles [heathens] seek. For your heavenly Father knows that you need all these things. But seek first the kingdom of God and his righteousness, and all these things shall be added to you' (Matt. 6:25,32-33).

All of life is to be regulated by a true understanding and view of ultimate reality (God), and from that flows the system of righteous values — as taught in the Scriptures. Moral behaviour is rooted in, and dependent upon, right values. Values derived from, and rooted in, materialism, on the other hand, will lead inevitably to modified morality and behaviour. Sinners adjust moral principles to suit their objectives in life; a materialist will forfeit his integrity for financial gain. Francis Schaeffer foresaw the day when morality would be determined by a fifty-one per cent vote — that is, people would determine what is right by popular majority opinion. Political candidates and leaders would receive support if they gave the people what they wanted and left them undisturbed. The two factors which would determine morality, he believed, are personal peace and affluence. Certainly, this was evident in public reaction to the scandal which surrounded the Clinton administration!

Some today preach a gospel of prosperity — they claim that God wants his people to be rich. If someone is not rich, it is evidence, they say, of a lack of faith. The promise of material prosperity and physical well-being has tremendous appeal and generates great enthusiasm. (Generally, those who seem to prosper most from that doctrine are the preachers!) While the Old Testament speaks of material blessings which were inherited and possessed under the old covenant, the New Testament teaches that spiritual resources and blessings are inherited in Christ. A church or person can easily claim, like the church at

Laodicea, to be 'rich ... wealthy, and [in] need of nothing' and, at the same time, be completely unaware that they are 'wretched, miserable, poor, blind, and naked' (Rev. 3:17). Similarly, like the church at Smyrna, a person might be poor but have the Lord's encouragement, comfort and assurance that he is rich (Rev. 2:9). Dr Noel Weeks says, 'Our temptation is not to seek material blessings by way of obedience, but through the way of disobedience.'[3]

'Let not the rich man glory in his riches.' Though materialism holds tremendous attraction and power, God's people must 'set [their minds] on things above, not on things on the earth' (Col. 3:2). They must get their system of values from the Word of God.

3. The danger of falsehood

When John Bunyan painted that graphic portrait of a godly preacher to which I referred in chapter 12, he emphasized that the *first* thing a new convert needs is the wise instruction and counsel of a godly pastor and teacher. 'This is,' he said, 'the only man whom the Lord of the place whither thou art going hath authorized to be thy guide in all difficult places.' At three important points in his wonderful allegory, Bunyan introduces the man whom he has described; he is named 'Evangelist'. In Bunyan's understanding, the work of an evangelist is quite different to what is depicted by that term in the twenty-first century: evangelism is a pastoral responsibility (Eph. 4:11; 2 Tim. 4:5). Evangelist is first seen in the City of Destruction warning sinners to 'flee from the wrath to come'. Next, he approaches Mt Sinai to rebuke and correct Christian for having deviated from the path. And, finally, as Christian and Faithful enter Vanity Fair, Evangelist is portrayed as encouraging the pilgrims in the face of danger, persecution and martyrdom. If Evangelist were to fail in one or more of these aspects of ministry, he would be unfaithful to his divine calling and fail to meet the criteria which the Scriptures, and Bunyan, require. One of God's gifts to his church is that of faithful teaching pastors (Eph. 4:11).

Having attended a theological college in which the authority and sufficiency of the Scripture were denied and all the essential doctrines of the Christian faith were interpreted according to naturalistic presuppositions, I have experienced something of the subtlety, attraction and power of error. Most of my classmates turned aside from the faith and, as a result, sought to make people comfortable in their sin rather than warning them to 'flee from the wrath to come'. God, in his mercy, spared me from embracing the error taught in that college through godly counsel and a difficult situation. My first weekend in the pastoral minis- try included a leaders' meeting on the Saturday afternoon and four worship services on the Sunday. Upon returning to my quarters on Saturday evening, the landlady informed me that I had a funeral to conduct on Monday. It was, by far, the worst funeral I have ever had to conduct; a young father had reversed his truck over his two-year-old son. That was the first of three funerals in the first two weeks of my ministry. Though difficult, it was a tremendous experience in that it made me realize how worthless liberal theology is — I had been ill-prepared and ill- equipped to minister to people in such times of crisis. That experience drove me to seek the finest theological education available. (Wherever did we get the idea that faith is established through the study of falsehood?) Having embraced contemporary notions concerning God and his Word, my teachers at that first college, with one possible exception, were not authorized by the King to guide pilgrims — much less instruct the next generation of preachers; they did not 'have [their] eyes toward heaven, the best of books in [their] hand, nor the law of truth on [their] lips'.

Falsehood or error, particularly in religious matters, has tremendous power and attraction for us as sinners. Some ideas are attractive because they engender pride and self-confidence; they lead us to believe that we are 'gods knowing good and evil'. Truth can be manipulated to suit particular ends and enable us to live as we please with an easy conscience. As we have seen previously, sinners do not 'like to retain God in their knowledge' (Rom. 1:28); in order to avoid and exclude him, the truth is skilfully modified and manipulated. Because falsehood masquerades as truth, it can be very subtle; one can embrace it unwittingly. The Scriptures are, therefore, full of warnings about being deceived and led astray; falsehood is destructive. Jesus described Satan as 'a murderer from the beginning, [who] does not stand in the truth' (John 8:44).

In his inimitable style, A. W. Tozer says, 'There are areas of Christian thought, and because of thought then also of life, where likenesses and differences are so difficult to distinguish that we are often hard put to it to escape complete deception. Throughout the whole world error and truth travel the same highways, work in the same fields and factories, attend the same churches, fly in the same planes and shop in the same stores. So skilled is error in imitating truth that the two are constantly being mistaken for each other. It takes a sharp eye these days to know which brother is Cain and which is Abel. It is therefore critically important that the Christian take full advantage of every provision God has made to save him from delusion.'[4]

Like a bank teller, God's people need to be so familiar with the genuine article (the truth) that they are not deceived by counterfeits. We need to study and meditate on the Word of God — not some substitute! 'Wise men' pride themselves in their ability to discern and understand without God's revelation.

How do we discern the true prophet from the false?

Because so many persuasive voices present all kinds of convincing arguments, how can we tell the difference between the truth of God and the wisdom of men? How do we discern whether a person is sent from God with the truth or if he is an impostor? Two passages in Deuteronomy address this question — passages which need to be applied in the church today!

The first passage is *Deuteronomy 13:1-5*, which says, 'If there arises among you a prophet or a dreamer of dreams, and he gives you a sign or a wonder, and the sign or the wonder comes to pass, of which he spoke to you, saying, "Let us go after other gods — which you have not known — and let us serve them," you shall not listen to the words of that prophet or that dreamer of dreams, for the LORD your God is testing you to know whether you love the LORD your God with all your heart and with all your soul. You shall walk after the LORD your God and fear him, and keep his commandments and obey his voice, and you shall serve him and hold fast to him. But that prophet or that dreamer of dreams shall be put to death, because he has spoken in order to turn you away from the LORD your God, who brought you out of the land of Egypt and redeemed you from the house of bondage, to entice you from the way in which the LORD your God commanded you to walk. So you shall put away the evil from your midst.'

In today's setting, the person described in this passage is a persuasive, eloquent speaker who comes to town and does sensational signs and wonders. People are impressed and stand in admiration and awe. Some have been proved to be fraudulent in the 'signs' which they perform, but the text says that 'the sign or wonder comes to pass'. This man actually performs miracles and the conclusion to which many come is that he has been sent from God. The children of Israel should not have needed this warning; the magicians in Egypt gave adequate proof that wicked men can perform signs and wonders. While signs and wonders might impress people, they do not necessarily prove anything. According to God's Word, signs and wonders are not the primary, nor the final, test of a genuine prophet.

The primary test by which all 'prophets' must be judged (in the sense of discerning) is the Word of God. Is his message concordant with the law of God? Does his message cause people to love the Lord God with all their hearts and souls and cling to him? Does his message cause people to bow down and worship the living God — are they 'lost in wonder, love and praise'? If the

prophet is from God, the people had better listen to him; if he is
not from God, he should be stoned! (That is what God thinks of
false prophets!)

The second passage which we need to consider is *Deuteronomy 18:9-22*. All of us, no doubt, are curious to know what the
future holds. Many people consult the daily horoscope to learn
what the stars have to say and what kind of day they can expect.
Others go much further and consult palm-readers, fortune-tellers
and mediums. On one occasion my wife and I watched two
women in a shopping centre trying to learn their fortune from a
slot machine! An intense desire to get a glimpse into the future
has led many people to try just about anything. It is incredible
what some people believe in! This passage lists some of the
ancient means employed by people in their attempts to learn the
future; these include witchcraft, soothsaying, interpretation of
omens, sorcery, spells, consulting mediums and spiritists and
calling up the dead (Deut. 18:10-11). Of all the falsehood
promulgated in the church in the past century, at least, probably
more error has arisen concerning eschatology than anything else.
Just about anyone can speculate on the end times, voice his
opinion, and people will listen — people want to know about the
future!

God in his wisdom has disclosed everything we need to
know. The prophetic books of the Bible were not written to
satisfy our curiosity, or even to set out the sequence of events. As
I said elsewhere, I used to think I knew all about eschatology; the
more I have studied Isaiah, Ezekiel, Daniel and Revelation, the
more I am convinced that these things are written to comfort us
by assuring us that when conditions are at their worst, God is
still on his throne. There are, for example, terrible things
described in the book of Revelation — the pouring out of vials of
wrath, plagues, death, judgement, and the like. When prospects
appear dismal and one is tempted to despair, the message comes
through loud and clear: 'Look up! The Lord is still on the
throne.' Frankly, I am not too concerned about the details; it is
sufficient to know that God is sovereign, that he has all things

under control, and he will always do what is right, good and just. Since I don't know what the future holds, I must walk humbly with my God each day that he gives me.

This passage contains an important prophecy concerning Christ. God says, 'I will raise up for them a Prophet like' Moses. When John the Baptist appeared, the Pharisees interrogated him, asking, 'Are you the Prophet?' (John 1:21). When the disciple Philip found Nathanael, he said, 'We have found him of whom Moses in the law ... wrote — Jesus of Nazareth' (John 1:45). Though many prophets had appeared in Israel over the centuries, none of them was recognized as the fulfilment of the prophecy of Moses. Ironically, when the Prophet came, they did not recognize or acknowledge him.

In keeping with that great prophetic pronouncement in Deuteronomy, a crucial question appears: 'How shall we know the word which the LORD has not spoken?' (Deut. 18:21). I remember hearing a 'faith healer' boast that between sixty to seventy per cent of his prophecies had come to pass; no doubt he thought that was a reasonable passing grade. Had he known the Scriptures, his claim would have condemned him. The test of a true prophet, according to this passage, is one hundred per cent. *Everything* a true prophet declares comes to pass because he speaks for God and God doesn't guess or make any mistakes — His word is accurate — not just ninety-nine per cent of the time but *always!*

Why did God speak through prophets?

Another important question arises: why did God call prophets to deliver his Word? Why didn't he speak directly to men as the need arose? Some today claim to receive direct revelation ('The Lord told me ...'); in doing so, they place themselves on an equal basis with the prophets and apostles.

Noel Weeks says, 'Those who ask why God does not reveal himself more openly to man have overlooked who God is and who man is... The Bible tells us that a day is going to come when

God will reveal himself to everyone. We call that day the day of judgement, and the Bible says that man's reaction will be to flee in fear... Can God reveal himself and man not be destroyed?

'God has a solution for this problem. God's word and revelation do not come directly to man, but through another man, a prophet. When Israel responded in fear to God's speaking on Mount Sinai, God had pity on them. He arranged to communicate not directly to them, but through a mediator, Moses... That gives the unbeliever a problem. He desires information because he does not know the secret things that are hidden in the plan of God. So mediums appear as a non-Christian substitute for the prophet... All these things are attempts to put something in the place of what God has planned, and that is why they are wrong.'[5]

The safeguard against falsehood

Falsehood takes many forms and expressions; no matter what the form it takes, it is exceedingly dangerous because it results in deviation from following the Lord. To remain true, we need, like the Bereans, to '[receive] the word with all readiness, and [search] the Scriptures daily to find out whether these things [are] so' (Acts 17:11).

A. W. Tozer says, 'The Christian cannot be certain of the reality and depth of his love until he comes face to face with the commandments of Christ and is forced to decide what to do about them... False tests can only lead to false conclusions as false signs on the highway lead to wrong destinations.'[6]

God is faithful, not only in instructing his people in his precepts, but also in warning of dangers along the way.

Moses warns of judgement for disobedience

Having reviewed and expounded the law in the body of the book of Deuteronomy (chapters 4:44 - 26:19), Moses concluded by charging the people to 'Keep all the commandments which I command you today' (Deut. 27:1). He directed them to assemble on the two mountains (Mt Ebal, the mountain of curse, and Mt Gerizim, the mountain of blessing) located in the middle of the land and separated by a very narrow valley. Moses instructed six tribes to assemble on Mt Gerizim and six tribes on Mt Ebal to affirm the blessings and the curses relating to their obedience or disobedience to the law.

Those two mountains stood in the centre of the land as a perpetual reminder that if the people were obedient to the law, they would be blessed. If they were unfaithful, they would come under the curse of God. Twelve specific areas in which the law could readily be broken are listed in the last half of chapter 27. All the people were required to affirm their commitment to the law by saying 'Amen' to each of those curses. On the other hand, at the beginning of chapter 28, six blessings are pronounced on those who 'obey the ... LORD [their] God' (Deut. 28:2).

The blessings and the curses carried tremendous significance for Israel — far beyond what those concepts might convey in contemporary society. The curse related back to the fall of Adam. At that point, Satan was cursed by God; essentially, that meant he was banished from the favour of God. The blessing, on the other hand, meant to have God look with favour upon his people; the concept is expressed in the benediction to be pronounced by Aaron:

The LORD bless you and keep you;
The LORD make his face shine upon you,
And be gracious to you;
The LORD lift up his countenance upon you,
And give you peace

(Num. 6:24-26).

To be cursed by God, then, was to have him turn away his face; to be blessed meant to have God's smile of approval.

The concluding affirmation which Israel had to make on Mt Ebal concerned obedience to the law: 'Cursed is the one who does not confirm all the words of this law' (Deut. 27:26). Significantly, the apostle Paul quotes this in his letter to the Galatians (Gal. 3:10). He shows that we could never be justified by the works of the law because we, as sinners, cannot obey it fully. Because we have all failed, we stand under the wrath and curse of God. In the same context, the apostle quotes another statement from Deuteronomy. He says that anyone who is hanged on a tree is 'accursed of God' (Deut. 21:22-23). The death of Christ on a Roman cross was a stumbling-block to the Jews; they believed that Messiah would be blessed by God, not cursed! When Messiah came, he was hung on a tree; he was cursed by God — the Father turned his face away and forsook his Son. He bore the curse on behalf of those who were disobedient and had transgressed the law — so that they might not be forsaken and cursed by God but rather enjoy his smile of approval.

Because Mt Ebal was the mountain of curse, the Israelites were instructed to erect a stone altar at the summit for a sacrifice. That altar prefigured the sacrifice on Mt Calvary. In the mid-1980s, archaeologists discovered an ancient altar on Mt Ebal which they believed was the one erected by Joshua. Only an acceptable sacrifice could remove the curse!

As I have pointed out, the book of Deuteronomy is Moses' farewell address to Israel. At this point, the people had not yet entered the land — they had not conquered the cities or partaken of the fruits of the land. Moses was concerned to warn them against the pitfalls of disobedience and wilful neglect of God's law. How well God knows the human heart! Moses, being a prophet, spoke of the future — and he did so accurately! The Spirit of God revealed to him what would happen centuries later. When God's people are disobedient, he brings plagues, diseases, and the like, to chastise them, to warn them and to awaken them to their peril. In his mercy, God sends disasters to warn them of worse things to come if they forget him, ignore his law and persist in their wicked ways.

Moses prophesies, therefore, that '... all these curses shall come upon you and pursue and overtake you, until you are destroyed, because you did not obey the voice of the LORD your God, to keep his commandments and his statutes which he commanded you. And they shall be upon you for a sign and a wonder, and on your descendants for ever. Because you did not serve the LORD your God with joy and gladness of heart, for the abundance of everything' (Deut. 28:45-47).

Specifically, 'The LORD,' he says, in chapter 28, 'will bring a nation against you from afar, from the end of the earth, as swift as the eagle flies, a nation whose language you will not understand, a nation of fierce countenance, which does not respect the elderly nor show favour to the young... They shall besiege you at all your gates until your high and fortified walls, in which you trust, come down throughout all your land... You shall eat the fruit of your own body, the flesh of your sons and your daughters whom the LORD your God has given you, in the siege and desperate straits in which your enemy shall distress you... Then the LORD will scatter you among all peoples, from one end of the earth to the other, and there you shall serve other gods... And among those nations you shall find no rest, nor shall the sole of your foot have a resting place; but there the LORD will give you a trembling heart, failing eyes, and anguish of soul' (Deut. 28:49-50,52-23,64-65).

God's faithfulness revealed in his judgements

After the conquest of Canaan, Israel occupied the land for about 800 years. By that time, they had, as Moses predicted, forgotten the Lord, were serving other gods and living in disobedience to God's law. As he had threatened, God raised up the nation of Babylon, which swooped down like an eagle and carried the people off into captivity; this happened in 586 B.C.

The destruction and devastation of Jerusalem were terrible — as foretold, people actually ate their own children. When the Babylonians had finished, there was nothing left; they destroyed the buildings, the gardens and the people — Jerusalem was nothing more than a heap of rubble.

As the time of desolation drew near, some of the early writing prophets, like Isaiah, warned of impending judgement and urged the people to 'Seek the LORD while he may be found, [and] call upon him while he is near' (Isa. 55:6). Their warning, however, went unheeded. One prophet who lived through that terrible time of desolation and judgement was Jeremiah. Sometimes he is described as the 'weeping prophet' — like our Lord, when he looked at Jerusalem, he had plenty to weep over! Jerusalem was no ordinary city; its destruction was no incidental matter. This city was the place where God chose to put his name; it was the centre for his redemptive purpose for the world.

In spite of the fact that nothing immediately at hand gave Jeremiah cause for encouragement or optimism, he declared:

The LORD has done what he purposed;
He has fulfilled his word
Which he commanded in days of old

(Lam. 2:17).

In reading both Jeremiah and Lamentations, it is quite evident that the prophet had the book of Deuteronomy in mind; he uses many of the same phrases and expressions. For example, in Jeremiah 21:8, he quotes Deuteronomy 30:15,19: 'Thus says the LORD: "Behold, I set before you the way of life and the way of death."' While the devastation of the people and the land was something to weep over, in effect he says, 'I can't find fault with God; he has simply done what he said he would do.' Jeremiah states in no uncertain terms that God is serious about his Word; he keeps, not only his promises, but also his threats.

As we have seen, the theme of Deuteronomy is the faithfulness of God. Jeremiah takes up that theme; he says that:

Through the LORD's mercies we are not consumed,
Because his compassions fail not.
They are new every morning;
Great is your *faithfulness*
                    (Lam. 3:22-23, emphasis mine).

Undoubtedly, Jeremiah had that great declaration of Moses in mind:

The Rock! His work is perfect,
For all his ways are just;
A God of *faithfulness* and without injustice,
Righteous and upright is he
                    (Deut. 32:4, NASB, emphasis mine).

When the Babylonian Captivity took place, many people, no doubt, had serious questions and asked, 'Why has God allowed this to happen to us? After all, I thought that God was a God of love and compassion.' 'What has happened to that covenantal promise which he made with our father Abraham? Has God forgotten what he promised to do?'

Moses had answered these kinds of objections: 'Now it shall come to pass, when all these things come upon you, the blessing and the curse which I have set before you, and you call them to mind among all the nations where the LORD your God drives you, and you return to the LORD your God and obey his voice, according to all that I command you today, you and your children, with all your heart and with all your soul, that *the LORD your God will bring you back* from captivity, and have compassion on you, and gather you again from all the nations where the LORD your God has scattered you... And the LORD your God will circumcise your heart ... to love the LORD your God with all your heart and with all your soul, that you may live' (Deut. 30:1-3,6, emphasis mine).

God's purpose was still being fulfilled; his people would be restored. He would circumcise their hearts and cause them to love him with all their heart and soul. That is accomplished, of course, only in Christ. Because God promised to restore his people, Jeremiah expresses hope. After experiencing the devastation of Jerusalem, he says that his strength and hope have perished (Lam. 3:18). No sooner are the words out of his mouth, however, than he recalls the fact that the mercies of the Lord never cease; therefore, he has hope (Lam. 3:21). His hope is sure and steadfast because it was based on the immutable Word of God. Again, he says:

'The LORD is my portion,' says my soul,
'Therefore I *hope* in him!'
The LORD is good to those who wait for him,
To the soul who seeks him
(Lam. 3:24-25, emphasis mine).

God is faithful; he will fulfil his Word. In speaking of the judgement pronounced against Eli, Matthew Henry says, 'It is he that pronounces the judgement, from whose bar there lies no appeal and against whose sentence there lies no exception. It is he that will execute the judgement, whose power cannot be resisted, his justice arraigned, nor his sovereignty contested.'[7] Earlier he writes, 'Divine threatenings, the less they are heeded, the surer they will come and the heavier they will fall... God will not go back from what he has sworn, either in mercy or judgement.'[8]

Moses praises God for his faithfulness

Picture again the scene as Moses bids farewell to the Israelites. Having declared God's future purposes for Israel, he cannot contain himself; he bursts into a song of praise to God (Deut. 32). Significantly, the thought which seems to be prominent in his mind and in his song is that of the *rock*. Before he smote the rock at Rephidim, God said that he himself would stand on it.

Moses understood that in smiting the rock, he was in effect smiting his God. Significantly, Paul says that the rock was Christ (1 Cor. 10:4). On the second occasion, he was instructed to speak to the rock; instead he smote it (Num. 20). For that one act of disobedience, he was not permitted to lead the people into the promised land. Without question Moses understood the significance of what he had done. In this song, he speaks of God as 'the Rock' (Deut. 32:4). Though he must have had deep regret over his own disobedience, nevertheless, that aspect is not reflected in his song. His song is one of gratitude and praise; he knew that God is faithful!

18.
The infinite, eternal and unchangeable God

In the February 1998 issue of *Reader's Digest*, an article appeared entitled, *When Your Child Asks About God*.[1] As one might expect, the article reflected popular contemporary thinking. The notion that ideas of God are 'based on belief — not scientific proof' is taken for granted and parents are encouraged to help their children to 'connect with God'. One must get children comfortable, so we are told, with 'God' words, religious symbols and those Bible stories which give images (such as 'Jonah and the whale') that 'God is with us through all life'. When children become teens, parents should avoid lecturing and 'remember that "questioning and rebelling are healthy and fine"'. Popular though those sentiments are, they reveal all too plainly the emptiness and futility of the world's concept of God and of religion.

When I read that article, I was reminded of Francis Schaeffer's comments concerning Sir Julian Huxley (1887-1950), who, 'though he was an atheist, [believed] that somehow or other — against all one might expect — a person functions better if he acts *as though God exists*. "So," the argument goes, "God does not in fact exist, but act as if he does!" ... In other words, according to Huxley, you can function properly only if you live your whole life upon a lie.'[2] According to Huxley, believing a lie is beneficial because it gives people a reference point — even though the reference point does not exist. Thank God, a much more objective and far better basis for faith in God exists. God cannot be put into a test tube, of course, but everything that is put into a test tube reveals something of his wisdom and power. God cannot be proved by science, but science confirms his existence.

Similarly, the hand of God is evident in history — apart from God, history, like science, loses all direction and purpose. Because God, in his sovereignty, providentially governs all things, history is 'his story'. God 'made his ways known to Moses, his acts to the children of Israel' (Ps. 103:7). Over the past century, attacks against God have been waged on these two fronts — science and history! In order to dismiss God from their thinking, men must distort the evidence of science and reconstruct the events of history. To what lengths sinners will go to avoid responsibility to their Maker!

No matter how concerted the effort or ingenious the attempt, God cannot be excluded by altering or manipulating the facts; to exclude him inevitably means the collapse of history and science. As we have seen, men do not like to retain God in their thinking; hence, as a last resort, modern men have endeavoured to destroy truth. When truth is made relative and subjective, facts do not matter — everything depends on how each individual perceives it. God has, however, revealed himself as the 'God of truth' (Deut. 32:4). Jesus Christ is 'the truth' (John 14:6); the Holy Spirit is 'the Spirit of truth' (John 16:13), and God's 'word is truth' (John 17:17; Ps. 119:142,151). God is the source of truth. He does not simply speak the truth; he is the truth — that is, he is true in his nature and being. Because he is eternal, 'his truth,' as the psalmist says, 'endures to all generations' (Ps. 100:5). (Incidentally, by way of contrast, in John 8:44 Jesus describes Satan as 'a murderer from the beginning, [who] does not stand in the truth, because there is no truth in him... He is a liar and the father of [lies]'.) Because truth is inseparably linked to the character of God, it has to be destroyed if men are to rid themselves of God. To destroy truth, however, is to destroy the foundation of life; life is impossible without truth. In one sense, the purpose of redemption is to make God's people true — as King David said, 'You desire truth in the inward parts' (Ps. 51:6).

God is not a nebulous entity, an abstraction about which we have vague and uncertain ideas, or a mysterious force to which we need to connect somehow — even if we are unsure of who or what he/she/it is. The true and living God has revealed himself clearly and unmistakably in his work of creation, in his works of providence, in his acts of history, through his servants, the prophets — through whom he gave the Scriptures — and, supremely, through his Son, Jesus Christ, the Lord. All his works reveal his wisdom, power and righteousness. He is, therefore, worthy of adoration, worship and praise. The desire and pursuit of everyone who has come to know God through Jesus Christ is not to 'connect' with him, but to get to know him personally and intimately. And, to know him, one must use the means of grace that he has ordained — particularly the use of the Scriptures in which he has revealed himself. God's people need to take time to 'be still, and know that [he is] God' (Ps. 46:10). To know him is to love him; to love him is to obey him; to obey him is to serve him; to serve him is to enjoy his presence and blessing.

In writing the foreword to David Hagopian's book, *Back to Basics*,[3] R. C. Sproul says, 'Reformed theology has little, if anything in its doctrine of God that differs from broader Christianity. On the other hand, the most distinctive dimension of Reformed theology is its doctrine of God. How can both statements be true? The answer is that the Reformed doctrine of God is not distinct considered *by itself*. What distinguishes the Reformed doctrine of God is its relentless application to all other doctrines. For example, Reformed theology is not satisfied to say that God is sovereign. It insists that this sovereignty extends to God's plan of salvation... In a word, the doctrine of the nature and character of God is basic to all theology.'

The knowledge of God is not only basic to all theology; it is basic to all life (that is, if the two can be separated!). Christians have a distinctive world view in which God is the centre and the circumference, the beginning and the end, of all things. He is not an appendage to be added to secular pursuits and activities; to glorify him in home and family life, in work and leisure and in recreation and entertainment is the objective and purpose of Christianity. In other words, what a person believes about God and how intimately he knows God will affect how he behaves and everything he does. The greatest and most urgent need in the church today is for professing Christians to understand who and what God is — and to apply that knowledge rigorously to daily life.

The unity and progress of doctrine in the Pentateuch

Having considered the themes concerning God and his redemptive work, it is important that we see the unity and progress of doctrine within the books of Moses. Hence, one aspect of this summary chapter is to show the progressive development of doctrine within these foundational books. These important relationships will reveal how wonderful, comprehensive and cohesive biblical truth really is.

Throughout this book, I have referred frequently to the catechism definition of God; I have done so because it is a classical statement and it expresses the biblical truth concerning God so well. It is a definition well worth committing to memory: 'God is a Spirit, infinite, eternal, and unchangeable, in his being, wisdom, power, holiness, justice, goodness, and truth.'[4]

Having taught Old Testament Survey in Bible college for several years, I began each year with the themes concerning God from the books of Moses — as I have used them in this work! It was several years, however, before it dawned on me how appropriately and wonderfully they relate to the catechism definition. In the table below, I want to show that relationship.

God is a Spirit; infinite, eternal, and unchangeable in his ...

Being and wisdom	**Genesis — the sovereignty of God** In creation, in his works of providence, and in choosing his people, God's being and wisdom are displayed.
Power	**Exodus — the power of God** In judging the Egyptians, redeeming his people, giving his law, and manifesting his presence, God revealed his great power.
Holiness	**Leviticus — the holiness of God** In depicting the heinousness of sin and its awful consequences and in showing the means of approach to God, he has shown his purity and holiness.
Justice and goodness	**Numbers — the goodness and severity of God** In providing for the needs of his people, in protecting them, in going before them, and in his patience with them, God revealed his abundant goodness and loving kindness. In judging Korah and Balaam for their wickedness, on the other hand, God executed his justice.
Truth	**Deuteronomy — the faithfulness of God** In keeping his covenant, in instructing in the principles of life, and in warning of dangers ahead, God demonstrated his faithfulness.

The work of the Trinity seen in the Pentateuch

While writing this book, I was sharing something of its content with a church leader; in the course of our conversation, he asked me if I thought there was any evidence for the Trinity within the Pentateuch. When I replied in the affirmative, he gave a somewhat cynical smile as he expressed his opinion that evidence for the Trinity cannot be found in these books.

If there are three persons in the Godhead, as the Scriptures teach and we categorically affirm, it would be surprising indeed if God had not revealed something of his tri-unity in this foundational material. Surely, in his self-disclosure, God would not have overlooked such a fundamental and necessary truth. We are not disappointed. Undoubtedly, the doctrine of the Trinity would escape our notice if it were not for the further revelation in the rest of Scripture. Because we have the advantage of looking at the books of Moses in the light of the complete Word of God, the doctrine of the Trinity is clearly present in these foundational books.

As we have seen, the Scriptures show that all three persons of the Godhead were involved in the work of creation. While God must be distinguished from his works, he cannot be kept separate from them. In other words, there is a sense in which God is known by what he does. We could summarize the content of this book as 'Themes concerning God and his redemptive work' because the character of God is seen so clearly in his great work of redemption. In this work, he has not only told us of his grace, mercy and love; he has demonstrated and proved it by what he has done.

The best overview, or summary, of redemption in the New Testament is possibly the first major paragraph of Ephesians (Eph. 1:3-14 — which, incidentally, is all one sentence in Greek). It teaches that *God the Father* chose us (v. 4), *God the Son* redeemed us (v. 7) and *God the Holy Spirit* sealed us (v. 13). Our redemption is, in other words, the work of all three persons of the Godhead. God the Father *planned* redemption; God the Son *purchased* redemption, and God the Holy Spirit *applies* the redemption purchased by Christ.

In the books of Moses, the hand of God the Father is evident in planning and initiating the redemption of his people. As we have seen (and shall see in the concluding chapter), God the Son is prominent through types and illustrations throughout these books. While mention is made of the role of the Spirit of God in creation (Gen. 1:2), not much more is said specifically concerning him in these books. That does not mean, however, that the Holy Spirit is absent or ignored. We must remember that the Spirit inspired Moses to write these things and, as we learn in the New Testament, his role is not to speak of himself but to glorify the Lord Jesus (John 16:14). He is, nevertheless, active in the redemptive work of God's people — both in the books of Moses and in the rest of Scripture. What is revealed concerning the work of each of the three persons of the God-head in the books of Moses?

1. The work of God the Father

God the Father formally initiated his redemptive plan by calling Abraham and making his covenantal promise to him. When God called to Moses from the burning bush and, later, re-deemed the Israelites from Egyptian bondage, it was all in keeping with and the fulfilment of that covenantal promise. Beginning with Genesis, it is evident that God, the Father, planned and initiated the redemption of his people.

2. The work of God the Son

Throughout these books of Moses, much of what we have seen typifies and illustrates the redemptive work of Jesus Christ, God the Son. The Passover, the Exodus, the giving of the manna, the smitten rock, the altar of sacrifice, the ministry of the high priest, the appointed feasts of Israel, and much more, all point to the person and work of Christ in purchasing the redemption of his people.

3. The work of God the Holy Spirit

As the children of Israel left Egypt, they were met at 'the edge of the unknown' by the visible presence of God — the Shekinah glory — God met them and went before them. He provided light for the Israelites while keeping the Egyptians in darkness. In spite of the disobedience and rebellion of the people, the presence of God remained with them throughout the forty years of wilderness wandering. Surely, this is typical of the work of God the Holy Spirit in guiding and leading his people. Even the great redemptive themes in these books suggest the roles of each of the persons in the Godhead.

The redemptive work of the triune God in the Pentateuch

Father Planned and initiated redemption	Genesis	Made his *covenant* with Abraham and *chose* a people for his name.
Son Purchased redemption	Exodus Leviticus	God's people *redeemed* from bondage. God's people brought into *communion* with God.
Spirit Applies redemption	Numbers Deuteronomy	God's *presence, provision, protection* and *guidance*. God's gracious *instruction* in his Word.

The corporate aspect of redemption

If any aspect is omitted or neglected, redemption is incomplete. While our redemption is planned, initiated, purchased and applied by God, that does not relieve us of responsibility. As I pointed out, Leviticus is the central book of the Pentateuch. Genesis and Exodus teach that redemption is due to God's gracious work alone. Numbers and Deuteronomy, on the other hand, teach the responsibility of those whom God has redeemed. Genesis and Exodus teach the *principles* of faith and obedience. Numbers and Deuteronomy reveal the *practice* of faith and obedience. Though God himself has planned, purchased and applied redemption, those who are redeemed are required to trust God with all their heart and to walk in obedience to his law. Leviticus, of course, stands in the middle and shows the basis and blessing of communion with God.

While God redeems his people individually, there is a corporate dimension which must not be overlooked. In the early days of my ministry, I was captivated by the book of Ephesians. For several months, I preached from that wonderful book everywhere I went – so much so that a dear old saint who could never remember my name referred to me as 'the man from Ephesus'! In my youthful zeal to make application of the truth to my personal life, I sometimes read Ephesians in the first person: 'Blessed be the God and Father ... who has blessed *me* ... just as he chose *me*...' To be sure, there was blessing in making that personal application, but one day the truth dawned on me that the book of Ephesians was not written to '*me*'; it was, rather, written to '*us*'.

The two paragraphs which constitute chapter 2 of that epistle show that our redemption has two important aspects. On the one hand, we 'who were dead in trespasses and sins' (v. 1) are made 'alive together with Christ' (v. 5). Through identification with Christ in his death, resurrection and exaltation, sinners are reconciled to God. As wonderful as that is, it is only one aspect of redemption. The second paragraph (vv. 11-22) shows that sinners, through the blood of the cross, are reconciled to God's people, 'the commonwealth of Israel,' and are no longer 'strangers [to] the covenants of promise' (v. 12). Those who are redeemed by the blood of Christ 'are no longer strangers and foreigners, but fellow citizens with the saints and members of the household of God' (v. 19). This corporate dimension of redemption is not merely desirable or optional; God's great purpose is to construct a living temple in which he himself dwells (vv. 20-22). While the books of Moses do not ignore God's work with individuals, the focus is on the corporate nature of redemption. Numbers, in particular, it will be remembered, emphasizes the importance of leadership, order and discipline. Hence, the importance of the corporate body of God's people is seen. The

church is the object of God's redemptive work: 'Christ ... loved
the church and gave himself for her' (Eph. 5:25).

As finite beings, it is not uncommon or unusual for us to
abandon tasks which we begin — a hobby is set aside because we
lack time or resources; the reading of a book is left unfinished
because of lost interest; or a job or marriage is abandoned
because it is undesirable or appears to have no future. Thank
God, he does not abandon what he begins (though judging by
human standards, he would have plenty of reasons to do so!)
What he begins, he carries to completion: '... being confident of
this very thing, that he who has begun a good work in you will
complete it' (Phil. 1:6). And his work is always 'very good'!

What effect does all this have on us?

Candidates running for political office these days often assure
the voters that they will not allow their personal beliefs to
influence their political decisions. Such claims appeal to the
gullible public because they sound unbiased and unprejudiced.
Those who make such claims, however, are either ignorant,
terribly naïve, or outright deceitful. While many people are
influenced by such claims, reporters and commentators don't
believe them; in the US, for example, everyone knows that the
choice of a president will determine what kind of justices will be
appointed to the Supreme Court. Of course a person's belief
affects his behaviour — creed can never be separated from
conduct! What an individual knows and believes will dictate
what he does. It is imperative, therefore, that we know the truth
concerning God. When that truth has been truly learned, it will
result in a permanent change of behaviour.

How, then, does the knowledge that we have gained from the
Pentateuch concerning God and his redemptive work affect and
change our behaviour? I want to conclude this chapter by asking
some pertinent questions for personal consideration and
practical application.

1. The effect on worship

How does the knowledge of the sovereignty of God, the power of God, the holiness of God, the goodness and severity of God and the faithfulness of God affect worship?

When I hear of skydivers dropping into times of worship, of clowns riding bicycles backwards down the church aisle, of preachers wearing baseball uniforms to mark the beginning of the baseball season, and many other novel activities, I fear that some churches, at least, have forgotten the meaning of worship. Such activities, which appear to be designed to attract and entertain people, would seem to be totally incongruous with the reverence and awe with which God should be approached. It is not only novel activities that are cause for concern; some churches have settled into dull, monotonous ritual (both formal and informal) which is equally tragic.

Should not the knowledge of our God cause us to prepare our hearts and minds in advance and to approach him with reverence and godly fear? Ought not praise of God through music be dignified – in keeping with his majestic holiness – and should it not express the loftiest thoughts possible? While posture is not always indicative of the condition of the heart, is it not appropriate to kneel before our Maker as an expression of adoration and to concur with the congregational petitions with a hearty 'Amen'? In public prayer, why is the 'Lord's Prayer' not used as the pattern for the content of prayer instead of a repetitious formality? Since the Bible is God's authoritative Word, should we not give careful attention to Scripture reading and to the exposition of it? Should we not be prepared to accept 'reproof and correction' as well as sound doctrine and 'instruction in righteousness'? (see 2 Tim. 3:16). In our giving, should we not bring our offerings cheerfully, regularly, consistently, proportionately and systematically – as the Scripture requires? (see 2 Cor. 9). Ought we not to respond in willing obedience to his commandments, in love for the brethren and in compassionate concern for those who are without God? The knowledge of God should result in greater love towards him and his people. It should make us more serious, more committed and determined to do his will and more desirous of closer communion with him.

2. The effect on prayer and the Christian's devotional life

How does the knowledge of God affect one's prayer and devotional life?

Having endured numerous church prayer meetings where the concerns and requests centred around the physical illnesses and unemployed status of various members of the congregation, I am convinced that this is another area where God's people need to examine themselves and make some radical changes. How does the knowledge that God is sovereign, powerful, holy, good, just and faithful affect our prayer?

The implications for our prayer life

God is sovereign	He is in complete control of all things and is able to do above and beyond anything we can ask or think (Eph. 3:20).
God is powerful	What God has promised, he will perform. There is no limitation to his power. Nothing is impossible with God. (see, e.g., Gen. 18:14; Matt. 19:26).
God is holy	Everything God does is governed by his righteous character; he is righteous in all his ways. 'Whate'er my God ordains is right; holy his will abideth.'[5] We can trust his judgement in all things — he never will deceive us.
God is good and just	This is cause for thanksgiving and praise. Both the blessing of his provision and the adversity of his chastisement are for our benefit and growth.
God is faithful	He answers the prayers of his people. He is true to his promises.

Much more could be said; the point is that the knowledge of who and what God is should affect our prayer significantly. If we were to use what is commonly called the 'Lord's Prayer' as a pattern for prayer instead of reciting it as a liturgy, our prayer would undoubtedly take on a new dynamic. What a privilege Christians have to be able to approach the sovereign God and address him as 'Father'! Recently, I visited a church in which the prayer meeting took on a fresh dynamic through the practical use of the Lord's Prayer; it was refreshing indeed, to hear and participate in prayers focused on the greatness and glory of God.

3. The effect on evangelism and missions

How does the knowledge of God affect evangelism and involvement in missions?

The knowledge of God should cause Christians to pray for the honour of 'thy name', the interests of 'thy kingdom' and the fulfilment of 'thy will' before asking for 'daily bread'. And, when petition is made for daily bread, the motive should be to have the physical strength and material resources to glorify God's name, advance his kingdom and do his will on earth. In other words, the knowledge of God brings the realization that our purpose on earth is to worship and serve him. Those who know God will make him known.

A missionary vision does not come by looking at missions any more than conviction of sin comes by looking at sin. Undoubtedly, there is nothing wrong with looking at missions; multitudes of young people take short-term trips and many of them make a worthwhile contribution – though some leaders have questioned whether the tremendous expense could not be used more effectively. Human need is great everywhere, but human need is not the primary motivational factor for missions; true missionary motivation comes from a personal knowledge of the 'Lord of the harvest'. To know him is to respond in love to him by obedience to his commission – and the response is not conditional or short-term!

Those who are called by the sovereign God know that they have been *sent* by the King of kings and Lord of lords. There is no greater task or privilege. As they face opposition and persecution in seeking to rescue the perishing from the dominion of Satan, they know that they are 'kept by the power of God' (1 Peter 1:5) and, therefore, are *safe*. Those who have learned that God is faithful depend on his promises knowing that their needs will be *supplied*: 'My God shall supply all your need according to his riches in glory by Christ Jesus' (Phil. 4:19). Those who know God do not take his blessings for granted but realize that God has blessed them so that they, in turn, might be a blessing to others. To know the majesty, glory and grace of God must create a desire to make him known!

4. The effect on the education of children

How does the knowledge of God affect the education of children?

One of the greatest tragedies in modern history was initiated, so I am told, in New Zealand. New Zealand was the first country to implement free, compulsory and secular education. A nation with such a rich Christian heritage should have known that any subject divorced from God loses its foundation, purpose and direction. If, as the Scripture affirms, the fear of the Lord is the beginning of knowledge and wisdom (Prov. 1:7; Ps. 111:10), education from which God is excluded becomes non-education or anti-education — it excludes the one foundational factor which gives education meaning and purpose. The fallacy and flaw of secular education has begun to be manifest in many educational institutions. Because education has divorced multitudes from their Maker, many have been left spiritually empty with a deep sense of personal alienation and purposelessness. They no longer know truth from falsehood, right from wrong, or good from bad. Their belief, or lack of it, has resulted in corruption, immorality and violence. Social disintegration is the inevitable result — and it is taking place at an accelerating pace!

For education to be Christian, every subject must be circum-scribed by, and permeated with, the knowledge of God — not just secular subjects with a few Scripture verses added and taught in a morally positive context! The purpose of true Christian education is to teach children the biblical world view so that they do not think in terms of worldly success, material prosperity, or personal comfort. It is to teach them to think and work in terms of eternity for the glory of God.

5. The implications for the way we live

How does the knowledge of God affect the issues of everyday life?

While teaching an adult Sunday School class, a friend of mine found himself embarrassed; he had made two columns on the blackboard and asked the class to enumerate characteristics of worldly people. The class responded by citing such things as materialism, pleasure-seeking, selfishness, pride, greed, and the like. In the other column, he began to list characteristics of Christians. The class members admitted that they too were materialistic, that they sought pleasure, were selfish, proud and greedy. The two columns were practically identical and he did not know what to do. On Monday morning, he came to my office and asked, 'What *is* the difference?' Tragically, the lifestyle of many professing Christians these days does not reflect biblical values or priorities. Sadly, not many are willing to sacrifice comfort, time, resources, or life, to fulfil the purpose for which God has left his people on this earth. Surely, if God is all that he has declared and demonstrated himself to be, he deserves the best!

My eldest daughter is married to a fine Christian man who has a good job with excellent fringe benefits. While they are not wealthy, they enjoy a comfortable life. Some time ago, she said to me, 'We have everything we need. We have a good income, adequate insurance and a comfortable home. When I go to the store, I really don't need to look at the price; if we need it, I buy it. If anything were to happen to my husband, I would be a wealthy widow. All the bases are covered; we do not have to trust the Lord for any practical need.' And then she added, 'I miss those times when we didn't know where our next meal was coming from and we had to depend on the Lord to provide the necessities of life or get us out of what appeared to us to be an impossible situation.' It is a wonderful experience to see the Lord send ravens with food because it reveals, not only his ability, but also his loving care. He never fails!

In Western society, at least, many Christians, it seems, know little, or nothing, about trusting God in daily circumstances or for practical needs. Even Christian organizations, institutions and mission agencies depend more on 'legal tender', it seems, than on the Lord in financial and practical matters. Christians must not be presumptuous or reckless, of course; they must, however, learn to prove the sufficiency of the Lord. Perhaps one reason why many churches adopt the 'Faith Promise Plan' in missions is because this is the only way some can prove the reality and goodness of God in providing above and beyond what can reasonably be expected. Those who know him know that he is trustworthy; he never fails!

Besides trusting the Lord for physical and material needs, many people experience times of crisis in which they need to know God's presence and prove his power and goodness. Recently, two popular Christian psychologists were discussing people's problems on the radio; at one point, they heartily agreed that Christians who experience grief or adversity of one kind or another must learn to forgive God. While that idea might appeal to carnal men, it reveals all too plainly an unbiblical and pathetic concept of God. To suggest that God needs to be forgiven implies that he is not righteous in all his ways, that he offends his people and that he has done wrong. How has God offended his creatures that he needs to be forgiven? Job's knowledge of God was limited, but he knew better than that. He declared, 'Though he slay me, yet will I trust him' (Job 13:15). With David, he knew that 'As for God, his way is perfect' (Ps.

18:30). Those who know that God is sovereign, powerful, righteous, faithful, just and good know that they can trust his judgement in every circumstance; they know that they can commit their lives into his hands with confidence knowing that he has all things under control. As I stated at the outset, we need to get to know God in this, the day of opportunity, before the day of adversity comes when our faith is tested. We need, therefore, to ask ourselves, 'How well do we know God? Would our knowledge of God carry us through difficult times of testing, trial, or persecution? Would the knowledge of God sustain us if we were taken to the gallows for our faith?' A true knowledge of God will affect every aspect of life profoundly.

Are we known by God?

When John Bunyan concluded his great allegory, *Pilgrim's Progress*, he did not end with Christian entering the Celestial City and his welcome by the King. The final scene depicts a man named Ignorance crossing the river with very little difficulty because Vain-hope, the ferryman, was there to help him over. Ignorance approached the city presuming that he would be welcomed with open arms; instead, he was taken and cast out. Bunyan concludes by saying, 'Then I saw that there was a way to Hell even from the gates of Heaven, as well as from the City of Destruction.' In other words, while we need to get to know God, we need also to make sure that God knows us. As our Lord warned in his Sermon on the Mount, on the Day of Judgement many will claim to belong to him and tell of all the wonderful works they have done for him, but he will declare, 'I never knew you; depart from me' (Matt. 7:23).

What a difference the knowledge of God makes! What a glorious day it will be when 'the earth shall be full of the knowledge of the LORD as the waters cover the sea'! (Isa. 11:9). O Lord, be pleased to hasten that great day!

19.
'Beginning with Moses'
Christ in the Pentateuch

When young men appear before presbytery for examination for ordination, one of my favourite questions is based on the occasion when Jesus walked the road to Emmaus with those two perplexed disciples on the evening of his resurrection. The disciples had failed to recognize him and were surprised that he seemed to be unaware of the events which had taken place in Jerusalem. I remind the candidates that Luke tells us that Jesus said, 'O foolish ones, and slow of heart to believe in all that the prophets have spoken! Ought not the Christ to have suffered these things and to enter into his glory? And *beginning at Moses* ... he expounded to them in all the Scriptures the things concerning himself' (Luke 24:25-27, emphasis mine).

My question is: 'What do you think Jesus might have told them about himself from the writings of Moses?' This question does not appear on any of the lists of topics that young men generally study in preparation for ordination; often it catches them by surprise and they do not know how to answer. I do not ask the question to confuse them, or to make the examination difficult; I ask it because it is a fair question and it reveals a lot about their acquaintance with, and understanding of, the foundational books of the Bible. Every minister of the gospel should be well acquainted with the answer. What do the books of Moses teach concerning Christ?

Before considering the answer, I want to turn to some other references in the New Testament to show that this is not an isolated comment. As if to reinforce the point, Luke repeats it. Jesus had revealed himself to the disciples, ate with them, and then said, 'These are the words which I spoke to you while I was still with you, that all things must be fulfilled which were *written in the Law of Moses* and the Prophets and the Psalms *concerning me*' (Luke 24:44, emphasis mine).

In other words, every part of the Old Testament reveals the Lord Jesus Christ. Our Lord had expounded the Old Testament to his disciples while he was with them; now, Luke tells us, 'He opened their understanding, that they might comprehend the Scriptures. Then he said to them, "Thus it is written, and thus it was necessary for the Christ to suffer and to rise from the dead the third day"' (Luke 24:45-46). The inference is that the Old Testament Scriptures concern the death and resurrection of our Lord.

The apostle John records the calling of Nathanael. 'Philip,' we are told, 'found Nathanael and said to him, "We have found him of whom *Moses in the law*, and also the prophets, wrote — Jesus of Nazareth"' (John 1:45, emphasis mine). Philip was aware of the fact that Moses had written of the Messiah.

John records also the occasion when Jesus was censored by the Jews for healing a blind man on the Sabbath. Our Lord responded by saying, 'Do not think that I shall accuse you to the Father; there is one who accuses you — Moses, in whom you trust. For if you believed Moses, you would believe me; for *he wrote about me*. But if you do not believe his writings, how will you believe my words?' (John 5:45-47, emphasis mine).

Similarly, in his defence before King Agrippa, the apostle Paul said, 'To this day I stand, witnessing both to small and great, saying no other things than those which the prophets and *Moses said* would come — *that the Christ would suffer*' (Acts

26:22-23, emphasis mine). Paul said that what he was preaching
was no new doctrine; it was precisely what Moses had taught.

And, finally, in the last recorded occasion of Paul's ministry,
he was under house arrest in Rome. We are told that many
people 'came to him at his lodging, to whom he explained and
solemnly testified of the kingdom of God, persuading them
concerning Jesus from both the Law of Moses and the Prophets,
from morning till evening' (Acts 28:23, emphasis mine). Why
didn't the apostle turn to the book of Romans? It had been
written long before his imprisonment in Rome and it explains
the gospel comprehensively and systematically. Why did he go
back to Moses and the prophets? He did so because the Old
Testament is foundational to our faith. We cannot understand
fully the meaning and significance of the person and work of the
Lord Jesus Christ if we do not begin with the writings of Moses.

What do we find concerning Christ in the Pentateuch?
Actually, there is so much to discuss that our treatment will be a
survey, at best; I have simply listed and categorized some of the
most obvious matters. More excellent detailed works on the
subject are available. While I have to be selective, there are not
many passages which do not refer to the Lord Jesus in some way.

I. Direct prophecies concerning Christ

Genesis 3:15

Immediately after the fall of Adam and Eve, God said to Satan:

> ... I will put enmity
> Between you and the woman,
> And between your seed and her Seed;
> He shall bruise your head,
> And you shall bruise his heel.

This is the first ray of hope for disobedient, rebellious man; the deliverer will crush the head of the serpent but, in doing so, his heel will be bruised. The first word concerning the Redeemer involves conflict and suffering. In this context, we are told that '... for Adam and his wife the LORD God made tunics of skin, and clothed them' (Gen. 3:21). That meant, of course, that animals had to be slain.

In his discussion of the sacrifices of Leviticus, Andrew Bonar says, 'We cannot but believe that these fuller institutions in Leviticus are just the expansion of what Adam first received... If so, may we not say that the child Jesus, wrapped in his swaddling clothes, was, in these ceremonies, laid down at the gate of Eden?'[1]

Jesus was the 'Lamb slain from the foundation of the world' (Rev. 13:8) — we should not be surprised to find him announced to Adam and portrayed in the sacrificial victim at the gate of the garden.

Genesis 12:1-3

In the course of his great redemptive plan, God called Abraham and promised that in him 'all the families of the earth [would] be blessed'. As we have seen previously, when God gave that promise to Abraham, he preached 'the gospel' to him (Gal. 3:8). That same passage says that when God spoke of blessing the nations through the seed of Abraham, he was specifically referring to Christ. According to the book of Revelation, when all things are accomplished, a great multitude of people from every tribe, family, people and tongue will be gathered around the throne worshipping the Lamb (Rev. 5:9; 7:9). What God promised Abraham, he will accomplish and fulfil. God has one great eternal plan centred in the person and work of his Son, Jesus Christ.

Genesis 49:10

God revealed to Jacob that:

> The sceptre shall not depart from Judah,
> Nor a lawgiver from between his feet,
> Until Shiloh comes;
> And to him shall be the obedience of the people.

Some scholars believe that the word 'Shiloh' means 'Man of peace'. The hope of Israel that Messiah would come from the tribe of Judah began with this promise.

Deuteronomy 18:18

God told Moses, 'I will raise up for [Israel] a prophet like you from among their brethren, and will put my words in his mouth, and he shall speak to them all that I command him.' There were many Hebrew prophets that came after Moses but none was recognized as the fulfilment of this promise until John the Baptist appeared. The priests and Levites asked John, '"Are you *the* prophet?" And he answered, "No!"'' (John 1:21, emphasis mine). John announced Jesus, however, as 'the Lamb of God who takes away the sin of the world' (John 1:29).

Later, when Jesus stepped from the crowd on the great day of the feast and declared, 'If anyone thirsts, let him come to me and drink' (John 7:37), some of the people said, 'Truly this is *the Prophet*' (John 7:40, emphasis mine). In his triumphal entry into Jerusalem, the multitudes said, 'This is Jesus, *the prophet*' (Matt. 21:11, emphasis mine). The people understood that the promise given to Moses referred to someone greater than Elijah, Isaiah and all the other prophets.

2. The Mosaic system

The law

The moral law of God is exceedingly important because it is basic to everything. Justification, for example, is based on justice; divine justice must be fully satisfied for sinners to stand before God but there can be no justice if there is no law. Several passages of Scripture tie the Lawgiver to the Saviour (e.g., Isa. 33:22; James 4:12). Jesus gave the law, he kept the law, he died under the law and he will judge according to the law. As he himself declared, he did not come to do away with the law but to fulfil it (Matt. 5:17).

'When the fulness of the time had come, God sent forth his Son, born of a woman, born *under the law,* to redeem those who were under the law, that we might receive the adoption as sons' (Gal. 4:4-5, emphasis mine).

Our Lord lived a sinless life and thereby kept all the requirements of the law on our behalf. On the cross, he paid the penalty for the broken law in our place. He fully satisfied all the demands of the law for us.

The tabernacle, priesthood and sacrifices

The tabernacle, the priesthood and the sacrifices were a 'copy and shadow of the heavenly things' (Heb. 8:5). Moses was instructed to be precise in making the tabernacle exactly as God had prescribed. Similarly, the details of the sacrifices and the function of the priests in the sanctuary were to be carried out exactly according to God's instructions.

Since the sacrifices and the priesthood were discussed briefly in the overview of Leviticus, it is not necessary to repeat that material. I want to re-emphasize the point, however, that the *only* acceptable way to approach God in all his majesty and purity is on the basis of an appropriate sacrifice and through the mediation of an acceptable high priest. Jesus Christ has offered up himself 'a sacrifice to satisfy divine justice, and reconcile us to God'.[2] Because we have 'a great High Priest who has passed through the heavens', we may 'come boldly to the throne of grace' (Heb. 4:14,16). He is now seated at the right hand of God where 'he always lives to make intercession for [us]' (Heb. 7:25). That is, he pleads the case of those who embrace him by faith on the basis of his righteous life and substitutionary sacrifice. All his work is ended; it is complete. 'It is finished!' It is little wonder that Jesus instructed those disciples on the road to Emmaus from Moses and showed them that it was necessary for the Christ to suffer these things and to enter into his glory.

3. Events in the Pentateuch

Creation and the Flood

The similarity of the first verse of Genesis to that of the Gospel of John is unmistakable. It appears as though John had the creation in mind as he takes his reader through a series of successive days in the ministry of Jesus. John understood that the work of creation and the work of redemption have many parallels. At the outset, he says that the Word, the Lord Jesus, was involved in the work of creation: 'All things were made through him, and without him nothing was made that was made' (John 1:3). Our Lord was actively involved in creation. It is worthy of note also that the apostle Peter relates Noah and the Flood to our salvation and the judgement to come (1 Peter 3:18-20; 2 Peter 2:5). Jesus himself related his Second Coming to the days of Noah (Matt. 24:37; Luke 17:26-27).

The Passover

As we have seen previously, the institution of the Passover was the beginning of a new life for ancient Israel. When the shed blood was applied to the door of the house, the angel of death passed by God's people. The Passover anticipated and illustrated the work of Christ whereby we enter into new life. The apostle Paul makes a direct identification; he says, 'Christ, our Passover, was sacrificed for us. Therefore let us keep the feast, not with old leaven, nor with the leaven of malice and wickedness, but with the unleavened bread of sincerity and truth' (1 Cor. 5:7).

The Exodus

God took his people to the edge of the Red Sea, where they were trapped between the armies of Pharaoh and the sea; they were in a hopeless predicament. Moses told the people to 'Stand still, and see the salvation of the LORD, which he will accomplish for you today' (Exod. 14:13). On that occasion, God's presence was light to his people and darkness to the Egyptians. God opened the sea and they marched through as on dry ground. Throughout the Old Testament, that great deliverance was recognized as the salvation of his people. The psalmist says:

> He saved them for the his name's sake,
> That he might make his mighty power known...
> And redeemed them from the hand of the enemy
> (Ps. 106:8,10).

Their salvation could not be attributed to the wisdom or ingenuity of man, but solely to the power and mercy of God. What a graphic picture it is of our redemption through the work of Jesus Christ on Calvary!

The manna and the rock

Having entered into the wilderness, the Israelites were hungry and grumbled against the Lord; Moses and Aaron told them that 'In the morning you shall see the glory of the LORD' (Exod. 16:7). Next morning, they found manna on the ground like frost. They did not know what it was, however; Moses told them, 'This is the bread which the LORD has given you to eat' (Exod. 16:15). They were to gather according to their need. For the forty years in the wilderness, the manna was given daily in abundance; there was plenty for all.

In his discourse on the bread of life, Jesus said, '*I am the bread of life*. He who comes to me shall never hunger... *I am the bread* which came down from heaven... *I am the bread of life*. Your fathers ate the manna in the wilderness, and are dead. This is *the bread* which comes down from heaven, that one may eat of it and not die. *I am the living bread* which came down from heaven. If anyone eats of *this bread*, he will live for ever; and the bread that I shall give is my flesh, which I shall give for the life of the world' (John 6:35,41,48-51, emphasis mine).

To reinforce this truth, Jesus took bread at the Last Supper and said to his disciples, 'This is my body which is broken for you' (1 Cor. 11:24). In giving instructions concerning the observance of the Lord's Supper, the apostle Paul says, 'As often as you eat this bread and drink this cup, you proclaim the Lord's death till he comes' (1 Cor. 11:26). As wheat is ground into flour to make bread, our Lord's body was broken to provide life and sustenance for us. As bread provides nourishment for the body, so our Lord is essential to the nourishment of the soul.

Following the account of the giving of manna in Exodus 16, the Israelites encamped at Rephidim but there was no water. Again they grumbled. God said to Moses, 'Go on before the people, and take with you some of the elders of Israel. Also take in your hand your rod with which you struck the river, and go. Behold, I will stand before you there on the rock in Horeb; and you shall strike the rock, and water will come out of it, that the people may drink' (Exod. 17:5-6).

Those ancient Israelites 'all drank the same spiritual drink. For they drank of that spiritual Rock that followed them, and *that Rock was Christ*' (1 Cor. 10:4, emphasis mine). The giving of the manna and the smiting of the rock are in successive chapters in Exodus; significantly, they are found in successive chapters in John's Gospel also. In his discourse on the bread of life Jesus declared, 'I am the bread of life. He who comes to me shall never hunger' (John 6:35). In the next chapter, Jesus stepped from the crowd on the great day of the feast and declared, 'If anyone thirsts, let him come to me and drink' (John 7:37). Those Old Testament events pointed to the Saviour who came to give us life, to nourish and satisfy the hunger and thirst of our souls. As we watch a world that is growing more and more desperate for something to satisfy the soul, how important and urgent it is that we direct them to the bread of life and the water of life! Our Lord alone is able to satisfy the hunger of the soul and quench one's spiritual thirst.

The brass serpent

After spending forty years of wilderness wandering, the new generation of Israelites were anxious to possess the land. Hence, they launched an attack against the King of Arad. Overall it was a successful campaign but some Israelites were captured (Num. 21:1). Having gained the victory, however, they became impatient. Again, they complained against God and Moses because all they had to eat was manna and there was no water. They had not learned to trust the Lord or to be content with his provision.

Because of their complaining, the Lord sent a plague of serpents; a large number of people were bitten and many people died. 'The people came to Moses, and said, "We have sinned, for we have spoken against the LORD and against you; pray to the LORD that he take away the serpents from us." So Moses prayed for the people. Then the LORD said to Moses, "Make a

fiery serpent, and set it on a pole; and it shall be that everyone
who is bitten, when he looks at it, shall live' (Num. 21:7-8).

James says that 'No man can tame the tongue. It is a unruly
evil, full of deadly poison' (James 3:8). In other words, the
tongue is like the bite of a serpent. In all of God's dealings with
sin, the punishment is always appropriate to the offence. And
how appropriate the remedy is! Jesus said to Nicodemus, 'As
Moses lifted up the serpent in the wilderness, even so must the
Son of man be lifted up' (John 3:14). That old serpent, the devil,
is the author of sin; he beguiled and deceived Eve. As a result,
the plague of sin is upon the whole race. When our Lord was
nailed to that cross by wicked hands, he 'who knew no sin
[became] sin for us'. On that cross, he bore our sins in his body
'that we might become the righteousness of God in him' (2 Cor.
5:21).

The nomination of the cities of refuge

While the cities of refuge were not established until the land had
been occupied, Moses declared that six of the forty-eight cities
settled by Levites were to be designated as places of refuge (Num.
35:9-15). The three cities east of the Jordan river are named in
Deuteronomy 4:41-43. All six cities are identified in Joshua
20:7-8 as:

Western
    Kadesh — 'Holy'
    Shechem — 'Shoulder'
    Hebron — 'Company'

Eastern
    Golan — 'Circle'
    Ramoth — 'Height'
    Bezer — 'Strong'

These cities were evenly distributed throughout the land and the roads leading to them were to be kept free of obstacles or obstructions which might hinder or injure a person who was fleeing for his life. These cities were a place of safety, they were free and they were near. If a person had committed murder, he was to be tried and, if found guilty, executed. If he were guilty of involuntary manslaughter, he could remain in the city of refuge until the death of the high priest. Evidently, the psalmist had the city of refuge in mind when he wrote, 'God is our refuge and strength, a very present help in trouble' (Ps. 46:1). The author of Hebrews applies the city of refuge to Christ when he speaks of those 'who have fled for refuge to lay hold of the hope set before us' (Heb. 6:18).

These are some of the events which our Lord could have discussed as he walked with those two perplexed disciples to Emmaus. One other area needs to be mentioned.

4. People

Joseph

A little book written for children which I treasure greatly is entitled, *Joseph and a Greater than Joseph* by Wallace Guilford.[3] After the narration of events in Joseph's life, Guilford concludes each chapter by drawing parallels between Joseph and Christ. It is a fascinating and profitable little book. The life of Joseph illustrates the life of our Lord in numerous ways. He was, for example, loved by his father and hated by his brothers. After being subjected to humiliation and life in Egypt, he finally emerged as the ruler. He saved his brethren and gave them an inheritance far beyond what they deserved.

344 KnowKnow your God

Moses

As we have seen from Deuteronomy 18, Moses was the greatest
of the Old Testament prophets. He was more than a prophet,
however. A prophet is one who represents God to the people.
On more than one occasion, Moses acted as a priest in repre-
senting the people before God; he was their mediator. Probably
the greatest occasion of intercession, apart from that of our Lord,
is found in Exodus 32. Moses had been up on Mt Sinai receiving the law; while he was gone, the people made the golden calf,
worshipped it and declared it to be the god that had delivered
them from Egyptian bondage. What an offence that was to the
wisdom, power and holiness of God! Indeed, their offence
against God was so great that he threatened to destroy them.
Moses, however, pleaded for them. This is one of the most
remarkable passages of Scripture in that Moses could not finish
his prayer – he was lost for words and the sentence is unfinished: 'If you will forgive their sin...' (Exod. 32:32). Moses
offered to bear the penalty of their sin himself; he said, '... but if
not, I pray, blot me out of your book which you have written' –
what a graphic picture he is of our Lord Jesus!

Aaron

In answer to the question, 'How does Christ execute the office of
a priest?' the *Shorter Catechism* says, 'Christ executes the office of
a priest, in his once offering up of himself a sacrifice to satisfy
divine justice, and reconcile us to God; and in making continual
intercession for us.'[4]
    According to Hebrews, Christ, as our great High Priest, has
'offered one sacrifice for sins for ever' (Heb. 10:12). The function of the Old Testament priesthood was never ended, of
course, 'For it is not possible that the blood of bulls and goats
could take away sins' (Heb. 10:4). Having offered a perfect
sacrifice, the Lord Jesus 'sat down at the right hand of God'
(Heb. 10:12). His work was complete and fully accomplished.

The office and function of the high priest included intercession; he represented people before God. Seated at God's right hand, Christ now makes continual intercession for his people. While Moses was frequently on his face before the Lord interceding for the people, Aaron also pleaded with God on their behalf; possibly the most dramatic occasion is recorded in Numbers 16. The people murmured against the punishment of Korah, Dathan and Abiram, and God threatened to destroy them. Moses told Aaron to take a censer with fire from the altar, put incense on it and go quickly among the people to make atonement for them and stop the plague. Aaron, we are told, ran with the incense and stood between the living and the dead and the plague stopped. The burned incense, says Matthew Henry, was 'not to purify the infected air, but to pacify an offended God'.[5] Aaron was a type of Christ, who came into the world to make an atonement for sin and to turn away the wrath of God from us and who, by his mediation and intercession, stands between the living and the dead.[6]

Isaac

One can scarcely imagine that Jesus failed to direct the attention of those disciples to Isaac. Like the Saviour, Isaac was a miracle child; Sarah was past the age of childbearing. Of particular importance, however, is the occasion when God told Abraham to take his son Isaac and offer him as a sacrifice on Mt Moriah (Gen. 22). (Incidentally, and significantly, Mt Moriah was the site where the temple was built later — and where the Mosque of Omar stands today!) As Abraham was about to offer Isaac, God directed his attention to a ram caught in the bushes. When he had offered the sacrifice, Abraham named the altar 'Jehovah-Jireh', which means, 'The Lord will provide.' Abraham learned the principle of substitution. What God spared Abraham, however, he did not spare himself. 'He ... did not spare his own Son, but delivered him up for us all' (Rom. 8:32).

Know your God

While the discovery of the truth concerning the sovereignty of
God, the power of God, the holiness of God, the goodness and
severity of God and the faithfulness of God is tremendously
important, it must never be forgotten that there is an important
difference between knowing *about* God and knowing God
personally. The only way to know God is through Jesus Christ;
he is the full, final and complete revelation of God. 'No one has
seen God at any time. The only begotten Son ... has [revealed]
him' (John 1:18). The books of Moses not only provide the
foundational truth concerning the being and character of God;
they also reveal how God is known personally. When the Lord
Jesus came to this world, no one who knew the writings of
Moses should have failed to recognize him; everything pointed to
him. The problem was not with the revelation, of course, but
with the blindness of men's eyes and the hardness of their
hearts. God revealed his Son so fully and completely because he
is the only hope of eternal life. After those two perplexed disciples had their eyes opened to recognize Jesus, '... they said to
one another, "Did not our heart burn within us while he talked
with us on the road, and while he opened the Scriptures to us?" '
(Luke 24:32).

In an age when many professing Christians have been
influenced greatly by the culture and, as a result, fail to understand the uniqueness and exclusiveness of Jesus Christ, the need
to 'know your God' is urgent. While the Scriptures teach us
many things about God, ultimately, the only way to know him in
a personal way is through Jesus Christ. Truly, 'This is eternal
life, [to] know you, the only true God, and Jesus Christ whom
you have sent' (John 17:3).

Notes

Introduction
1. *Westminster Shorter Catechism*, Question 1.
2. Matthew Henry, *Matthew Henry's Commentary on the Whole Bible* (Fleming H. Revell Company, Old Tappen, New Jersey, n. d.), vol. II, p.326.
3. Gene Edward Veith, 'Forbidding Evangelism', *World* Magazine, 5 June 1999, pp.24-5.
4. Henry, *Commentary*, vol. I, p.112.

Chapter 1 — God's own introduction to his Word
1. Francis Schaeffer, *Genesis in Space and Time* (Intervarsity Press, Downer's Grove, IL, 1972), p.9.
2. *Westminster Shorter Catechism*, Question 1.
3. *Ibid.*, Question 16.
4. Henry, *Commentary*, vol. I, p.28.
5. *Ibid.*, p.43.
6. John Hardon, *The Catholic Catechism; a Contemporary Catechism of the Teachings of the Catholic Church* (Doubleday, NY, 1975) p.100.
7. See, for example, Harvey Cox, The *Secular City* (MacMillan, Old Tappen, NJ, 1990).
8. Malachi Martin, *The Keys of This Blood; the Struggle for World Dominion between Mikhail Gorbachev and the Capitalist West* (Simon & Schuster, NY, 1990).
9. From Charles Wesley's hymn, 'Love Divine, All Loves Excelling'.

Chapter 2 — The sovereignty of God in his work of creation
1. Quoted by R. C. Sproul in *Not a Chance* (Baker Books, Grand Rapids, 1994) p.177.
2. Sproul, *Not a Chance*, p.177.
3. D. L. Moody, *Notes from my Bible* (Morgan and Scott, London, n. d.), p.8.
4. Linleigh J. Roberts, *Let Us Make Man* (Banner of Truth, Edinburgh, 1986).
5. *Westminster Shorter Catechism*, Question 6.
6. *Ibid.*, Question 4.
7. *Ibid.*, Question 9.
8. Moody, *Notes from my Bible*, p.8.
9. *Westminster Shorter Catechism*, Question 1

Chapter 3 — The sovereignty of God in his works of providence
1. Colin Brown, *Philosophy of the Christian Faith* (Tyndale Press, London, 1969), p.75.
2. Warren Young, *A Christian Approach to Philosophy* (Van Kampen Press, Inc., Wheaton, 1954), p.210.
3. B. G. Ranganthan, *Origins* (Banner of Truth, Edinburgh, 1988).
4. Rabbi Kushner, *When Bad Things Happen to Good People* (Avon Publishers, New York, 1981).
5. Francis Schaeffer, *How Should we then Live?* (Fleming H. Revell Company, Old Tappen, New Jersey, 1976), pp.194-6.
6. *Westminster Shorter Catechism*, Question 11.
7. A. W Pink, *Gleanings From Genesis* (Moody Press, Chicago, n. d.), p.145.
8. *Ibid.*, p.142
9. Griffith Thomas, *Genesis* (Grand Rapids: Wm B. Eerdmans Publishing Co., 1969), p.238.
10. Henry, *Commentary*, vol. I, p.48.
11. *Ibid.*, p.65.
12. *Ibid.*
13. *Ibid.*, p.109.
14. Thomas Watson, *The Lord's Prayer* (London: Banner of Truth Trust, 1962), p.167.
15. John Flavel, *The Mystery of Providence* (Edinburgh: Banner of Truth Trust, 1963), Part III, ch. 11.
16. *Ibid.*, p.182.

Chapter 4 — The sovereignty of God in choosing his people
1. *Westminster Shorter Catechism*, Question 19.
2. *Ibid.*, Question 20.
3. *Ibid.*

Chapter 5 — The power of God in judgement
1. Caroline Jones, *The Search for Meaning, Book Two* (Australian Broadcasting Corporation, Crow's Nest, NSW, 1990), p.xii.
2. Maurice Roberts, *The Thought of God* (Banner of Truth Trust, Edinburgh, 1993), p.215.
3. Henry, *Commentary*, vol. I, p.302.
4. *Ibid.*, p.291.
5. *Ibid.*, p.307.
6. *Ibid.*, p.308.
7. *Ibid.*, p.302.
8. *Ibid.*, p.302.
9. *Ibid.*, p.308.
10. *Ibid.*, p.310.

Chapter 6 — The power of God in redemption
1. Maurice Roberts, *The Thought of God*, p.104.
2. Henry, *Commentary*, vol. V, p.1137.

3. *Ibid.*, vol. I, p.318.
4. *Ibid.*, p.320
5. *Ibid.*, p.318.
6. *Ibid.*, p.319.
7. *Ibid.*, p.320.
8. *Ibid.*, p.321.
9. *Ibid.*, p.328.
10. *Ibid.*, p.329.
11. *Ibid.*, vol. II, p.16.
12. Author unknown.
13. Arthur W. Pink, *Gleanings in Exodus* (Moody Press, Chicago, n. d.), p.107.
14. Henry, *Commentary*, vol. I, p.318.

Chapter 7 — The power of God in revelation
1. Henry, *Commentary*, vol. I, p.358.
2. Pink, *Gleanings in Exodus*, p.154.
3. *Ibid.*, p.155.
4. A. W Tozer, *Knowledge of the Holy* (San Francisco: Harper and Row, Publishers, 1985), p.1.
5. *Ibid.*, p.7.
6. Henry, *Commentary*, vol. I, p.358.
7. *Ibid.*, p.363.
8. *Ibid.*
9. *Westminster Confession of Faith*, Chapter 19, Pt 4.
10. John Newton, *Letters of John Newton* (Banner of Truth Trust, London, 1960), p.40.
11. *Westminster Shorter Catechism*, Question 3.

Chapter 8 — The power of God's presence
1. *Westminster Shorter Catechism*, Question 3.
2. Pink, *Gleanings in Exodus*, p.180.
3. Henry, *Commentary*, vol. I, p.383.
4. See for example, W. G. Moorehead's, *The Tabernacle* (Kregel Publications, Grand Rapids, 1957).
5. Pink, *Gleanings in Exodus*, p.190.
6. Linleigh J. Roberts, *Let Us Make Man*, chapter 14.
7. Henry, *Commentary*, vol. III, p.410.
8. *Ibid.*
9. *Westminster Shorter Catechism*, Question 1.
10. Pink, *Gleanings in Exodus*, p.181.
11. Vern Poythress, *The Shadow of Christ in the Law of Moses* (Wolgemuth & Hyatt, Publishers, Inc., Brentwood, Tennessee, 1991), p.10.
12. Henry, *Commentary*, vol. I, p.422.

Chapter 9 — The barrier to communion with God
1. Newton, *Letters*, p.40

2. J. I. Packer, *Among God's Giants* (Eastbourne: Kingsway Publications, 1991), p.389.
3. *Westminster Shorter Catechism*, Question 14.
4. *Ibid.*, Question 18.
5. *Westminster Larger Catechism*, Question 150.
6. *Ibid.*, Question 151.
7. *Westminster Shorter Catechism*, Question 19.
8. See chapter 2, note 4 for details.
9. G. Campbell Morgan, *The Answers of Jesus to Job* (Westwood, NJ: Fleming H. Revell Company, 1967), p.26.
10. The title of Jonathan Edwards' famous sermon.

Chapter 10 — The basis for communion with God
1. *Westminster Shorter Catechism*, Question 19.
2. *Ibid.*, Question 20.
3. Henry, *Commentary*, vol. I, p.449.
4. Andrew A. Bonar, *A Commentary on Leviticus* (The Banner of Truth Trust, London, 1966 [first published 1846]).
5. *New Trinity Hymnal* (Great Commission Publishing), p.246.
6. Henry, *Commentary*, p.498.
7. *Trinity Hymnal*, No. 127.
8. *Westminster Shorter Catechism*, Question 25.
9. Henry, *Commentary*, vol. I, p.489.
10. *Ibid.*, p.490.
11. *New Trinity Hymnal*, No. 305.

Chapter 11 — The blessing of communion with God
1. *Westminster Shorter Catechism*, Question 4.
2. *Ibid.*, Question 1.
3. Henry, *Commentary*, vol. I, p.539
4. *Ibid.*
5. *Ibid.*
6. *Ibid.*, p.552.
7. *Ibid.*, p.553
8. *Westminster Shorter Catechism*, Question 4.

Chapter 12 — The importance of leadership, order and discipline
1. *Westminster Shorter Catechism*, Question 4.
2. John Bunyan, *The Pilgrim's Progress* (Barbour Publishing, Inc., Uhrichsville, Ohio, 1985), p.46.
3. *Ibid.*, p.25
4. Gordon Keddie, *According to Promise* (Evangelical Press, Darlington, 1992), p.17.

Chapter 13 — The importance of faith and obedience
1. John Calvin, *Commentaries on the Last Four Books of Moses*, vol. 2, p.449.
2. Henry, *Commentary*, vol. I, p.606.

3. *Ibid.*, p.607.
4. *Ibid.*, p.622.
5. *Ibid.*, p.624.
6. *Ibid.*, p.630.
7. *Ibid.*, p.658.
8. *News & Views*, McKenzie Study Center, February 1998, vol. 15, No. 2.

Chapter 14 — Serious challenges to faith
1. *Westminster Shorter Catechism*, Question 18.
2. George Bush, *Notes on Numbers* (James & Klock Publishing Co, Minneapolis, 1976), p.231.
3. Henry, *Commentary*, vol. I, p.259.
4. *Ibid.*, p.639.
5. *Ibid.*, p.642.
6. *Ibid.*, p.639.
7. *Bush, Notes on Numbers*, p.237.
8. *Henry, Commentary*, vol. I, p.643.
9. Bush, *Notes on Numbers*, p.234.
10. Bunyan, *Pilgrim's Progress*, p.26.
11. Henry, *Commentary*, vol. I, p.661.
12. *Ibid.*, p.674.
13. *Ibid.*, p.687.
14. *Westminster Shorter Catechism*, Question 4.

Chapter 15 — God's faithfulness in keeping his covenant
1. Edmund Clowney, *The Unfolding Mystery* (P & R Publishing, Phillipsburg, NJ, 1988), p.89.
2. Henry, *Commentary*, vol. I, p.765.
3. Campbell Morgan, *The Messages of the Books of the Bible* (Hodder and Stoughton, London, n. d.), vol. 1, p.94.
4. O. T. Allis, *God Spake by Moses* (Presbyterian & Reformed Publishing Company, 1951), p.129.
5. Henry, *Commentary*, vol. I, p.726.
6. Quoted by Ravi Zacharias, *Deliver us from Evil* (Word Publishing, Dallas, 1996) p.xvii.
7. Allis, *God Spake by Moses*, p.130.
8. Sidlow Baxter, *Explore the Book* (Zondervan Publishing House, Grand Rapids, 1967), vol. 1, p.212.
9. Morgan, *The Messages of the Books of the Bible*, p.92, emphasis mine.
10. Henry, *Commentary*, vol. I, p.742
11. *Westminster Shorter Catechism*, Question 14.
12. *Ibid.*, p.730.

Chapter 16 — God's faithfulness in instructing his people
1. Henry, *Commentary*, vol. I, p.751.
2. *Ibid.*, p.796.
3. *Ibid.*

4. *Ibid.*, vol. II, p.5.
5. *Ibid.*
6. *Ibid.*, vol. I, p.720.
7. Allis, *God spake by Moses*, p.137.
8. From John Rippon's *Selection of Hymns*, 1787.
9. Author unknown.
10. Henry, *Commentary*, vol. I, p.776.
11. *Ibid.*, p.774.
12. Allis, *God spake by Moses*, p.139.
13. Henry, *Commentary*, vol. I, p.776.
14. *Ibid.*, p.808.
15. *Ibid.*, p.552.
16. *Ibid.*, p.808.
17. *Ibid.*, p.552.

Chapter 17 — God's faithfulness in warning of dangers
1. Noel Weeks, *Gateway to the Old Testament* (Banner of Truth Trust, Edinburgh, 1995), p.246.
2. Henry, *Commentary*, vol. I, p.762.
3. Weeks, *Gateway to the Old Testament*, p.301.
4. A. W. Tozer, *That Incredible Christian* (Christian Publications, Inc., Harrisburg, PA, 1964), p.50.
5. Weeks, *Gateway to the Old Testament*, pp.285-6.
6. Tozer, *That Incredible Christian*, pp.133-4.
7. Henry, *Commentary*, vol. II, p.299.
8. *Ibid.*, pp.297-8.

Chapter 18 — The infinite, eternal and unchangeable God
1. *Reader's Digest*, February 1998, p.109.
2. Francis A Schaeffer, *The Complete Works of Francis A. Schaeffer, A Christian Worldview* (Crossway Books, Westchester, IL, 1982), vol. 5, p.370.
3. David Hagopian, *Back to Basics* (Presbyterian and Reformed Publishing, New Jersey, 1996) p.x.
4. *Westminster Shorter Catechism*, Question 4.
5. *Trinity Hymnal*, No. 94.

Chapter 19 — 'Beginning with Moses' — Christ in the Pentateuch
1. Bonar, *Leviticus*, p.31.
2. *Westminster Shorter Catechism*, Question 25.
3. Wallace A. Guilford, *Joseph and a Greater than Joseph* (Christian Press, Sydney, n.d.).
4. *Westminster Shorter Catechism*, Question 25.
5. Henry, *Commentary*, vol. I, p.645
6. *Ibid.*, p.646.